From Log-Cabin to White House

Also from Westphalia Press
westphaliapress.org

The Idea of the Digital University

Criminology Confronts Cultural Change

Eight Decades in Syria

Avant-Garde Politician

Socrates: An Oration

Strategies for Online Education

Conflicts in Health Policy

Material History and Ritual Objects

Jiu-Jitsu Combat Tricks

Opportunity and Horatio Alger

Careers in the Face of Challenge

Bookplates of the Kings

Collecting American Presidential Autographs

Misunderstood Children

Original Cables from the Pearl Harbor Attack

Social Satire and the Modern Novel

The Amenities of Book Collecting

Trademark Power

A Definitive Commentary on Bookplates

James Martineau and Rebuilding Theology

Royalty in All Ages

The Middle East: New Order or Disorder?

The Man Who Killed President Garfield

Chinese Nights Entertainments: Stories from Old China

Understanding Art

Homeopathy

The Signpost of Learning

Collecting Old Books

The Boy Chums Cruising in Florida Waters

The Thomas Starr King Dispute

Salt Water Game Fishing

Lariats and Lassos

Mr. Garfield of Ohio

The Wisdom of Thomas Starr King

The French Foreign Legion

War in Syria

Naturism Comes to the United States

Water Resources: Iniatives and Agendas

Designing, Adapting, Strategizing in Online Education

Feeding the Global South

The Design of Life: Development from a Human Perspective

From Log-Cabin to White House: Life of James A. Garfield

by William A. Thayer

WESTPHALIA PRESS
An Imprint of Policy Studies Organization

From Log-Cabin to White House: Life of James A. Garfield

Westphalia Press
An imprint of Policy Studies Organization
1527 New Hampshire Ave., NW
Washington, D.C. 20036
info@ipsonet.org

ISBN-13: 978-1-63391-425-4
ISBN-10: 1-63391-425-9

Cover design by Taillefer Long at Illuminated Stories:
illuminatedstories.com

Daniel Gutierrez-Sandoval, Executive Director
PSO and Westphalia Press

Updated material and comments on this edition
can be found at the Westphalia Press website:
www.westphaliapress.org

J. A. Garfield.

FROM

LOG-CABIN

TO

THE WHITE HOUSE

LIFE OF

JAMES A. GARFIELD:

BOYHOOD, YOUTH, MANHOOD, ASSASSINATION, DEATH, FUNERAL.

BY

WILLIAM M. THAYER,

AUTHOR OF "FROM PIONEER HOME TO THE WHITE HOUSE,"

With Eulogy

BY HON. JAMES G. BLAINE

New York:
HURST & COMPANY,
Publishers.

TO

ALL WHO HONOR TRUE MANHOOD,

This Volume,

PORTRAYING THE INDUSTRY, COURAGE, DECISION, ENERGY, PERSEVERANCE, AND NOBLE CHARACTER OF THE LATE PRESIDENT

JAMES A. GARFIELD,

IN HIS EARLY STRUGGLES FOR A LIVELIHOOD AND EDUCATION, AND HIS GRAND PUBLIC CAREER,

Is Sincerely and Affectionately Dedicated.

PREFACE.

EIGHTEEN years ago the author prepared a book for youth and young men upon the life of Abraham Lincoln, entitled THE PIONEER BOY, AND HOW HE BECAME PRESIDENT. The favorable reception of that volume carried it through thirty-six editions. After the nomination of General Garfield for the presidency, it was thought that a similar work upon his life would furnish one of the noblest examples of success to all who honor true manhood.

With the plan of making the volume not a work for the campaign, but a standard volume for the family for the years to come, months were employed in gathering and preparing the material.

The materials for the work were furnished by General Garfield; several of his early associates, two of whom were born in log-cabins near him; several of his teachers and pupils; the owner and captain of the canal-boat on which he served; and intimate friends of his manhood, — the most reliable sources of information possible. The materials forcibly impressed us with the similarity between the lives of President Lincoln and President Garfield.

Both of these statesmen were born in log-cabins, built by their fathers, in the wilderness, for family homes. Both were poor as mortals can well be. Both were born with talents of the highest order; but neither enjoyed early advantages of schools and teachers. At eight years of age Lincoln lost his mother; and when Garfield was eighteen months old he lost his father. Both worked on a farm, chopped wood, and did whatever else was needful for a livelihood, when eight years of age. Both improved every leisure moment in study and reading. Both read all the books that could be borrowed for miles around; and each was known, in his own township and time, as a boy of remarkable mental ability and promise. Both of them early displayed great tact and energy, turning a hand to any kind of labor, — farming, chopping, teaming, carpentering. In his youth, Lincoln ran a flat-boat down the Ohio and Mississippi rivers to New Orleans, eighteen hundred miles, on a trading expedition; Garfield, at about the same age, served on a boat of the Ohio and Pennsylvania Canal, driving mules and acting as steersman. Both were well known for their industry, tact, perseverance, integrity, courage, economy, thoroughness, punctuality, decision, and benevolence. Both taught school in the backwoods as soon as they knew enough to teach. Each of them studied law when pursuing another vocation for a livelihood,

— Lincoln a surveyor, and Garfield a teacher. Each became a member of the legislature in his native State before thirty years of age. Both served the country in war, when about the same age, — Lincoln in the "Black Hawk War," and Garfield in the "War of the Rebellion." Each was the youngest member of the legislature, and the youngest officer in the army when he served. The talents and eloquence of both made them members of Congress, — Lincoln at thirty-seven years of age, and Garfield at thirty-three; each one of them being the youngest member of the House of Representatives at the time. Both of them took high rank at once as debaters and eloquent speakers, as well as stalwart opposers of slavery. Both, also, won a reputation for wit and humor and geniality, making them popular with both sides of the House. Neither of them were candidates in the National Conventions that nominated them for the Presidency, — both were compromise candidates when it became apparent that union could be secured upon no others. Their names were introduced amid the wildest enthusiasm; thousands cheering, hats swinging, handkerchiefs waving, and the bands playing national airs. The nomination of each was hailed with demonstrations of joy throughout the country.

And now, the most remarkable of all coincidences in their lives we record with sadness, — both died in the Presidential office by the ASSASSIN'S SHOT. History has no parallel for this amazing fact. We search in vain the annals of all countries for a kindred record. Beginning life in the obscurity of the wilderness, and ending it on the summit of renown! Their first home a log cabin! their *last*, the White House! Beloved by a trusting nation, and shot by the assassin!

A more inspiring example to study and imitate cannot be found in the annals of our Republic. As a model of whatever belongs to noble traits of character, heroic achievements, and the highest success fairly won, we present him in this book.

W. M. T.

FRANKLIN, MASS., 1882.

NOTE. — This book has been revised, greatly enlarged, and embellished with new portraits and illustrations, and is printed from new electrotype plates.

CONTENTS.

CHAPTER I.

FIRST DAY AT SCHOOL.

CHAPTER II.

BEFORE SCHOOL-DAYS.

CHAPTER III.

GETTING ON.

CHAPTER IV.

TRIALS AND TRIUMPHS.

CHAPTER V.

BOY FARMER.

CHAPTER VI.

SUNDAY IN THE WOODS.

CHAPTER VII.

HIGHER UP.

CHAPTER VIII.

BOY CARPENTER.

CHAPTER IX.

BARN-BUILDING.

CHAPTER X.

A BLACK-SALTER.

CHAPTER XI.

A WOOD-CHOPPER.

CHAPTER XII.

A CANAL BOY.

CHAPTER XIII.

TRIUMPHS ON THE TOW-PATH.

CHAPTER XIV.

THE TURNING-POINT.

CHAPTER XV.

GEAUGA SEMINARY.

CHAPTER XVI.

AFTER VACATION.

CHAPTER XVII.

KEEPING SCHOOL.

CHAPTER XVIII.

THIRD YEAR AT SCHOOL.

CHAPTER XIX.

THE ECLECTIC INSTITUTE.

CHAPTER XX.

STUDENT AND TEACHER.

CHAPTER XXI.

IN COLLEGE.

CHAPTER XXII.

RETURN TO HIRAM.

CHAPTER XXIII.

FROM PEACE TO WAR.

CHAPTER XXIV.

TOP OF THE LADDER.

CHAPTER XXV.

IN THE WHITE HOUSE.

CHAPTER XXVI.

ASSASSINATION.

CHAPTER XXVII.

DEATH — FUNERAL CEREMONIES.

CHAPTER XXVIII.

EULOGY.

FROM LOG-CABIN TO WHITE HOUSE.

CHAPTER I.

FIRST DAY AT SCHOOL.

RUMOR came to the log-cabin that a school would open soon at the village, one-and-a-half miles distant. It was only a rumor at first, but the rumor grew into fact in the course of a week.

"Jimmy must go, mother," said Thomas, who was nearly thirteen years old, a boy of heroic spirit and true filial and fraternal devotion.

"Yes, Jimmy must go," responded his mother, with such a smile as lights up the face of those mothers only who think what a treasure and joy there is in the little three-year old; for Jimmy had not yet reached his fourth birthday. "I wish you could go, Tom, also," she added.

"I wish I could, too," the thoughtful lad replied; "but the potatoes would hardly be dug, and the corn would hardly be harvested, nor the winter rye be put in, if I should go. The girls and Jimmy can go, and my work will get us food and clothes." The last sentence was spoken with so much interest, as if the son and brother found his highest pleasure in being able to run the little farm alone, while his sisters and precious little brother could attend the school together, that his good mother could scarcely suppress her honest pride over the unselfish and noble boy. Her maternal pride came very near making a demonstration and applying some pet names to Thomas, but her excellent judgment, which usually ruled, guided her into a wiser course, and she let the occasion pass with only a few well-chosen words of approval.

"It is a good chance for Jimmy," added Thomas, after a moment had passed, in which remark his mother saw the "heap" of love he had for his little brother; and every one else would see it now, too, could they understand the circumstances. More than one person had remarked that Thomas thought a "heap" of James.

It was a busy time in the cabin, preparing the children for school. The girls and Thomas went to school before the family removed to Orange, so that it was not a new thing to them. Besides, their mother had taught them much. She had made no special effort to teach James, except to tell him Bible stories, and answer his multitudinous questions in her instructive way. Still, James knew nearly all his letters, and was better versed in Bible history than most children of his age at the present day. The stories of the Ark, Cain and Abel, Joseph, Ishmael, Isaac, Jacob, Absalom, Daniel, the Bethlehem Babe, and many others, were familiar to him at that time. The little fellow possessed a remarkable memory, and he was bright and sunny, the light and joy of the log-cabin. It would not suffice to say that his mother thought that he was particularly a bright and talented boy; for mothers are quite apt to think very well of their offspring. But when we add that Thomas and his sisters, and the neighbors also, regarded James as a very precocious and promising lad, the reader may safely conclude that the hero of this volume was none of your simple-minded "children of the woods"—neither a juvenile drone nor ignoramus. He was just the little fellow to make music at home or in the school-house.

"Jimmy can't walk half the way," said Thomas; "he will be tired to death before he hardly gets out of sight of home."

"I'll see to that," replied his sister, with an air of assurance that indicated her plans were all laid. "Jimmy won't be tired."

"What is going to prevent it?" inquired Thomas.

"You'll see," answered his sister, somewhat evasively, though Thomas knew by her appearance that there was real significance in what she said.

"Well, what's up now?" added Thomas, sure that some project was in her head.

"Nothing is up, except Jimmy; he will be *up*—on my back," answered the brave girl, who had resolved to spare her lively little brother's legs by carrying him to school.

"Carry Jimmy to school!" exclaimed Thomas; "you will be more tired than he will be to walk. It is a bigger load than our great-grandfather carried in the Revolutionary war. You'll get sick of that."

"It won't be the first thing I am sick of that I have done," was all the girl's reply.

We did not mean to tell this resolute maid's unpoetical name; but we desire to say something about her, and so we must tell her name. It was MEHETABEL. The name was load enough to carry to school without adding the burden of Jimmy. Mehetabel was fifteen years old, just such a strapping girl as would grow up in the woods, among tall trees; but she did not merit such a name as that. It sat upon her better at fifteen than it could have done in babyhood, undoubtedly. Just think of a baby bearing the name of MEHETABEL! We have looked for its origin, and find that it belongs to the old Jewish dispensation, and ought to have been dumped into oblivion with its lumbering ceremonials. But, somehow, it slid over into the new dispensation, and after the lapse of eighteen hundred years and more it now confronts us in Ohio!

Well, the first day of school arrived, and MEHETABEL took her two burdens — her name and her brother — and trudged off to school. Jimmy was mightily pleased with his new mode of conveyance, and so were the whole family; and they made a jolly morning of it in starting off the pioneer troop, who were only forty-six years distant from the White House. The log-cabin smiled as it had not smiled since that terrible day of sorrow, of which we shall soon speak. Thomas was the happiest boy in Ohio on that blessed morning, although he did not know it; and he went to work with fresh vigor and determination, splendid fellow that he was. While the children are in school, and Thomas is driving work on the farm, and the good mother is having a lonely day in the cabin, with her spinning-wheel, we will stop to tell how this family came to be in the woods of Ohio, and add some definite information about the father.

In the year 1799 Thomas Garfield was a farmer in Worcester, Otsego County, N. Y. That year a son was born to him, to whom he gave the name of Abram. Thirty-two years afterwards, this son Abram became the father of James A. Garfield.

Before Abram was two years old, his father suddenly sickened and died, leaving his wife and several children penniless, — a sorrow that was singularly repeated in the life of Abram, who died, as we shall see, when James was less than two years of age, leaving his wife and four children to battle with the hardships of life. It was not possible for Abram's mother to keep the family together and provide for so many mouths; so a neighbor, James Stone, took Abram into his family, and reared him as one of his own children.

When the lad was ten years old, widow Ballou removed into the neighborhood, from New Hampshire. Mrs. Ballou had a daughter, Eliza, about a year younger than Abram, a very bright, promising girl. Abram and Eliza became playmates, and thought very much of each other.

Eliza was fourteen years old when her mother conceived the idea of emigrating to Ohio, which was then the "Far West," and great stories were told about its prolific soil and future wealth. Emigrants from New York, and also from the New England States, were removing thither in considerable numbers. James Ballou, her son, now a young man, saw emigrant wagons passing through New York, or starting from it, their destination being Ohio, and became more enthusiastic than his mother to go. At last she decided to remove thither, sold her little farm, packed her household goods into an emigrant wagon, and with her children started for the West. Abram was a lonely boy when Eliza left, and the two separated regretfully.

It was a long and tiresome journey of six weeks,—a trip that could be accomplished now in twelve hours. The family were in the wagon, except when the wagon was stuck in the mud, and they were compelled to unload, and, with levers, lift it out. The roads were fearfully bad, without a bridge over a single river; so they had streams to ford, swamps to wade, and quagmires to avoid, enough to test the courage and patience of the most experienced woman and the bravest girl. On the way James shot game, so that there was no lack of food. At length they reached Zanesville, Muskingum County, one of the oldest settlements in Ohio at that time; and there they settled.

About five years later Abram Garfield took the "Ohio fever," as it was called, or else the memory of the fair-haired maiden inspired him to nobler deeds, and he, too, started for the West,—a young man of twenty years, hopeful, fearless, ambitious, and smart. He found work in Newburg, near Cleveland. Cleveland was then only a small collection of log-cabins, containing about one hundred people. Newburg was newer and more isolated. But, for some reason, the young adventurer selected the latter place for his home.

It is quite evident that he not only worked, but cast about to learn something of the maiden he could not forget. For he learned, after a time, that the Ballou family were at Zanesville, whither he wended his way on a visit, as soon as possible. The family gave him a hearty greeting, especially Eliza, who had grown into a winsome damsel of almost nineteen. That Abram was glad to see her would be a tame way of stating the fact. If Eliza had constituted all the "Far West" there was at that time, Abram would have been fascinated by the country, making no account at all of New York in the comparison. Without stretching out the tale into a "long yarn," it will suffice to say, that Eliza just filled Abram's eye, and in less than two years from that time became his wife. They were married February 3, 1821, and repaired at once to his chosen home, Newburg, where a log-cabin, eighteen by twenty feet, containing but one room, awaited them. It was a very humble abode, but true love put as much happiness into it as could have been there if it had been a palace. The cabin was destitute of sash or glass, though places for three windows, covered with greased paper, admitted light. Greased paper was a common substitute for glass, and was the "stained-glass" of that day. The furniture was manufactured by her noble husband, of whom she was as proud as he was of her; and it was the latest style of that region, therefore fashionable. It consisted of several three-legged stools, a puncheon table, a bed in one corner, constructed of poles and slabs, a frying-pan, one iron pot, two wooden plates, with knives and forks to match, and a "Dutch oven," which was simply a kettle with a rimmed cover, on which live coals were laid. Here James A. Garfield's father began life in earnest, and here he lived nine years, during which time three of his children were born. He tilled the soil, and also at two different times took contracts on the Ohio and Pennsylvania Canal, which was in process of construction.

The young adventurer was not satisfied, however. His growing family demanded larger provision for the future, so he purchased fifty acres of land, at two dollars an acre, in Orange, Cuyahoga County, seventeen miles from the first home of his wedded life. He selected this locality because Amos Boynton, whose wife was sister to Mrs. Garfield, had purchased a tract there; and the families could remove thither together. One log-cabin was erected first, in which both families lived, thick as "three in a bed," until another cabin could be built. When these cabins were built the nearest neighbor was seven miles away. It was January, 1830, when Abram Garfield removed to this new home in the wilderness. His cabin was larger and more substantial than the one he left. It was twenty by thirty feet, made of unhewn logs, notched and laid one upon another, in what boys call the "cob-house" style, to the height of twelve feet or more in front, and eight feet or more on the back side. The spaces between the logs were filled with clay or mud, making a warm abode for winter, and a cool one for summer.

The chimney was constructed of wood and mud,

rising from the roof like a pyramid, smallest at the top. The roof was covered with slabs, held in place by long weight-poles. The floor was made of logs each split into two parts and laid the flat side up, hewn smooth with an axe. There was a loft above to which the family ascended by a sort of permanent ladder in one corner of the cabin. The children slept upon the floor of the loft, on straw beds. The only door of the dwelling was made of plank; and three small windows furnished all the light possible, though not so much as was needed. This, briefly, was the pioneer home in which James A. Garfield was born, on the 19th day of November, 1831, and from which he went forth to his first day at school, as already described.

Abram Garfield was a tall, heavy, handsome man, capable of great endurance; just the man to plunge into a wilderness to make a home and clear land for a farm. He possessed the strength, will, and wisdom for such an enterprise. His brain was in fair proportion to his body, large and active, making him a strong-minded man; and, under other and more favorable circumstances, he might have made a broad and deep mark on his day and generation. But he thought of little except his family in that day of hardship and want, and so he chose a home and occupation where honor and fame were out of the question. But, with all his physical strength, the loving husband and father was not exempt from the attacks of disease. One day, in the midst of his hard toil, he heard the alarm of "Fire in the forest." Forest fires were common in summer time, and often large tracts of woods were burned over; and sometimes pioneer cabins were destroyed, and the crops on little farms in the wilderness were injured.

"It is coming this way certainly," said Mr. Garfield, with some anxiety, after satisfying himself as to the danger. "I'm afraid it will make trouble for us. Mehetabel, run to the house with my axe, and bring me the shovel."

The girl was assisting her father. Within five minutes Mr. Garfield had the shovel, and Mrs. Garfield, and all the children except the baby, were out to watch the fire.

"We must fight it," said Mr. Garfield, "or only ashes will be left of our home at sundown."

"I fear as much," replied Mrs. Garfield. "These forest fires are terrible."

"Mehetabel, you and Thomas follow me;" and he ran across the house-lot to the edge of the woods to prevent the fiery demon from attacking his habitation.

Thomas and his sister followed. The fire reached the spot almost as soon as they did, and the battle with it began. It was a long and hard fight. Mr. Garfield met the enemy with all the vigor of a father contending for his children. He fully realized what their situation would be if the sun should go down upon the ruins of their home, and the thought impelled him to superhuman efforts. For nearly two hours, in the burning sun of a hot July day, he fought the fire with his strong arm. Sometimes the battle seemed to turn in favor of the fiery element, and again the resolute pioneer appeared to have the advantage over it. At last, however, the fire was conquered, or rather, was prevented from devouring the little cabin and desolating the crops, though it swept on beyond the farm, whither the wind drove it.

Thoroughly heated and exhausted, Mr. Garfield sat down upon a stump to rest, and enjoy the cool, refreshing breeze that sprang up from the West. He did not dream that he was exposing his health by sitting, covered with perspiration, in that cool wind. But that night he was seized violently by congestion of the throat, and his stout frame writhed in pain, threatening speedy dissolution. As early in the morning as possible, Mehetabel was posted away to Mr. Boynton's, and Thomas to a neighbor in another direction, for their assistance. There was no physician within many miles; but one of the neighbors summoned claimed to possess some medical knowledge, and the patient was passed over into his hands, substantially, after he arrived. He applied a blister, thereby aggravating the disease, and hurrying the sick man to his grave. Mrs. Garfield did all that true love and remarkable efficiency could do to save her husband, but her tender and faithful ministrations were fruitless; he sank rapidly, and at last died without a struggle. His last words were, looking upon his children, and then addressing his wife:

"I have planted four saplings in these woods; I must now leave them to your care."

Oh, what a dark pall settled upon that abode! A happier family never dwelt in a palace than was found in that cabin. And now the burden of sorrow that rested upon the widowed wife and fatherless children was gauged by the greatness of bereaved affection. Little James was but eighteen months old when his father died — too young to understand the irreparable loss, or to feel the pangs of grief that well-nigh crushed other hearts. It was well that his baby spirit could not take in the sorrow of that hour; there was anguish enough in that stricken home without adding his touching wail thereto.

The neighbors came, what few there were (only four or five families within a radius of ten miles), and sympathized and wept with the widow and fatherless ones. With their assistance the lifeless remains were closed in a rough box, and borne out through the low doorway, and buried in a corner of the wheat-field near by. No sermon, no remarks, no prayers, except the silent prayers that went up for grace from aching hearts! Reader, you will never know, you never *can* know, nobody can ever know, except by the dreadful experience, what the death and burial of a loved one is in the wilderness, amid the gloom and silence of primeval forests. That bereaved widow still lives, and after the lapse of nearly fifty years she bears the marks of that great sorrow. A kind Providence that "tempers the wind to the shorn lamb" has wonderfully sustained her, and she has found her Saviour to be as "the shadow of a great rock in a weary land." Still the brow of almost eighty years is furrowed by the severity of that affliction.

An incident should be recorded here. It occurred a short time before Mr. Garfield's death; and he was reading a volume of Plutarch's "Lives," with James in his lap. The latter could speak the words, "papa," "mamma," and others. "Say Plutarch," said his father. James repeated it very distinctly. "Say it again," continued Mr. Garfield. James repeated it plainly, as before, and continued to repeat it. Looking up to his wife, Mr. Garfield remarked, with a true father's love and pride, "Eliza, this boy will be a scholar some day!"

Winter was approaching; and winter in the wilderness, especially when the stalwart arm upon which loved ones depend for support and defence is palsied in death, is not calculated to dispel gloom from a dwelling. Could human experience be more dreary than when a woman is left a widow, alone with her children, in a wilderness swept by wintry storms; and that affliction intensified by extreme poverty, so that economy and careful planning are needful to keep the wolf of hunger from the door? What a winter it was! The snow lay deep and heavy upon the earth, burying the sacred mound in the corner of the wheat-field out of sight, and the high winds moaned through the naked forests as if wailing for the dead. The howl of wolves and the cry of panthers never sounded so terrible as they did during those long, desolate, wintry nights. The children, realizing the loneliness of their situation, now that their strong protector was dead, would lie awake at night to listen tremblingly to the howls and cries of these hungry animals, at the very door of their cabin. Sometimes it seemed to them that the panthers knew their courageous father was lying dead in the wheat-field, and so they ventured to come to the very door to moan and cry, as famishing children cry for bread. Baby James, however, slept on, oblivious alike to the sorrows and perils of the hour. God was keeping him against the night of national danger, when he would listen to the yell of the wolves of plunder at the door of the republic. That winter, alone in the almost pathless forest, with the warring elements and beasts of prey uniting to make desolation more desolate, could not have had more sad thoughts, bitter tears, hours of loneliness, and blasted hopes, crowded into it than were the natural outcome of the direful situation.

It seemed to the weary ones that spring would never return; but it did, after a long, never-to-be-forgotten winter. And spring swept away the snow and ice, and the streams ran singing again, and the dead things of the field and forest returned to life, save only the dead in the corner of the wheat-field. There was no resurrection there; and so hope was not revived in the cabin, and a gloomy outlook made even spring-time sad. There was no money in the house, and there was a debt on the farm. Food, also, was running low; and the widowed mother might hear her children cry for bread. What could she do? Leaving the children still at school, we will continue the story of her sufferings.

CHAPTER II.

BEFORE SCHOOL-DAYS.

N her strait Widow Garfield sought the advice of neighbor Boynton, whose real kindness had been a solace to her heart. He said :

"No woman with four children can carry on a farm like this alone, and support her family. I see no possible way out of your trouble except to sell your place and return to your friends."

"And leave my husband in the wheat-field ?" responded Mrs. Garfield. "Never ; I can't do that."

"But what else can you do?" continued the neighbor.

Looking at the circumstances squarely, with her accustomed good sense and courageous spirit, she answered :

"When I have sold, paid the debts and the expense of removal to my friends, I shall have little or nothing left, and that, too, without a rod of land on which to raise corn to make a loaf."

"Your friends could help you," suggested the neighbor.

"I can never cast myself upon the charity of

iends," Mrs. Garfield replied, with an emphasis that showed she meant what she said. "So long as I have my health I believe that my Heavenly Father will [illegible] these two hands so as to support my children. My dear husband made this home at the sacrifice of his life, and every log in this cabin is sacred to me now. It seems to me like a holy trust, that I must preserve as faithfully as I would guard his grave."

The heroism that came out through these words was worthy of a Revolutionary matron; and the woman's fortitude fairly drew tears from the eyes of the neighbor.

"Then you would not sell your farm any way?" added the neighbor, inquiringly.

"Not all of it," she replied. "Part of it might go, enough to pay the debt."

"I never thought of that," answered the neighbor. "Perhaps that is the way out of your trouble. Better think that over, and I will. I'll look about, too, and see what can be done by way of selling part of it."

The neighbor left, and Mrs. Garfield went immediately to a greater than he, where she had often been in her want and woe for counsel. On her knees in one corner of the cabin she laid her case before God. and promised to follow His guidance if He would only make duty plain. God did make it plain as day to her. She arose from her knees without a doubt in her heart. She was happier than she had been any time since death darkened her home. She felt like singing the twenty-seventh Psalm: "The Lord is my light and my salvation; whom shall I fear? the

Lord is the strength of my life; of whom shall I be afraid?"

Calling Thomas, who was not quite eleven years old, but now the only male dependence on the farm, she laid the case before him, as if he had been a man of thirty years, and the resolute and trusty boy replied:

"I can plough and plant, mother. I can sow the wheat, too, and cut the wood, milk the cows, and do heaps of things for you."

"You are a small boy to do so much," responded his mother; "but with my help perhaps it can be done. God has promised to be with the widow and fatherless. I don't feel that I can move away from this place."

"We needn't," Thomas said, quickly. "I want to live here, and I will work real hard."

"Not too hard, my son, lest there be two graves instead of one in the corner of the wheat-field," answered Mrs. Garfield, with much emotion. "We must finish the fence around the wheat, and that will be very hard work; but I think that I can split the rails, and together we can set the fence."

"And I can finish the barn, I know," added Thomas. His father had partially fenced the wheat-field, and had been putting up a small barn, which was nearly completed.

And so the whole subject was canvassed, and plans laid, in the full expectation of remaining on the pioneer farm. Nor did the widow have to wait long to sell a portion of her land. Settlers were coming into that part of Ohio occasionally, and one of them heard, through the neighbor spoken of, that Mrs.

Garfield would dispose of part of her land. He lost no time in finding her humble abode, and at once bargained with her for twenty acres, paying cash for the same. With this money she paid all the debts, although it took the last dollar to remove this incumbrance.

Spring was fairly upon them when the sale was effected, so that she and Thomas proceeded at once to put the little farm in order. He procured a horse of the nearest neighbor, who was generous enough to offer him the use of the animal, and prepared the ground for wheat, corn, and potatoes, and a small garden for vegetables. It was truly wonderful to witness the tact and endurance of this boy-farmer of ten years, toiling from early morning till night set in, his young heart bounding with delight over his ability to assist his widowed mother. Without any assistance, except such as his mother, and sister of twelve years, rendered, he did the planting and sowing in a style that assured a good harvest in the autumn.

At the same time his mother prepared the fence for the wheat-field. She found trees in the forest already felled, and she split the rails, every one of them, severe as the labor was, sometimes almost exhausting her strength, and always making a large draft upon her nerves. But the necessity was laid upon her, and she stopped not to inquire, as she did in the case of Thomas, whether there might not be another grave in the wheat-field at no distant period. Before July the house-lot, which was the small plat of cleared land sowed and planted, was fenced in, and the little farm was doing well. There was no school for Thomas and his sisters to attend, so that he had all the time there was from morning until night to labor, and wait — wait for the seed to grow. He did his work, apparently, with as much ease and efficiency as a young man of twenty would have done it.

But another trial awaited the afflicted family. Food was becoming scarce, and no money to purchase more. An examination satisfied the widow that the corn would be exhausted long before harvest unless the family were put upon a daily allowance. So, without speaking of this new trial to her children, she counted the number of weeks and days to harvest-time, and estimated the amount of corn that would be required each day. To her surprise and grief, a fair daily allowance would exhaust the bin of corn before harvest. She took in the situation at once, and, bravely and quickly as a general on the field of battle, decided she would forego supper herself that the children might have enough. For a while the devoted mother lived upon two meals a day, though working harder than she had ever worked any previous summer; for she assisted Thomas on the farm to the extent of her strength, and even beyond her strength.

A few weeks elapsed, and the doting mother discovered some mistake in her calculations, and she was startled to find that the present daily allowance of corn would consume the last ear before the new crop could be gathered. Without a murmur, and with a martyr spirit, she resolved to forego dinner; and from that time until harvest she indulged in but one meal a day. All this self-denial was practised in a manner to conceal it as much as possible from the children. They were growing and hearty, and Thomas especially needed substantial food, since he was doing almost a man's labor. Seldom was a pioneer family found in more straitened circumstances in mid-summer than was Widow Garfield's in the year 1834. Had not the spirit of a Revolutionary matron presided over that cabin, and the grace of Him who does not suffer a sparrow to fall without his notice sustained the presiding genius, the history of that family would have closed that year in the forests of Ohio.

But the harvest came, and a blessed harvest it was! The crops were abundant, and of excellent quality. Want fled at the sight of the bending sheaves and golden ears. The dear mother had come off conqueror in her long contest with the wolf of hunger, and her heart overflowed with gratitude to the Great Giver. The twenty-third Psalm had new significance in that log-cabin, — "The Lord is my shepherd, I shall not want," etc., — and the grateful mother repeated it over and over, from day to day, as the real language of her soul in the hour of deliverance from distressing want. The first full meal which the abundant harvest brought was a benison to that household, and never again did hunger and starvation threaten to destroy them.

We have told the reader somewhat about the father of this family, and now that so much has been said of the mother we need to say more. We stop here to record briefly some facts of her early history.

She was a descendant of Maturin Ballou, a Huguenot of France, who was driven from that country on the revocation of the edict of Nantes. He joined the colony of Roger Williams and came to America, settling in Cumberland, R. I. There he built a church, which still stands, and is carefully preserved as a relic of the past. It is known as the "Elder Ballou Meeting-house." When it was built there were no saw-mills in the country, and no nails, and few tools to work with, so that the old "meeting-house" is a great curiosity. Its galleries and pews are hewn out of solid logs, and put together with wooden pegs. Even its floor was hewn out of logs, and fastened down with wooden pegs. Here Maturin Ballou preached the gospel while he lived, and was followed by his son, then his grandson, then his great-grandson, and so on to the tenth generation. A race of preachers sprang from this pioneer minister. In one family of the Ballous, the father and four sons were clergymen; then followed three grandsons, one great-grandson, and one great-great-grandson, all from one branch. There were also many lawyers, doctors, and other public men among the Ballous, eminent for their talents and remarkable force of character. Some of them figured in the American Revolution, both as officers and privates, as heroic and efficient in war as they were renowned in peace. They were a conscientious people, and one of them, who preached in the old meeting-house about the year 1775, would not receive any salary for his services. He protested against being a "hireling." And yet he was so poor that one of his sons was forced to learn to write upon "birch-bark, in lieu of paper, and use charcoal, instead of pen and ink." This son was the celebrated

Hosea Ballou, founder of Universalism in the United States. His father broke away from the Cumberland fold before Hosea was born, and removed to New Hampshire, where he settled. A cousin, James Ballou, emigrated thither with him, married, and became the father of Eliza Ballou, who, as we have seen, is the mother of James A. Garfield.

It is not difficult, therefore, to discover the origin of Mrs. Garfield's (mother of James) great fortitude, indomitable perseverance, tact, talents, and large executive ability. Were she otherwise, she would not fairly represent the long line of illustrious ancestors whose record is found upon two hundred years, and more, of our nation's history.

In the spring of 1835, a family moved into the vicinity, which proved of great benefit to the Garfields. They had sewing to be done, and Mrs. Garfield was glad of the opportunity to do it. A boy was needed, also, to plough and chop occasionally, and Thomas found it a good opportunity to earn a little money for his mother. It was additional sunshine let into the log-cabin.

It was an era when Thomas brought home the first money that he earned. A happier boy never crossed a threshold than he was when he handed the avails of his labor to his mother, saying:

"Now the shoemaker can come and make Jimmy a pair of shoes."

"Certainly," answered his mother; "and he will be indebted to you for the first pair of shoes that he ever wore. You'll never be sorry."

"I never expect to be sorry," replied Thomas

"Jimmy ought to have had a pair a long time ago, and he would have had a pair if there had been any way for me to earn them."

"Well you can send word to the shoemaker as soon as you please," continued his mother; "the quicker the better."

James was three and a half years old at that time, and he had not known the luxury of a pair of shoes, no, not even in the winter. To come into the possession of the first pair of shoes, in these circumstances, was an event of great importance. To a child in the woods, it was like the accession of a fortune to a poor man, now. Be assured, reader, that Jimmy greeted the advent of the shoemaker with hearty good-will when he came; and he came very soon after the shoe question was settled, for Thomas lost no time in securing his services.

Then, in that part of the country, shoemakers did not have shops of their own, but they went from cabin to cabin, boarding with the families while they were making shoes for the members. In this case, the cobbler boarded with Mrs. Garfield, and his board paid part of the cost of the shoes. Shoemakers were not experts in the business, at that time and in that region, so they required much more time to produce a pair of shoes; and when they were completed, no one could say that their beauty added to their value. They answered every purpose, however, in a region where fashion was at a discount.

The acquisition of that pair of shoes elated the little possessor more than an election to Congress did less than thirty years thereafter. He was rich now, and well equipped for pioneer life. He could defy the snows of winter as well as the stubs of summer.

One thing more should be told here. Abram Garfield and his noble wife were Christians. Before removing to Orange, they united with a comparatively new sect, called Disciples, though Campbellites was a name by which they were sometimes known, in honor of the founder of the sect, Alexander Campbell. Their creed was very short, plain, and good. It was as follows:

1. A belief in God the Father.

2. That Jesus is the Christ, the Son of the living God, the only Saviour.

3. That Christ is a Divine Being.

4. That the Holy Spirit is the Divine agent in the conversion of sinners, and in guidance and direction.

5. That the Old and New Testament Scriptures are inspired of God.

6. That there is future punishment for the wicked, and reward for the righteous.

7. That God hears and answers prayer.

8. That the Bible is the only creed.

With such decided opinions, of course their cabin home was dedicated to God, and the Bible was the counsellor and guide of their life. The voice of prayer was heard daily in the rude abode, and the children were reared under the influence of Christian instruction and living.

It has taken us so long to relate the history of this family previous to Jimmy's first day at school, that we must now hasten to meet the children, on their return, as told in the next chapter.

CHAPTER III.

GETTING ON.

RS. GARFIELD was making her spinning wheel hum when the children came home. She was obliged to economize her time, in order to clothe her family with goods of her own manufacture. The spinning-wheel and loom were just as indispensable to pioneers, at that time, as a "Dutch oven" was. The age of factories had not come, certainly not in that part of the country. In New England, even, factories were in their infancy, then, — small affairs.

"Oh, such a good time as we have had!" exclaimed Mehetabel, as she came rushing into the cabin with James and her sister.

"Twenty-one scholars," added her sister, under considerable excitement. "Mr. Lander's children were there, and they have twice as far to go as we have. They have to walk over three miles."

"And how did Jimmy get on at school?" inquired their mother, as soon as there was a place for her to put in a word.

"He liked it," answered Mehetabel; "he said his letters; and he asked the master how he knew that letter was R."

"Just like him," ejaculated Thomas, laughing outright. Thomas had just come in, leaving his work when he saw the children return. "The master will have enough to do to answer all his questions. What did the master tell him?"

"He told him that he learned it was R at school, when he was about as old as he was," replied Mehetabel. And Thomas was giving Jimmy a toss in the air, by way of sport, while she was relating the facts, and Jimmy himself was making a most vigorous attempt to embellish the occurrences of the day from his imperfect vocabulary.

"How did you like your ride, Jimmy?" inquired Thomas.

"I liked it," was the child's answer, uttered in a gleeful way.

"You liked it better than Hit did, I guess."

"I liked it well enough," responded Mehetabel.

"Wer'n't you awful tired?"

"I wasn't tired much."

"Did you carry him all the way?"

"Pretty much. He walked a little of the way home. He isn't much of a load."

"Did he sit still in school?"

"Pretty still. He left his seat once, and went over to scrape the acquaintance of another boy opposite."

"What did the master say?"

"He took him by the hand and led him back, looking at us, and smiling; and he told him that each boy and girl had his own seat in school, and he must keep it."

"You are a great one, Jimmy," exclaimed Thomas, tossing the little midget into the air again. "You will make music for them in school."

"Well, children, I am glad that you like your school so well," remarked their mother, who had been listening to the prattle with maternal interest. "You must make the most of it, too, for we can't expect many school advantages in these woods. Poor opportunities are better than none."

Ohio schools were of the poorest class then, short and miserable. The teachers knew but little to begin with, and children had to travel so far to school that their attendance was limited to certain parts of the year. In many schools, reading, spelling, and writing were the only branches taught. Geography and arithmetic were added to the studies in some schools. All of these branches were pursued in the school which the Garfield children attended. Teachers in the new settlements, at that time, were usually males; it was not supposed that females could teach school well. That females make the best teachers, as a class, is a recent discovery.

The books used in the best pioneer schools of Ohio were Webster's Spelling-book, the English Reader, Pike's and Adams' Arithmetic, and Morse's (old) Geography. The Garfields possessed all of these. They had, also, the Farmer's Almanac, and a copy of Davy Crockett's Almanac, which was found, at one time, in almost every cabin of the West. Reading-books were scarce then throughout the country, in comparison with the present time; in the wilds of Ohio they were not so plenty as panthers and wolves.

Many of the few books found there related to exciting adventures with beasts of prey, hair-breadth escapes on perilous waters, and the daring exploits of pirates and rascals; and they were illustrated with very poor pictures. Three or four volumes, besides the Bible and school-books, constituted the whole literary outfit of the Garfields. They had more brains than books, as the sequel will abundantly prove.

The village where the school was located was not much of a village, after all. In addition to the log school-house, eighteen by twenty feet, there was a grist-mill, and a log-house, in a part of which was a store, the other part being used for a dwelling. The place is now known by the name of Chagrin Falls, and derived its singular name from the following fact: A bright Yankee began the settlement, attracted thither by the stream of water. He removed to the place in the winter time, when the stream was swollen and swift, and he erected a saw-mill. But when the summer came the stream dried up, and his hopes dried up with it. His *chagrin* was so great over his *dry* enterprise that he named the locality as above, in order to warn his Yankee relations against repeating his folly.

We cannot delay to rehearse much that transpired in school during this first term that James attended. Two or three matters of special interest only can be noticed.

We have said that James was very familiar with Bible stories; and we have intimated too, that he was very inquisitive. His questions often created a laugh in school, both teacher and scholars enjoying their originality and pertinency very much. The fact was, James meant to understand things as he went along, and so his active brain put many inquiries over which the school was merry. They were not merry because his questions were pointless and childish; far otherwise. They were merry because such a little fellow showed so much brightness and precocity by his inquiries. Scholars and teachers came to regard him as a sort of prodigy.

One day, at noon, an older scholar set him upon the table, saying:

"Now, Jimmy, you be master and ask questions, and we will be scholars and answer them."

"Take your seats, then," responded Jimmy, by way of consenting, his bright eyes sparkling with delight.

The pupils took their seats in glee.

"Now go ahead, Jimmy," cried out Jacob Lander. "Don't ask too hard questions."

Jimmy immediately began on his hobby—Bible questions.

"Who made the ark?"

"Noah," answered a half dozen voices.

"Who told him to make the ark?"

"God," replied several.

"What for did God want he should make the ark?"

There was a pause; no one answered. It was one of Jacob Lander's hard questions, that James should have avoided. After waiting in vain for an answer he answered it himself.

"To save his self and family in."

"Save from what?" cried out Jacob.

"From the flood," replied James.

"Who was the oldest man?" James continued.

"Methusaleh," several answered.

"How old was he?"

Nobody could tell, and so James told them.

"Who was the meekest man?"

"Moses," was the prompt answer.

"Who had a coat of many colors?"

"Joseph," equally prompt.

"Who was swallowed in the Red Sea?"

Nobody replied. He told.

And thus, for ten or fifteen minutes, this child of not quite four years interrogated the scholars around him, presenting one of the most marvellous scenes on record, whether in wilderness or city. From his earliest years his memory was very remarkable, embracing and retaining stories, facts, and whatever he heard, with unusual accuracy. He acquired very much information in school by listening to the recitations of other and older pupils. Nothing was more common, during his first term at school, than for him to repeat at home something he had learned from the recitations of older scholars. Then, too, nothing escaped his notice. His faculty of observation was ever on the alert. Language, manners, apparel, methods of work, conversation, almost everything attracted his attention; so that he was ever surprising friends, from his childhood, by the amount of information he possessed.

He was a great imitator, too. Children differ very much in this regard. James was one in whom this faculty appeared to be large by inheritance. It was encouraging to behave well in his presence, it was perilous and doubly wicked to set a bad example before him. Coupled with his observation, this quality made him sharp and critical, for one of his years.

"School will keep through the winter," said Mehetabel to her mother, as she came home one day, near the close of the term. "Jacob's father is raising the money to pay the master."

"How did you learn? I have not heard of it,' answered Mrs. Garfield.

"Several of the scholars said so; and they are all going."

"Going to have a vacation?" inquired her mother.

"Yes; two or three weeks; school will begin in December for the winter."

"I am very glad indeed that you can have such an opportunity to attend school," continued her mother.

"Then I can go, can I?"

"Yes; you can all go except Jimmy. He cannot go so far in the winter; and it will be too hard for you to carry him through the snow."

"Will Tom go?"

"I hope so; he has worked very hard that the rest of you might go, and now he should go."

Ten minutes afterwards Thomas was discussing the matter, and presenting reasons why he could not attend.

"I shall find enough to do taking care of the cows and chopping wood, even if there is no snow to shovel, which is not very likely."

"But we must let some things go undone, if possible, that you may learn when you can," suggested his mother. "In this new country you must take education when you can get it."

"I can study at home evenings and stormy days," replied Thomas.

"That is what Jimmy must do — study at home," continued Mrs. Garfield. "He has a good start now, and he can make a good reader before next summer."

The result was that Thomas did not attend the winter term, nor James. Their two sisters went, and Mrs. Garfield instructed James and assisted Thomas somewhat in his studies.

Long winter evenings in the woods were favorable for study by the light of the blazing fire, that made the cabin more cheerful even than it was in daytime. Pioneers could not afford the luxury of a tallow candle or an oil lamp. Sometimes they adopted a substitute for both — the pitch-pine knot. But usually, in winter, pioneers depended upon the light of the fireplace. Fireplaces were very large, so as to admit logs four feet long, with a quantity of smaller fuel in like proportion. When the mass of combustible material was fairly ablaze, the light and heat penetrated into every corner of the cabin; and the heat below greatly modified the excessive cold of the loft above.

That winter was a memorable one for James. He made decided progress in spelling and reading before the next summer came, with its hot days and growing crops. It was after the winter was over and gone, and the warm sunlight was bathing the forests and gladdening the earth, that James came into possession of a child's volume somehow, — either it was a present or was borrowed of a neighbor,—from which he derived much real pleasure. One day he spelled out and read aloud the following line:

"The rain came pattering on the roof."

"Why, mother!" he shouted, under visible excitement, "I've heard the rain do that myself."

"You have?"

"Why, yes, I have," he continued, as if a new revelation were made to him. And then he read the line over again, with more emphasis and louder than before:

"The rain came pattering on the roof."

"Yes, mother, I've heard it just so!" and the little fellow appeared to be struggling with a thought larger than ever tasked his mind before. It was the first time, probably, that he had learned the actual use of words to represent things, to describe objects and events—the outside world on paper.

From that time James was introduced into a new world,—a world of thought. Words expressed thoughts to him, and books contained words; and so he went for books with all his mind, and might, and strength. There was nothing about the cabin equal to a book. He preferred the "English Reader" to anything that could be raised on the little farm. He revelled in books—such books as he could find at that time when there was a dearth of books. Day after day the "English Reader" was his companion. He would lie flat upon the cabin floor by the hour, or sprawl himself out under a tree, on a warm summer day, with the "English Reader" in his hand, exploring its mines of thought, mastering its wonderful knowledge, and making himself familiar with its inspiring contents. This was before the lad was five years old; and he was scarcely six years old when he had committed to memory a great portion of that "Reader." Other volumes, too, occupied much of his attention, though none to such an extent as the "English Reader." Such was his childish devotion to books that his mother could scarcely refrain from prophesying, even then, an intellectual career for him. She knew not how it could be done, — all the surroundings of the family were unfriendly to such an experience, — but somehow she was made to feel that there was a wider, grander field of action for that active, precocious mind.

CHAPTER IV.

TRIALS AND TRIUMPHS.

E can have a school-house nearer to us," remarked Mrs. Garfield to Mr. Boynton. "For the sake of my James, I wish we could have."

"There are scarcely enough families yet to make such a change," replied Mr. Boynton; "some of them would have to go as far as they do now."

"That is very true; but more families would have a shorter distance to go than they have now. I think that fact is worth considering."

Mrs. Garfield was giving utterance, for the first time, to thoughts that had been in her mind for several months. In her own mind she had numbered the families which might be induced to unite in erecting a log school-house upon one corner of her farm. She continued:

"Suppose you inquire of Mr. Collins and others, and learn what they think about it. If eight or ten families will unite, or even eight families, we can have a school nearer home. I will give the land on which to build the house; and three days' labor by seven or eight men will complete the building. It is not a long or expensive job, and it is just the time to start now, if the thing is to be done."

"Perhaps it can be done," Mr. Boynton answered thoughtfully. "The more I look at it, the less difficult it seems. I will consult the neighbors you mention, and others, too. I should be as pleased as anybody to have it done." And as he spoke the last sentence he turned towards home.

Without recording the details of this new enterprise, we need only say, that it was very easily accomplished; and before winter set in, a log school-house stood on the Garfield farm. Neighbors welcomed the project, especially because it would be an advantage to Widow Garfield, whom they very much respected, and to whom their warmest sympathies had always been tendered in her affliction.

"Now you can go to school by your own conveyance," said Thomas to Jimmy, one day after the school-house was finished. "You won't have to make a beast of burden of Hit any longer. You will like that, won't you?"

James assented; when his mother added:

"Your master is coming from New Hampshire, where I was born. You will like him; and he is to board here to begin with."

Mrs. Garfield had four children, and Mr. Boynton six, to go to school,—ten in all from two families.

It was through Mrs. Garfield's influence that the school-house was built; and then, it was through her influence that a school-master was imported from New Hampshire. The school-house was twenty feet square, with puncheon floor, slab roof, and log benches without backs,—large enough to accommodate twenty-five scholars. Teachers always "boarded round," dividing the time equally among the families; and it was considered quite an advantage to a family of children to have the "master" board with them.

By hard labor, assisted by his mother and sisters, Thomas harvested the crops in the autumn, cut and hauled wood, and did other necessary work, so that he could attend the winter term of school with his sisters and James. He had everything about the farm in fine order when December and the school-master, whose name was Foster, arrived. They came together, and one was about as rough as the other. The "master" was a young man of twenty years, uncouth in his appearance, large and unwieldy, but a sensible sort of a Yankee, who had picked up considerable knowledge without going to school or reading much. On the whole, he was full as much of a man as pioneers could expect for the small wages they were able to pay. He was kind-hearted, of good character, and was really influenced by a strong desire to benefit his pupils.

He took up his abode at the beginning of school with Mrs. Garfield, and slept in the loft with Thomas and James. At once his attention was drawn to James, as a very precocious child. Good terms were established between them; and when they started off together for the school-house, on the first day of school, the teacher said to him, putting his hand kindly on his head:

"If you learn well, my boy, you may grow up yet and be a general."

James did not know exactly what a general was, but then he concluded that a general must be some great affair, or a school-master would not speak so favorably of him. The remark fastened upon the lad's mind; somehow he felt, all through the day, that he was beginning just then to make a general, whatever that might be. It was not out of his mind for a minute: and he labored somewhat upon the point, how long a time it would take to make him into a general. However, he knew that there was one being who stood between him, and all learning, and all the future,—and that being was his mother. What he did not know, she would know. As soon as he reached home, after school, he inquired:

"Ma, what's a gen'ral?"

"What's what?" his mother answered, not comprehending his question.

"What's a gen'ral?" James repeated, somewhat more distinctly.

"Oh, I see now—a general!" she answered; "that is what you want to know."

"Yes; the master said I might make a gen'ral if I learn."

"That is what put it into your head, then," continued his mother, laughing, "You don't know whether you would like to be one or not, I suppose: is that it?"

"I want to know what it is," James replied.

"Well, I will tell you, my son, for your great-grandfather fought in the Revolutionary War under a general. You ought to know something about that, and something about your ancestors, too, as well as about a general."

She proceeded to tell him about his paternal ancestors: "How Edward Garfield came to this country from England, with John Winthrop, John Endicott, Francis Higginson, and many other Puritans, tc escape oppression at home, and settled in Watertown, Mass., which was as much of a wilderness then as Ohio was, when your father removed here. The Indians were his neighbors, and he bought land of them, and lived in peace with them. There he and his descendants lived, some of them removing into other towns, and many of them among the most influential citizens of that time. By and by, England, the mother-country, made war upon the people there, and the fight of Concord bridge occurred on the 19th of April, 1775. The soldiers of England wore red coats, glittering with brass buttons, and they carried guns with which to shoot down the farmers and people of Massachusetts Colony, unless they would surrender and obey the King of England. But the men would do neither. They seized their guns, determined to defend themselves, and shoot the red-coats rather than continue to be subject to the king. Your great-uncle, Abraham Garfield, was among the soldiers at Concord Bridge. This was the beginning of th Revolutionary War, in which our soldiers fought bravely for their rights, and your great-grandfather, Solomon Garfield, was one of them. Then our soldiers wore blue coats, trimmed with brass buttons, and they were led by generals who were the most distinguished men, like General Washington. The generals wore coats that shone with gold lace, and epaulets, or ornaments, on their shoulders, and hats like the one General Washington wears in the almanac picture, made showy with gold lace and a feather. Generals carried swords instead of guns; and they rode horseback, and led the soldiers into battle. I hope we shall never want any more generals in this country, for it is terrible to shoot down men as they do in war. But by study and learning you can make a man equal to a general, and be as honored, without killing your fellow-men.

"When the Revolutionary War was over, your great-grandfather removed into the State of New York, where he had a son whom he named Thomas. Thomas grew up to be a man, and was married, and had a son whom he named Abram; and this Abram was your father. Now, it will be easy for you to remember, that Solomon Garfield was your great-grandfather, a soldier of the American Revolution; that Thomas Garfield, a pioneer of New York state, was your grandfather, and Abram, his son, a pioneer of Ohio, was your father. There was no general among all your ancestors, though some of them were equal to generals. If you should ever become a general, you will be what no one of your ancestors ever was, as far back as we can trace them — two hundred and fifty years."

James listened to this recital with wonder. He scarcely knew before that he was connected with the world outside of the Ohio wilderness. Now, he clearly understood that his relations acted a conspicuous part in settling this country, and were people of much consequence. It was a new and inspiring thought to him. His cabin home was invested with new interest and more importance. How far his life was influenced by this revelation of the past, we cannot say, but there is no doubt that his active brain was stirred to nobler thought, and his young heart stamped by indelible impressions.

James believed in his teacher, and his teacher believed in him. There was mutual attraction from the outset. The teacher saw that the backwoods boy was a great man in embryo. He was glad to have such a scholar under his tuition. He was somewhat taken aback, however, by subsequent occurrences. The second day of school he established the following rule:

"Scholars cannot study their lessons and look about the school-room: therefore gazing about is strictly forbidden."

It was a novel rule to the pupils. It savored of more strictness than they had been accustomed to. It was a very difficult rule for James to observe. He acquired much information by his close observation. His two eyes and two ears were more than books to him. Besides, he had never undertaken to perform the feat of sitting bolt upright upon a log bench without a back, and looking down upon his book with steady gaze. It was a severe ordeal for a boy who never sat still in his life, and who evidently was not constructed upon the principle of sitting still. However, his heart accepted the rule, and he meant to do the best that he could with it. If he were to make a general, or something else as good, he must do as the "master" told him to do. As much as that was clear to him. But the first thing he knew, his eyes were *off* the book, and *on* the class reciting.

"James!" said the teacher pleasantly, "have you forgotten the rule so quick?"

"I forgot," was James' laconic reply; and down dashed his eyes upon his book. Not long, however. A taking answer to a question in the class on the floor brought up his eyes again, as if by magic.

"What! so soon forgetting the rule again, James?" exclaimed the teacher. "You have a very short memory."

James looked down upon his book abashed, but he made no reply. The fact was, he meant to mind the rule and do his best to please his teacher. But it was never intended that two such eyes and two such ears as James possessed should come under a rule like that. The teacher was unwittingly at fault here. He did not quite understand his pupil; and so he insisted upon the observance of the rule, and for two weeks continued to correct James, hoping that he would finally bring his eyes and ears into complete subjection. But his effort was fruitless. James was incorrigible, when he meant to be obedient, and he grew nervous under the discipline. He thought so much about keeping his eyes in the prescribed place that he could think very little about his lessons; and so he became comparatively dull and defective in his recitations.

At length, just before the teacher left Mrs. Garfield's for another boarding-place, he said to her, in James' presence:

"I do not want to wound your feelings, James is such a noble boy; but then I want to tell you—"

"Say on," replied Mrs. Garfield, quite startled by the solemn tone of the "master."

"James is not quite the boy in school that I ex pected."

"How so?" interrupted Mrs. Garfield, completely taken by surprise. "You astonish me."

"I know that you will be grieved, but I think it is my duty to tell you." And Mrs. Garfield could see that he shrunk from telling her, and she began to think that something awful had happened; still she repeated:

"Say on."

"Well, it is only this: James don't sit still, and he don't learn his lessons. I fear that I shall not be able to make a scholar of him."

"O James!" his mother exclaimed, as if the teacher had put a shot through her body. That was all she said; and it was uttered in a tone of agony that went straight to the little fellow's heart, as he stood looking and listening. She sent him to school that he might make a scholar, and now her hopes were dashed in a moment. No wonder that her response was an exclamation of disappointment and grief!

"I *will* be a good boy," ejaculated James, bursting into tears, and burying his face in his mother's lap. "I *mean* to be a good boy." And he never told more truth in a single sentence than he did in the last one. It never will do for a philosopher, however wise, to attempt to repress the centrifugal force of nature; and that was what the teacher was trying to do.

"Perhaps he can't sit still," at length Mrs. Garfield suggested; "he never was still in his life."

"I *will* sit still," was the boy's response, still sobbing as if his heart would burst, yet speaking before the teacher had time to reply.

"Perhaps so," answered the teacher, thoughtfully as if the grieved mother had awakened a new idea in him.

"I never knew him to fail of learning before," Mrs. Garfield continued; "never."

"I *will* learn, mother!" the boy shouted between his sobs.

"You mean to learn, I have no doubt," answered his mother. "Some boys do worse than they intend; perhaps that is the trouble with you."

"You dear child," said the teacher, putting his hand upon his head, touched by the lad's piteous appeals; "you and I are good friends, and I think we shall have no more trouble. I will try you again. So wipe up, and let us laugh and not cry."

The teacher saw his mistake. The child's mother had opened his eyes by her wise suggestion. In his mind he resolved to let the centrifugal force alone, and adopt another policy. So the subject was dropped, and James went to school on the following day, to sit still or not, as he pleased. The teacher resolved to leave him to himself, and see what the effect would be. The result was excellent. The boy did not sit still, of course he did not; but he was natural and happy, and his eyes fulfilled their function in roaming about more or less, and his ears heard what was going on in the school-house. The teacher could not make a blind and deaf boy of him, any way, and so he ceased to try. He allowed him to see and hear for himself; and it just filled the lad with happiness. It fired his ambition, and brought out his brilliant parts, so that he became the star of the school.

It was quite a number of days before Mrs. Garfield saw the teacher again, as he went to board with another family. Then he called to cheer the mother, whom he had so thoroughly grieved. Her first question was, as he entered her house, —

"How does James do now?"

"Oh, grandly," the teacher replied, in a tone that indicated great satisfaction in being able to speak so approvingly.

"I am so glad!" was the mother's only response; and her heart was healed.

"He is perpetual motion in school," continued the teacher, "but he learns; no scholar learns so fast as he does."

"Then you have given up your rule?" Mrs. Garfield remarked, inquiringly.

"Yes; I think you are right about him. Such a rule cramps him; he can't be himself under it. I guess he tried hard to obey it."

"Children are very unlike," continued Mrs. Garfield. "James is unlike my other children in his restlessness and energy, as well as in his precociousness. I hope that he will come out all right."

"Come out all right!" responded the teacher. "My word for it, he will make his mark in the world; you can depend on that."

"I hope so;" and Mrs. Garfield put her whole mother's heart into those last three words.

The restive nature of James was a theme of remark

frequently. Thomas sometimes complained of it. He lodged with James, and the latter would toss and tumble about, often awaking Thomas by his movements, kicking off the clothes, and thereby putting himself and brother to considerable inconvenience. Often he would turn over, and feeling cold after having kicked off the bedclothes, he would say in his sleep, —

"Tom, cover me up."

Thomas would pull the clothing over him, and lie down to his dreams, but only to repeat the operation again and again. It was said of James, twenty-five years after that time, when he had become a general, that, one night, after a terrible battle, he laid down with other officers to sleep, and in his restlessness he kicked off his covering; then, turning partly over, he said, —

"Tom, cover me up."

An officer pulled the blanket over him, and awoke him by the act. On being told of his request in his sleep, James thought of his good brother Thomas and of the little log-house in the woods of Ohio; and he turned over and wept, as he did in childhood when the teacher concluded that he could not make a scholar of him.

At the beginning of the school the teacher had said:

"At the close of the term I shall present this Testament (holding up a pretty Testament of rather diminutive size) to the best scholar, — best in study, behavior, and all that makes a good scholar."

It was a new thing to them, and it proved quite an incentive to most of the pupils. Several tried hard for it; but it was pretty well understood, before the term was half through, who would have the book. None were surprised when, at the close of the last day of school, the teacher said, —

"James! step this way."

James lost no time in obeying.

"This book," passing the Testament to him, "is yours. I think you have fairly earned it as the best scholar in school. I have no fault to find with any scholar; but your remarkable progress entitles you to the book."

The pupils were all satisfied; James was a happy boy, and his mother wept tears of joy.

From the time that James was permitted to be himself in school, his advancement was remarkable. Every teacher regarded him as a boy of uncommon talents, and every scholar was attracted to him as by magnetic influence. He read every book that he could beg or borrow; yet he was efficient to assist Thomas on the farm at six years of age. He went to school whenever there was a school; but that was only a few weeks in a year. He improved his evenings and leisure time at home, however, and all the books at hand were read over and over, until he was perfectly familiar with their contents. His mental appetite was always craving, nor was it ever gorged by excess of food. It appeared to be capable of appropriating and digesting all that the times and locality could furnish.

About this time the Garfield and Boynton children formed a kind of club for improvement in spelling. The spelling-book became the field of their exploits

They studied it enthusiastically, and drilled each other in its contents, as if they meant to master it. The result was great proficiency in spelling—all of them excelling their companions at school. The drill was of great advantage to them in spelling-matches, when the winter school was going; especially to James, who became quite an enthusiast in that branch. He was the best speller in school, when more than half the pupils were older than he. Some of them said that James could spell every word in the book correctly. Whether he could or not, in choosing sides for a spelling-match, James was sure to be the first one chosen.

CHAPTER V.

BOY FARMER.

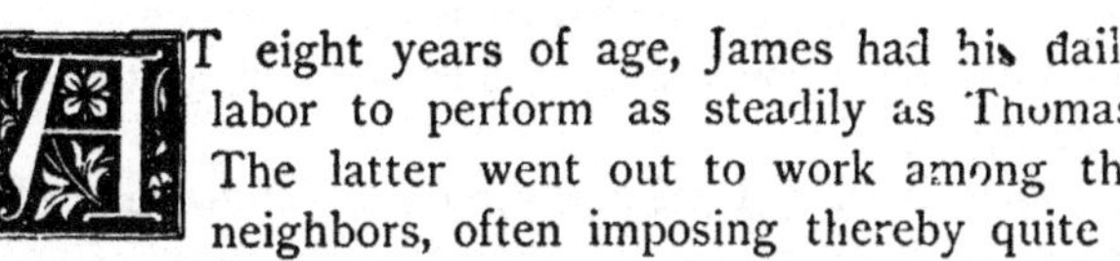

AT eight years of age, James had his daily labor to perform as steadily as Thomas. The latter went out to work among the neighbors, often imposing thereby quite a responsibility upon James, who looked after the stock and farm at home. He could chop wood, milk cows, shell corn, cultivate vegetables, and do many other things that farmers must do.

It was very great assistance to the family when Thomas could earn a little money by his labor. That money procured some indispensable articles, the absence of which was a real privation both to mother and children. They needed more money now than ever, because all must have shoes, and all must have books; and there were the teachers to pay, and occasional meetings at the school-house now were some expense. So that the earnings of Thomas just met a demand of the time, in which every member of the household shared.

"You are eight years old, my son, and Thomas is seventeen," said Mrs. Garfield to James. "Thomas was not eleven years old when your father died, and he had to take your father's place on the farm. You must be getting ready to take Thomas's place, for he will soon be of age, and then he will have to go out into the world to seek his fortune, and you will have to take care of the farm."

"I can do that," James answered.

"Not without learning how to do it," said his mother. 'Practice makes perfect' is an old and true proverb."

"I know that I can take care of the farm, if Tom could," interrupted James with some assurance.

"Yes, when you are as old as he," suggested his mother.

"That is what I mean, — when I get to be as old as he was."

"I hope that some day you will do something better than farming," continued Mrs. Garfield.

"What is there better than farming?" James asked.

"It is better for some men to teach and preach. Wouldn't you like to teach school?"

"When I am old enough, I should."

"Well, it won't be long before you are old enough. If you are qualified, you can teach school when you are as old as Thomas is now."

"When I am seventeen?" James responded with some surprise. All of his teachers had been older than that, and he could scarcely see how he could do the same at seventeen.

"Yes, at seventeen or eighteen. Many young men teach school as early as that. But farming comes first in order, as we are situated."

"And it is time to get the cows, now," remarked James, hurrying off for them, and terminating the conversation.

James was a self-reliant boy, just the one to take hold of farm work with tact and vigor. He scarcely knew what "*I can't*" meant. It was an expression that he never used. The phrase that he had just employed in reply to his mother, "*I can do that,*" was a common one with him. Once it put him into a laughable position. He was after hens' eggs in the barn, with his playmate, Edwin Mapes.

"Look here, Jim!" called out Edwin, at the same time exhibiting an egg that he had found.

"You're a lucky fellow," answered James, taking the egg.

"Suck it," responded Edwin; "some boys suck eggs."

"I never did," replied James.

"Nor I," answered Edwin, "but I could do it, I suppose."

"So could I, if other boys have done it," continued James in rather a characteristic way.

"You can't do it," challenged Edwin; "I stump you to do it."

Putting it in that way aroused the indomitable spirit of James, and he accepted the challenge.

"Here goes my first raw egg," he exclaimed as the yolk went into his mouth. He was very fond of boiled eggs, but the raw one proved nauseating, and would not down at his bidding.

"Sticks in your crop, don't it?" shouted Edwin, laughing heartily over the spectacle.

James was not in a condition to reply, but his action seemed to say:

"I said I could swallow an egg, and I will."

His stomach heaved, his face scowled, and Edwin roared: still James held to the egg, and made for the house as fast as his nimble limbs could take him, Edwin following after to learn what next. Rushing into the house James seized a piece of bread, thrust it into his mouth, chewed it up with the egg, and swallowed the whole together.

"There!" he exclaimed, "it's done."

He did what he said he would, and he felt like a conqueror. Edwin swayed to and fro with laughter; and, although forty years have elapsed since that day, it is not impossible for him to get up a laugh over it still. Mrs. Garfield looked on with curious interest, not comprehending the meaning of the affair until an explanation followed. Then she only smiled, and said "Foolish boy!"

He was a "foolish boy;" "foolish" just as many promising boys are "foolish" at times. But the spirit of the lad appeared through the "foolish" act. Nevertheless, the "*I can*" element of his character rather dignified the performance. The more we think of it, the more we are inclined to take back our endorsement of that word "foolish," because the act was an outcome of his self-reliance. When William Carey, the renowned missionary to India, was a boy, he possessed a daring, adventurous spirit, that expressed itself in climbing trees and buildings, and in going where, and doing what, few boys would do because of the peril. One day he fell from the top of a tree, on which he perched like an owl, and broke one of his legs. He was confined to the house and bed several weeks; but the first thing he did on his recovery was to climb that identical tree to its very top, and seat himself on the bough from which he had fallen, to show that the feat was not impossible. There is no doubt that his mother called him a "foolish boy," to risk his limbs and life again on a tree; but his admirers have ever loved to rehearse the deed, as proof of the boy's invincible, reliant spirit. No one who reads of Carey's immense labors for the heathen, his fearlessness in great danger, his hair-breadth escapes from death, his tact and coolness in every emergency, can fail to see that his "foolish" act of climbing the tree was a good illustration of the maxim, that "The boy is father of the man."

James was not egotistical or self-confident; these are no part of self-reliance. Nor was he proud, pride is no part of self-reliance. He was not conscious of having anything to be proud of. No boy was ever more simple-hearted and confiding in others than was he. He did not tell his mother that he could run the farm because he overrated his abilities; it was the honest expression of what he was willing to do, and what he thought he could do. It was the opposite of that inefficient, irresolute boyhood that exclaims, "I can't," when it ought to be ashamed to say it; and when a decided, hearty, "I can," would prove a trumpet-call to duty, rallying all the powers to instant action. This was one thing that encouraged his mother to expect so much of him when he should become a man. On one occa sion, after he began to labor on the farm, and quite a task was before him, she said to him:

"James, half the battle is in thinking you can do a thing. My father used to say, 'Where there's a will, there's a way;' repeating a proverb that is as old as the hills."

"What does that mean?" interrupted James, referring to the proverb.

"It means, that he who *wills* to do anything *will* do it. That is, the boy who relies upon himself, and determines to perform a task in spite of difficulties, will accomplish his purpose. You can do that?" And his mother waited for a reply.

"I can," James answered, with emphasis.

"Depend upon yourself. Feel that you are equal to the work in hand, and it will be easily done. 'God helps those who help themselves,' it is said, and I believe it. He has helped me wonderfully since your father died. I scarcely knew which way to turn, when he died; I scarcely saw how I could live here in the woods; and yet I could find no way to get out of them and live. But just as soon as I fell back upon God and myself, I took up the cross, and bore it easily. We have fared much better than I expected; and it is because I was made to feel that 'Where there's a will, there's a way.' God will bless all our efforts to do the best we can."

"What'll he do, when we don't do the best we can?" inquired James.

"He will withhold his blessing; and that is the greatest calamity that could possibly happen to us. We can do nothing well without his blessing."

"I thought God only helped people be *good*," remarked James, who was beginning to inquire within himself whether He helped farmers.

"God helps folks to be good in everything, - good boys, good men, good workers, good thinkers, good farmers, good teachers, good everything. And without his help we can be good in nothing."

James drank in every word, and looked very much as if he believed that he and God could run the farm successfully. His mother continued:

"If you do one thing well you will do another well, and so on to the end. You will soon learn that your own efforts are necessary to accomplish anything, and so you will form the habit of depending upon yourself, — the only way to make the most of yourself."

Such was the instruction that James received from the wisest of mothers, just when such lessons respecting self-reliance would do him the most good. It was on this line that he was started off in his boyhood, and he followed that line thereafter. He had no one to help him upward, and he had no desire to have anybody help him. Unlike boys who depend upon some rich father or uncle to give them "a good start," or upon superior advantages, he settled down upon the stubborn fact, that if anything was ever made out of him he must do it himself. Hard work was before him, and hard fare, and he expected nothing less. A statesman who rose from obscurity to eminence once said, "Whatever may be thought of my attainments, it must be conceded that I made as much out of the stuff put into my hands as was possible." That the germ of such an impulse must have taken root in

James' heart early, is quite evident from some remarks of his to young men after he was forty years old:

"Occasion cannot make spurs, young men. If you expect to wear spurs, you must win them. If you wish to use them, you must buckle them to your own heels before you go into the fight. Any success you may achieve is not worth having unless you fight for it. Whatever you win in life you must conquer by your own efforts, and then it is yours,—a part of yourself. . . . Let not poverty stand as an obstacle in your way. Poverty is uncomfortable, as I can testify; but nine times out of ten the best thing that can happen to a young man is to be tossed overboard, and compelled to sink or swim for himself. In all my acquaintance I have never known one to be drowned who was worth saving. . . . To a young man who has in himself the magnificent possibilities of life, it is not fitting that he should be permanently commanded; he should be a commander. You must not continue to be *employed;* you must be an *employer.* You must be promoted from the ranks to a command. There is something, young men, that you can command; go and find it, and command it. You can at least command a horse and dray, can be generalissimo of them and may carve out a fortune with them."

Another incident of James' early life illustrates the phase of his character in question, and, at the same time, shows his aptitude in unexpected emergencies. He was eight or ten years of age when it occurred, a pupil in school with his cousin, Henry Boynton. Sitting side by side, one day they became more roguish than usual, without intending to violate the rules of school. Sly looks and an occasional laugh satisfied the teacher, who was a sharp disciplinarian, that something unusual was going on, and he concluded that the wisest treatment would be to stop it at once.

"James and Henry!" he called out, loudly, "lay aside your books and go home, both of you."

A clap of thunder would not have startled them more. They looked at each other seriously, as if the result was entirely unexpected, and delayed for a moment.

"Don't dilly-dally," exclaimed the teacher; "both of you go home immediately."

"I will go," answered James. Henry said nothing; and both passed out. James made an express of his dexterous legs, shortening the distance from the school-house to home to about three or four minutes, and an equal time to return. Returning to school, he entered the room, puffing like an engine, and resumed his seat.

"James! did I not tell you to go home?" shouted the teacher, never dreaming that the boy had had time to obey the mandate.

"I have been home," answered James, not in the least disconcerted. He had obeyed his teacher promptly, though he took very good care that his mother did not see him when he reached the cabin.

"Been home?" responded the teacher, inquiringly, surprised that the boy had been home in so short a time.

"Yes, sir, I have been home," replied James; "you didn't tell me to *stay*."

"Well, you can *stay* here, now," answered the

teacher with a smile, thinking that was the best way to dispose of so good a joke. James remained, and was very careful not to be sent home again, lest the affair might not terminate so pleasantly. Henry sulked about the school-house for a while, and then went home and stayed the remainder of the day. That was the difference between the two boys. James saw the way out of the trouble at once, through the most literal obedience, and, believing that he was equal to the emergency, he started promptly to fulfil the command. He was neither sulky nor rebellious, but happy as a lark, lively as a cricket, and smiling as a morning in May. Such a little episode rather tightened the bond existing between the teacher and James. The former discovered more of that sharp discrimination and practical wit in the affair, for which he had already learned that James was distinguished.

James was now eleven years old, and Thomas was twenty. The district concluded to erect a frame school-house, and sold the old one to Thomas for a trifle. Thomas and James, assisted by their cousins, the Boynton boys, took it down, and put it up again directly in the rear of their mother's cabin, thus providing her with an additional room, which was a great convenience. Thomas did it in anticipation of leaving home when he should attain his majority.

CHAPTER VI.

SUNDAY IN THE WOODS.

IONEERS need a Sabbath full as much as anybody else," was Mrs. Garfield's remark to James, and her other children. "'Remember the Sabbath day to keep it holy,' is a commandment that must be kept in the woods as faithfully as elsewhere. In large towns and cities people prepare for this by building houses of worship, some of them with tall and handsome spires, pointing to heaven, with bells in the towers."

"What for do they want bells?" inquired James, to whom this announcement about houses of worship and bells was a revelation. Neither James nor the other children had seen a house of worship, or heard a Sabbath bell, and their mother touched upon a theme as new and fascinating as a novel when she described Sabbath scenes in large towns.

"The bells call people to worship promptly, by ringing at the time of meeting," Mrs. Garfield replied to James' question

"Bells would not be of much use to pioneers, who live so far apart, even if they could afford to have them," she continued.

"Wouldn't they sound splendid in the forests?" exclaimed James.

"Indeed they would," responded his mother; "and they would be good company, too. I imagine it would not be so lonesome if Sabbath bells echoed through the wilderness. But pioneers ought to be thankful that they can ever have preaching, under any circumcumstances whatever."

"I should like to live in a big town where they have meeting-houses with tall spires," added James.

"Perhaps you will some day," suggested his mother. "None of us will live to see them in this town, probably."

The last remark was rather of a damper upon James' aspirations, who scarcely expected, then, ever to find a home elsewhere. The foregoing conversation will derive significance from an acquaintance with the religious privileges of the family.

At the time of which we are speaking there was no stated preaching in the vicinity of the Garfield estate. The sect called Disciples held occasional services in school-houses and dwelling-houses. These occasional services began before the death of Mr. Garfield. As the latter, with his wife, had united with that sect before removing into the township of Orange, they were especially ready to welcome the itinerant preacher to their log-cabin, and to the school-house. Sometimes the meeting was at a cabin or school-house five, six, and even eight miles away. It was not unusual, in James' boyhood, for pioneers to travel six and eight miles to a religious meeting, on Sunday. They went with ox-teams and horse-teams, single and double, and some men and boys walked the whole distance. Often, in some sections, the father would ride horseback to meeting, with his wife on a pillion behind him, carrying her youngest child, the older children following on foot. The meagre religious privileges were highly valued, and there was much labor and hardship involved in availing themselves of them.

The preachers of that day were illiterate men,— good, but uncultivated. They were *pioneer* preachers, just as the settlers were *pioneer* settlers. They were well suited, perhaps, to the times and locality,— rough, sincere, earnest men, who found real satisfaction in travelling through the destitute country, usually on horseback, to do the people spiritual good. Occasionally there was a remarkable preacher among them, possessing great native ability, force of character, and singular magnetic presence. These were especially welcome, although any one of the number was received cordially. In their travels they called at all cabins, as pastors now make visits from house to house, their visits being chiefly of a religious character. They ate and lodged in cabins, wherever noon and night overtook them. The best fare that a cabin had was cheerfully set before them, and the best advice and sympathy the preacher could command were freely proffered. It is not possible for us, at this day, to say how great was the influence of this pastoral work. Men may read about it, and laugh over it now, but there can be no doubt that it provided a much needed and indispensable source of Christian power, influence, and enjoyment. It contributed largely to make pioneer life nobler, and, in an important sense, educational.

James enjoyed no better opportunities of religious worship than we have described, before he was ten years of age. Occasional worship was a privilege that he highly prized, as others did. He did not readily let slip an opportunity to attend public worship. And the impressions it left upon his heart were gauged by his deep interest in such occasions.

Whether there was any meeting or not, however, the weekly Sabbath was recognized in the Garfield cabin. No labor upon that day, except works of necessity, was the rule carefully observed. The Bible stood in the place of preacher. It was both read and studied. Mrs. Garfield's rule was to read four chapters daily on week days, and more on the Sabbath, when she formally expounded it in her sensible and thoughtful manner. The children asked questions as well as she. James was especially inquisitive about the Scriptures, and, after he learned to read, he read them much, both on the Sabbath and week days. Bible stories that he learned from his mother's lips, before he could speak plainly, became invested with new charms when he could read them at his leisure. He became so familiar with many narratives, that he knew just where in the Bible to turn to them; and he had a multitude of questions to ask about "God's book," as his mother reverently called it.

"How do you know that it is 'God's book,' mother?" he asked.

"Because it is not like any book that man ever wrote."

"You said once that Moses, Isaiah, David, Matthew, Paul, and others wrote it," recalling his mother's explanation of different books.

"Yes, that is true, they did write it; but they wrote as they were moved by the Holy Ghost. They could not have written it without God's help. They wrote just what God told them, by his Spirit, to write."

"And that is why you call it God's book?" James inquired.

"Yes; he is the author of it, although he directed men to write it, and guided them, also, in doing it."

"Are all the stories in it true stories?"

"Yes; every one of them."

"Is it true that Joseph had a coat of many different colors?"

"I expect it is."

"Why didn't he have a coat of *one* color? Would it not be easier to make such a one?"

"His father loved him more than he did his other children, and he made such a coat for him out of his partiality."

"Did he do right to love one of his children more than he did others?"

"No; he did not."

"Was his father a good man?"

"Yes. Some good men do wrong."

"If good men do wrong, how do you know them from bad men?"

"They don't do so many wicked things, nor so bad things, as bad men do."

"Can't good men stop doing bad things?"

"Yes; with God's help."

"Don't God always help them?"

"No."

"Why don't he?"

"Perhaps they don't deserve it."

"Can't men be good without his help?"

"No; and what is worse, they won't be."

"Why won't they?"

"Because they are so wicked."

"How can they be good, then?" meaning that he could not see how a good man could be a wicked man at the same time.

In this dialogue appears the inquisitiveness of James, as well as his discrimination and thoughtfulness. Often his mother was unable to answer his boyish questions about the Bible. Their depth and point confounded her. It was here, especially, that she had unmistakable proof of his remarkable talents. It was around the old family Bible that the chief interest of the Sabbath clustered in her rude home. It was to her family what a Constitution is to the State, and what character is to the individual. Largely it made up for the absence of books, teachers, money, and conveniences. It would be quite impossible to say how much unalloyed happiness it contributed to the family. Certainly, its wise teachings were so indelibly impressed upon James' heart that its contents were more familiar to him at forty years of age than they are to most Christian men, so that its figures, symbols, and laconic sentences adorned his public addresses, to the admiration of listeners.

It is probable that James and his brother and sisters received more real valuable lessons, to assist in the formation of good habits, and to establish noble purposes, in their western cabin, than the children of many Christian families do from the constant ministrations of public worship. The absence of religious advantages was a good reason for the best improvement of the few enjoyed. The mother, too, felt additional obligations to guide, instruct, and mould the hearts of her offspring, because there was so little outside of her cabin to aid her. For these reasons, perhaps James enjoyed better advantages to become distinguished than he would have had in the more populous and wealthy parts of the country.

When James was eight years old the Temperance Reformation was moving on with power. The New England States presented a scene of enthusiasm without precedent, and the interest spread into north-eastern Ohio. Even the cabins of pioneers were reached by the wave of influence for temperance. Mrs. Garfield was just the woman to welcome such a reform, and to appreciate its true value. The subject was a fitting one for the Sabbath, although it was not neglected on other days. As the handmaid of religion, it challenged her best thoughts and efforts.

"Drunkenness is a terrible sin," she said, "and I was always glad that your father had the same view of it that I have."

"Didn't he drink rum or whiskey?" asked James.

"Seldom; and he got out of patience with men intoxicated. He thought they were very weak men by nature."

"Why don't men stop drinking it when it is hurting them?" James inquired.

"It is difficult to say why they don't. Some think they can't do it."

"Can't stop!" James exclaimed, with surprise.

"It is said that they can't stop, — that they form such a terrible appetite that they can't control it."

"I would," responded James, with characteristic firmness.

"Better never begin to use intoxicating liquors; that is the only safe course. It is easier not to begin to go wrong, than it is to turn back and do better, after beginning."

"What do men drink liquor for?"

"It would be difficult to tell what some of them drink it for, I think. Most men drink it because they like it, I suppose."

"Does it taste good?"

"I suppose it does to those who like it."

"I should like to taste of some, just to see what it tastes like," added James.

"I rather you would never know how it tastes, my son. If you never taste it, you can never become a drunkard, that is certain. 'Look not thou upon the wine when it is red, when it giveth his color in the cup, when it moveth itself aright. At the last it biteth like a serpent, and stingeth like an adder.' Nothing could be truer than that."

"What is there in rum that makes it hurt people so?" continued James.

"There is alcohol in it, and it is that which makes

drunkards. It don't hurt any one to drink milk or water, does it?"

"Of course it don't."

"Well, there's the difference between these wholesome drinks and intoxicating liquors; there is no alcohol in the milk and water."

"What for do they put alcohol into them, if it hurts people?"

Mrs. Garfield explained the last question as best she could, assuring him that the alcohol was not put in, but was developed in the drink by an artificial process, and that men wanted to produce the alcohol in order to make money.

In this way the great reformatory idea of that day found a lodgment in the Garfield cabin. James did not obtain a very definite idea of the enormous evil of intemperance, living where he had no opportunity to observe it; but his idea was distinct enough to cause him to abhor the cause of the woe. His mother gave him facts enough respecting the curse of intemperance, that had come under her own observation, to show him that intemperance was a terrible evil, and his young heart was fully resolved to avoid the way to it.

Another lesson that made Sunday in the woods a memorable day to James, although it was prominent on other days also, was loyalty to the country. Mrs. Garfield's memory was full of facts respecting the sacrifices and sufferings of her ancestors to defend and preserve American Independence; and many an hour, as we have already intimated, was whiled away in recitals of their heroic deeds.

There is no doubt that James formed an exalted

idea of what we call LOYALTY from these stories that were so inspiring and marvellous to the young. It is often the case that indirect methods fasten upon the young mind so tenaciously that they outlast many lessons that have been imparted with the utmost care and hopefulness. It is certain that James derived an impulse from some source, in regard to loyalty, that contributed to make this virtue one of the most prominent elements of his character in manhood. Although his mother did not formally imitate the example of the father of Hannibal, who led his son to the altar of his divinity at eight years of age, and made him swear eternal hate to the enemies of Rome, yet she did what was tantamount to that, and what secured as effectually the devotion of her son to the defence of his country.

"Never be afraid to do what is right," Mrs. Garfield remarked. "The biggest coward in the world is the man who is afraid to do right."

"I shouldn't think men would be afraid to do right," remarked James.

"I shouldn't think *boys* would be afraid to do right," responded his mother, perceiving that James scarcely thought there was an opportunity for this sort of bravery in boyhood. "Boys don't dare to do right, sometimes."

"When?" inquired James, as if he questioned the truth of the latter statement.

"When they don't dare to obey their mothers or teachers because their companions don't want they should," answered his mother, intending to remind him of certain facts in his own boyish life.

"I thought you meant when I got to be a man," said James, with a look denoting that he was *hit.*

"I meant when a boy, as well. If you don't begin to stand up for the right when you are young, you never will when you are old. 'The boy is father of the man,' is a proverb as true as it is old. Then a cowardly boy is as contemptible as a cowardly man. Obey your mother and teacher, though all your companions laugh at you."

"I do," answered James.

"Yes, I think you do, generally; and I speak of it now, that you may give even more attention to it in the future than in the past, and grow more and more fearless to oppose wrong as you grow older. When you become a man you will meet with many more, and greater temptations, than you have now, and unless you have more decision and courage you will not be equal to the circumstances."

"Daniel's bravery got him into the den of lions," suggested James.

"Very true; and it was better for him to be in a den of lions, with God on his side, than a friend of the king, with God against him. If you are like Daniel in moral courage, I shall be satisfied. The lions could not devour him so long as God was his friend; and God is always the friend of those who stand by the right."

James never had other than royal lessons upon moral courage and kindred qualities. These things, which lie at the very foundation of stability of character and personal excellence, were ingrained into his early life. The Sabbath furnished a favorable opportunity for special efforts in this direction, though every day in the week bore witness in the same line.

We must not close this chapter without reference to one fact connected with the Garfield family that is worthy of particular attention. It was their "coat-of-arms." A coat-of-arms formerly was a "habit worn by knights over their armor. It was a short-sleeved coat or tunic, reaching to the waist, and embroidered with their armorial ensigns and various devices." The Garfield coat-of-arms consisted of a shield, with a gold ground, three horizontal crimson bars crossing it in one corner, over it a helmet with raised visor, together with a heart, and above the whole an arm wielding a sword, on which was inscribed the motto, *In cruce vinco* — "IN THE CROSS I CONQUER."

What we wish to say about this coat-of-arms relates to the motto. It tells of a courage that was born of faith in God, such as was found in the Ohio cabin, and without which the sorrows and hardships that invested its early history would have proved too much for flesh and blood. It is a grand spirit to brood over a human habitation, beneath whose roof childhood buds and blossoms into true life. It appropriates the Sabbath, Bible, and every other hallowed power that is accessible, to the "life that now is," because of another "life that is to come." It was this spirit that James nursed from his mother's breast, and inhaled from the domestic atmosphere that wrapped his boyhood, to arouse heroic qualities, and bend them to victorious work.

When James was about ten years old, his uncle, Amos Boynton, organized a congregation in the school-house, and took charge of it himself, when no minister was on the ground. Mr. Boynton was a man of excellent abilities, and a very devoted Christian man. He was more familiar with the Bible than any man in the township, and could repeat large portions of it. A copy of the Scriptures was his constant companion. He carried it with him into the field. If he stopped to rest himself, or his cattle, the brief time was spent in reading the Book of books. His familiarity with the Bible qualified him to conduct Sabbath services in the log school-house; and they were of great moral and spiritual advantage to the people. To James they were of as much real value as to any one.

At that time religious controversy ran high in northern Ohio. The Disciples were a new sect, and all other sects denounced them; while they, in turn, expressed themselves freely concerning the errors and follies of their opponents. James often heard discussions at home upon these controverted religious questions, in which his mother engaged with others. It was not unusual for preachers to refer to them in their sermons; and always, when preachers stayed at his mother's house, as they often did, these questions were discussed, and they made a deep impression upon the active mind of James. So bright a boy as he could scarcely fail to see that vast importance attached to subjects in which the ministers and his mother were so much interested. These controversies lent more or less importance to Sunday in the woods.

Among the topics discussed was Baptism, the

Disciples being immersionists. The extent to which James' mind was impressed by these discussions is learned from the following fact. Considerable political excitement prevailed in that part of Ohio in the "Harrison Campaign." The neighbors were all for Harrison,—Whigs,—and James had heard his mother say that his father was a Whig, and a great admirer of Henry Clay, and voted for him when he was a candidate for President. One day some neighbors were discussing politics in James' presence, when one of them asked him, in a sportive way, "Jimmy, what are you, Democrat or Whig?"

"I'm Whig; but I'm not *baptized*," answered James.

The subject of Baptism was so thoroughly impressed upon his mind, and the subject of Whigism, also, that the little fellow supposed he could not be a properly constructed Whig until he was baptized.

CHAPTER VII.

HIGHER UP.

ALLOO, Jim, now you will have to be a farmer in earnest! for I am going to Michigan," said Thomas, when he returned from Cleveland. "Got a place out there."

"Where?" inquired James, not understanding where it was that his brother was going.

"To Michigan," repeated Thomas. "It is more of a wilderness than Orange is."

"I know that," answered James. "What are you going to do out there?"

"Clearing," replied Thomas; "twelve dollars a month."

"You don't get so much as that, do you?" said James, to whom that amount of monthly wages seemed enormous.

"Yes, twelve dollars a month. It's hard work, early and late. Mother shall have a frame-house, now."

"Good!" was James' answer, given with evident satisfaction.

At this time James was twelve years old, and Thomas was twenty-one; a period that had been much discussed in the family, in anticipation of its arrival. There was a definite understanding, between Thomas and his mother, that the former should leave home at twenty-one, and James should run the farm. It was important that Thomas should be earning something abroad now that he had attained to his majority, and James was old enough to attend to affairs at home. Thomas went to Cleveland for the purpose of obtaining work, without any definite idea of what that work would be. Emigration to Michigan was increasing, and there was considerable excitement over the resources of that State, so that labor was in considerable demand for that section. The first opportunity that opened to Thomas he accepted without hesitation, and it was, as already announced, clearing land for a farmer in Michigan, at twelve dollars a month.

Thomas passed into the house with James to make known the result of his errand to Cleveland.

"I hope it will prove all for the best," remarked Mrs. Garfield, after hearing the report. "It's farther away than I expected."

"Yes, it is some distance; but that is of little consequence, after all. It is good pay."

"How far is it?" asked James, who was intensely interested in the change.

"I don't know exactly," answered his mother: "it's farther than I wish it was."

"Will you live in a log-house, Tom?" James continued.

"Yes; a cabin not half so large and good as this."

"How long shall you be gone?"

"Six months certain; perhaps longer."

"And you will have to take Tom's place on the farm," said Mrs. Garfield, addressing James. "That will be taking a step higher."

"I can do it," responded James, "though I am sorry Tom is going."

"We shall miss him sadly," remarked Mrs. Garfield. "It will be more lonesome than ever when he is gone; but we must make the best of it."

"It will be best all round, I am thinking," said Thomas, "if it is the way for you to have a frame-house, mother. I mean that shall come about."

"That will be nice, won't it, mother?" exclaimed James, who was thoroughly prepared to appreciate a real house, after twelve years' occupancy of a cabin.

"Yes, it will be nice indeed, almost too nice to prove a reality," replied his mother.

"It will prove a reality," remarked Thomas with decision.

Thomas had spent much time, during the last five years, in cutting and preparing lumber for a new house, hoping the time would come when his mother could command money enough to employ a carpenter to erect it. He had prepared sufficient lumber for the house when he became twenty-one years of age; but there was no money to pay a carpenter to put it up. Now Thomas saw the way clear for erecting the house after a while, and the prospect fired his ambition. He was willing to go to Michigan for that object alone; indeed, he rejoiced to go, if by so doing a frame-house could be secured.

Thomas was busy preparing to leave, and James was equally busy in attending to lessons that Thomas gave him about the work to be done on the farm. The ground was to be ploughed, the wheat sowed, the corn and potatoes planted, with all the etceteras usually belonging to the season's labor. Thomas had his directions to give concerning all these things, that his little brother might the more successfully perform farm-work. However, his time at home was limited, as his engagement required him to be in Michigan at an early date; and soon he was gone.

It was almost like making another grave in the corner of the wheat-field to part with Thomas. He had been the main stay of the family since the death of his father, and his mother had leaned upon him as mothers will upon a noble son; and now to miss his face and voice, and miss his counsels and labors, created a void in the home circle that brought tears to the eyes of all. It was a trying hour for James, to whom Thomas was both brotherly and fatherly. The most tender and loving confidence existed between the two. Thomas was proud of his gifted little brother, and James had perfect confidence in his efficient big brother. It was not strange, therefore, that James felt the absence of Thomas deeply, and deplored the necessity that compelled him to leave home. Nevertheless, he went to work upon the farm with a will. He knew how to labor, because he had labored much with Thomas for four years, and was often called the "boy-farmer;" but now he was a farmer in a more important sense, and must rely upon his own judgment, plans, and efficiency to a great extent. He was much higher up than before in the matter of care and responsibility.

Here, as well as anywhere, we may describe the scenery about the Garfield estate, for that may have had an important influence upon the life and character of James. He was the sort of boy who delights in beauty and grandeur, to whom a river, mountain, or wild forest was more attractive than they often are to older heads. A person reared in the locality describes the scenery as follows: —

"Orange township is situated in the south-eastern portion of Cuyahoga County, fifteen miles from Cleveland. It is now, and always has been, strictly a farming town. There is no village within its limits.

"Its surface is irregular and hilly, presenting some of the finest rural scenery to be found in this part of Ohio. On the north-east flows the Chagrin River, from which the land gradually rises towards the south-west for a distance of three miles. Looking east from this range of hills a grand view is obtained. The valley of the Chagrin, with its simple beauty, and the country for twenty miles beyond, are distinctly visible. All combine to form a picture that is strong, charming, and impressive. It was to a spot south of this chain of hills that the parents of General Garfield came in 1830."

We should have said that at this time, the "Western land speculation" was running high. People grew wild over the prospect of coining money out of the wild lands of Ohio, Michigan, Indiana, and Illinois. Men at the East bought thousands of acres of land in the West, that they never saw, and did not positively know that such land existed. Hundreds and thousands of people sold houses and lands in New England

and in the Middle States, and removed thither, to make their fortunes. Perhaps Thomas cherished a secret hope that somehow he should become a rich man in the woods of Michigan. It is certain that the opportunity to labor in that State came to him through the "Western land mania." We will leave him there, felling trees and clearing land for the Michigan farmer, while we look after James at home.

"Well, your farmer boy is making things lively," remarked a neighbor, who called upon Mrs. Garfield. "He's as handy as any of us with his tools."

"And works as hard, I guess," responded Mrs. Garfield.

"That is so; all of us work hard enough," rejoined the neighbor.

"Pioneer life is beset with hardships," continued Mrs. Garfield; "though its poverty is not so hard to be borne as poverty in a large town or city."

"Do you really think so?"

"Certainly I do."

"What makes you think so?"

"Why, don't you see that there are no rich around us to be compared with? We are not continually being reminded of our extreme poverty by the presence of those who can have all that money can buy."

"You think there is some satisfaction in all being poor together?" interrupted the neighbor, jocosely.

"Yes; that is about it. 'Misery loves company,' and I suppose that is true of poverty."

"Well, we are all poor enough, if that is all," continued the neighbor; "and on your theory we ought to be tolerably happy."

"We are, I think, as happy as the human race averages, and perhaps a little more than that. God averages human experience well, after all our fault-finding."

"There must be some satisfaction in thinking so; but I can't exactly accept that view. Pioneers have more than their full share of hardships and trials, in my opinion," replied the neighbor, just as James came in from the corn-field. Turning to him, by way of cordial salutation, he added,

"What do you think about it, James?"

"Think about what?"

"Whether pioneers have more hardships than other people?"

"I don't know much about it," answered James. "If I knew what hardships other people have I could tell something about it; but I don't."

James never spoke a truer word. He was born and reared in the forest. He had never seen even a village, much less a large town or city. He had seen but one or two frame-houses at that time; and these had just been erected in the vicinity. How could he understand that others enjoyed more than he did? He was a happy boy. He had his home, though it was a cabin. He had his mother, and brother, and sisters, and they were just as dear to him as home and brothers and sisters are to those who dwell in palaces. Perhaps they were more so: we incline to the belief that they were. He had a mother; and if any mother was ever worth more to a child than his was he did not know it, nor could he be made to believe any such thing So he was a contented boy. What other people, more highly blest, called hardships, he accepted as a matter of course. He scarcely knew that it was not as good as others enjoyed. Why should he not be a rollicking, wide-awake, happy boy? Hard work challenged his best endeavors now that his brother was gone; but hard work is not necessarily a hardship. Some rich men work more hours in a day to keep their money, than the poor man does to keep soul and body together. And often it is more annoying labor, straining the nerves, banishing sleep, fretting the disposition, and keeping up a continual fever of anxiety.

James did not call hard work hardship; he never thought of such a thing. He was never happier than he was during that season of severe toil after his brother left home. He had greater responsibility, but responsibility is not hardship. He felt more manly and competent; and he was both, now that the care of the farm and his mother rested on his shoulders. A close observer could see the honest pride of a noble heart cropping out through his manly bearing. Call it hardship to run the farm! He never dreamed of it; it was his delight. The language of singing expressed his daily experience far better than complainings. Under his homely jacket nestled a spirit that had not learned discontent. No! Neighbor Mapes put his question to the wrong party, when he said,—

"What do you think about it, James?"

James was not the passenger to awake. Break the slumbers of somebody who is happy only when he is asleep. James was happiest when he was awake, as mortals everywhere should be. And he never was more wide awake than he was on the farm during that season of excessive labor.

"Going to exchange work with Mr. Lamper," said James one day to his mother.

"How so?" inquired his mother.

"He wants an extra hand once in a while, and so do I; and then I want his oxen sometimes."

"You have seen him?"

"Yes; and have made the bargain."

"A good arrangement, I guess," added his mother. "Then, his head is older than yours, and he can show you some things about farming that you don't know."

"And 'Two heads are better than one, if one is a sheep's head,' I have heard you say a good many times," added James, in his lively way.

"If they are *pioneer* heads, it is so," rejoined his mother, whose opinion of pioneer life was more favorable than that of neighbor Mapes. "Pioneer life requires all the wisdom that can be got together to make life in the woods successful."

This reference to "life in the woods" was partly in a vein of pleasantry; for now the designation was scarcely appropriate. Nearly fourteen years had elapsed since Mrs. Garfield moved into that township, and great changes had been wrought in that time. Many settlers had moved into the township, and the unbroken forests had yielded to the pioneer's axe, and well-conducted farms dotted the landscape. Neighbors were near and many now, as compared with the distance and number of them ten years before. The pioneer stage had really passed, and it was not "life in the woods" that James was living. There was a saw-mill and an ashery in the vicinity; also a carpenter was added to the population of the town. All this brought a change that James, young as he was, could but notice.

The plan of exchanging work was one that James originated, and it proved of great value to him during the season. It lightened his labor when "Two heads were better than one," and gave him the use of the oxen when no other aid could be half so valuable. Then Mr. Lamper was glad to exchange labor with a boy who was equal to a man in his efficiency. James could turn his hand to any sort of work upon the farm, and had physical strength to endure almost any strain. His honest pride of character assisted him, too, more than ever in his work, as any sharp observer could see.

We cannot dwell upon the labors of that eventful season, except to add, that the farm did for James what a teacher did for some other boys. The celebrated engineer, and inventor of the locomotive engine, George Stephenson, said that he studied mechanics with his engine instead of a professor. Indeed, the engine was his professor, and taught him daily the most important lessons. He was eighteen years of age, and was running the engine in a colliery. On Saturday afternoons, when the workmen were released from labor, and were spending their time in rum-shops, or attending dog-fights, George took his engine to pieces, and cleaned and studied it. He could neither read nor write, but he could understand and appropriate the silent lessons of his engine; and these made him the renowned inventor of the locomotive. Well might he call the engine his teacher.

James might have called the farm his teacher. It taught him many excellent lessons. He extracted the most valuable knowledge from its soil. He evoked inspiring thoughts from its labor. His manhood developed under its rigid discipline. His mind enlarged its mental grasp. The season spent in the log school-house could not have pushed him higher up than did his experience on the farm. It was positive proof that work is discipline as much as study, and that it can do for boys, often, more than study to qualify them for the stern duties of life. James was more of a man at the close of that season than he was at the beginning of it.

He had little time to read during those months; and yet he never valued reading more. He was never more hungry for knowledge than he was during that period of constant labor. He thought much of going to school; and often the thought would force itself upon his mind, how can I get an education? Not that he formed any definite plan concerning it, or even considered that such a thing was possible; but the vague thought would sometimes arise. And then his mother frequently dropped remarks which showed the strong desire of her heart, that James might, at some future time, she knew not how or when, become a scholar. That such a boy should spend his life in tilling the earth appeared to her like wasting pearls.

"James, I hope that you will not always have to work on a farm." How often she remarked thus.

"What would you do if I shouldn't?" was James' thoughtful reply.

"I hardly know. 'It is not in man that walketh to direct his steps,' and I am glad of it. There is my hope, that some day you can get an education."

"I should like to, if it is best."

"I know it will be best, if you can do it. You can never know too much."

"I guess that is so," replied James, half humorously. "I couldn't ever know too much to work on a farm. There is more to learn about it than I could learn in many years."

"That is true, no doubt; but I have a strong desire that you should become a scholar; and sometimes the desire is so strong that I feel as if I could not be denied."

"I don't feel so."

"Wouldn't you like to study, and become a scholar?"

"Why, yes, I should like nothing better; but how can I do it?"

"I don't know, and that is what troubles me, though I ought not to be troubled. I know that God will open the way, if it is best, and I ought to leave it there; but, somehow, I can't help having anxiety about it."

"Well, it can't be at present," added James, as if perfectly satisfied with his situation.

Thus James was led on, and his mother, too, not knowing whither Providence was guiding them. James was going up higher all the while, although it scarcely seemed so to his doting mother. The Lord was laying a deeper foundation than could have been laid if she had had her own way. "A man's heart deviseth his way, but the Lord directeth his steps."

CHAPTER VIII.

BOY CARPENTER.

OM is coming!" was the shout Mrs. Garfield heard, as she caught sight of James bounding across the garden. "Tom is coming!" louder yet. One would have thought the boy had suddenly lost his reason, judging by his antics.

Sure enough! Looking from the cabin door she saw Thomas approaching, and James had already reached him in his pleasurable excitement. If James was glad to get hold of Thomas' hand, Thomas was equally rejoiced to get hold of James. The greeting was mutual and hearty. The big brother and the little brother made for the house, hand in hand, their tongues running glibly all the while.

"Are we going to have a frame-house now?" asked James, almost the first thing.

"Yes, we'll have a frame-house now, and let the hens keep house in the cabin," replied Thomas.

"It's just about good enough for them," remarked James in response. "It will make a good hen-house."

"Rather better accommodations than they have had," Thomas added; "and will compare well with our quarters when the house is done."

By this time mother and son stood face to face, James shouting:

"Going to have the frame-house now, mother!"

Mrs. Garfield found that she was a good deal like James, and when she saw that her Thomas was certainly coming, she forgot everything else, and hastened to meet him,—not as wildly as James, but very much as all fond mothers will do when they have not seen their good sons for seven months. She went across the house-lot at double-quick, and soon had hold of the big boy as firmly as he had hold of her. It was a glad meeting. Mothers and sons who dwell in palaces scarcely know what a luxury it was. Why, it more than paid for the long separation. The meeting paid principal and interest in full. The family were united again,—girls, boys, and mother,—one girl rather big now, twenty-three years old; and Thomas almost twenty-two, just the age of his father when the latter was married. Happy family!

They were hardly seated in the cabin, when Thomas flung a handful of gold into his mother's lap, saying:

"Now you can have a frame-house;" and the noble young man seemed to be perfectly satisfied, now that he was able to give his mother a better home. "We'll go about it at once."

"My! what a lot!" was James' exclamation when he saw the shining gold; and he proceeded to examine the treasure in his mother's lap.

"How much is there, Tom?" he asked.

"Seventy-five dollars, just."

"And you earned it all?"

"Every cent of it."

James read aloud the inscriptions on the new, bright coin, while he handled it in amazement that his own brother could make such a "pile." Things had not been conducted on a gold basis in that cabin, so that it was a new spectacle that suddenly broke upon James' delighted vision. He had not seen *gold* coin before, nor had he dreamed that such an article could come out of the Michigan woods. It is not strange, therefore, that the backwoods boy was considerably elated over the sight. What a mint was to him later, that seventy-five dollars in gold was to him then.

"Why don't you say something, mother?" exclaimed James, no doubt expecting that his mother would be as gushing as himself over the gold. The fact was, she could not have said anything if she had tried. What mother could in the circumstances? That great boy, as old as his father was when she became his bride, coming home with such proof of his filial love! Thinking of his mother more than he did of himself! Happy only in helping her! Who wonders that she sat mute as a marble statue? There was no language for such an occasion. All the Noah Websters in the world could not provide words for such a moment. A mother's heart, at such a time, defies expression. At least it was so with mother Garfield's heart. It could have taken that strapping son to itself, and folded him like a baby again, and covered him over with kisses, which would have been only a figure of speech, but language was out of the question. James saw the point as soon as her tears dropped upon the gold coin. He could not exactly understand it, though, for *he* felt like hurrahing instead of crying, and he knew that his mother was glad that she could have a frame-house, for he had often heard her express a wish of that kind. So he could not quite understand it. Readers! it was because he was like all the rest of the boys and girls — they do not understand the mystery of a mother's love.

The excitement of the hour passed, however, and the equilibrium of feeling and daily duties was re stored.

"I'm off again, mother, as soon as I get you into the new house," said Thomas. "There's plenty of work in Michigan, and I must be doing it."

"Well, you must manage it to suit yourself. I suppose that Mr. Treat can be had at any time to put the house up." Mr. Treat was the carpenter.

"I will find out. I can work with him, and we'll make a quick job of it."

"I'll work, too," said James. "I can carry boards, drive nails, and do other things."

"You can draw the sand, too, Jimmy," replied Thomas.

"Sand! What do you do with sand?" exclaimed James, forgetting that mortar was necessary. It was excusable, however, since he was familiar only with mud, that made the log-house tight.

"To make mortar with, of course; we must have mortar for plastering," Thomas answered. "I can get lime, brick, nails, and windows at Cleveland."

"And you'll take me along with you, I s'pose," suggested James.

"Yes; I can chuck you in most anywhere. Per haps I shall need your help."

James had not been to Cleveland, at that time. It was but a small place, of about a thousand inhabitants, though growing rapidly.

"How long will you be gone to Cleveland?" inquired James.

"One day only; can't spare any more time. A long day, perhaps."

"When shall you go?"

"Just as soon as I have engaged Mr. Treat."

Mr. Treat was seen and engaged at once, and Thomas and James made the trip to Cleveland for windows, nails, etc. Bricks were obtained subsequently, without going to Cleveland.

A few days only elapsed before the carpenter and Thomas were at work on the new house. James, too, was not a mere spectator. He was far more interested in the erection of the house than he would have been in a circus. It was an era in his life. All the spare moments he could snatch from the farm-work and care of the stock he devoted to the new house. He had drawn the sand before the carpenter began to frame the building.

"Here, Jimmy, I see you want to help," said Mr. Treat. "Just take this chisel and mallet, and put this mortise through as you have seen me do the others. I guess you can do it."

"Yes, I can do that," James answered, elated with the idea of being able to render assistance; and with mallet and chisel the mortise was hurried through.

"Give us another," exclaimed James, proud of his achievement.

"What!" responded Mr. Treat, "got that done so quick?"

"Yes, all done; look at it," answered James.

"And well done, too," said Mr. Treat, examining the mortise. "Pretty good for a boy."

"Can I do another?" continued James.

"Yes, a dozen if you want to;" and the carpenter started him on another mortise, and after that another, and another, until he had completed the sixth.

"You must try your hand at planing now," said Mr. Treat. "A small boy to shove a plane, but I guess you can do it. Here (arranging a board on his bench), try this, and see how you make it."

At that time planing machines were unknown, at least in that part of the country; all the planing was done by hand. In the newly-settled townships, like Orange, also, less planing was done; more rough boards were used. The frame-houses were of rude construction, having no particular style or comeliness, — just a comfortable place to live in, more comfortable and pleasant than log-cabins. Many of them could boast only of a single room below, — parlor, sitting-room, kitchen, and wash-room, all in one, — the second story remaining unfinished, and used for lodging, being divided into apartments by curtains. It was very little labor and small expense to erect such a dwelling. Others were somewhat more elaborate, having two, and even three rooms below, with sleeping-rooms finished above. The Garfield house contained three rooms below, and two above, unfinished. Hence, seventy-five dollars was ample to buy nails, bricks, lime, and other necessary articles, and to pay the carpenter in addition.

James went on with the planing very readily, for he had watched both Mr. Treat and Thomas in this part of the work until he comprehended the "knack," as the carpenter called it. As we have already said, his sharp observation was equal to a teacher, and it made him master of many things that he never could have known without this faculty. Captain Samuel Brown, a bridge-builder, lived on the banks of the Tweed, across which he desired to build a bridge. While he was studying the subject, he chanced to walk in his garden early one fine morning, when his attention was arrested by a spider's-web across his path. A careful examination of the web suggested to him the idea of a suspension-bridge, constructed by the use of iron ropes or chains, as the spider had built his light bridge. No indifferent gazer would take the hint of a suspension-bridge from the web of a spider, but sharp, discriminating observation took the hint.

James' keen observation enabled him to build many suspension-bridges over impassable places in his boyhood and youth, and, in comparison with some of them, his success with carpenter's tools is scarcely worth mentioning.

"I like this," said James, as he turned over the well-planed board to the carpenter, "*it's* fun!"

"You will not find much *fun* in it when you have kept at it all day," replied the carpenter. "It takes elbow-grease to do this work well."

"Elbow-grease!" repeated James; "what's elbow-grease?"

"It is *sweat*, that is pouring out of you now, Jimmy," the carpenter replied. "Can't do much at planing without putting sweat into it."

"Sweat alone won't run a plane," rejoined James, intimating to the carpenter that brains were needed as much as work.

"That is so," replied Mr. Treat; "but you understand what I mean. The most skilful workman will find hard labor in this business; and to do it well, he must be willing to sweat."

"If sweat is proof of doing it well, then the board is well planed, Mr. Treat, for I sweat enough," James added.

"You have done it well; I couldn't have done it better myself," replied Mr. Treat. "You were born to be a carpenter, I guess."

"I'd like to be one," interrupted James, "if I could be a good one."

"Well, you would make a good one, my boy, judging from the work you have done. Perhaps you will be a boss-carpenter before you are twenty-one. Who knows?"

"I couldn't be that without a chance," remarked James, intimating that a chance was scarcely possible for a boy in his circumstances.

"Of course not; but where there's a will there's a way."

"That's what mother says."

"And that is what overcomes difficulties," continued Mr. Treat. "But there are more boards (pointing to a pile on the ground) if you want to do more of this sort of work."

Another board was laid on the bench, and James continued to drive the plane for an hour and more. He was general errand-boy when he was about the building, so that he could not use plane or chisel long, without interruption. It was, "Go here," and "go there;" "get this," and "get that;" to all of which demands he cheerfully responded.

The raising of the house was a grand affair to James. It was the first house-raising he ever attended, and it was a great novelty. He was sent to notify the neighbors of the event on a given day, and to solicit their assistance. The neighbors were thoroughly glad that Mrs. Garfield was going to have a new house, and many were their praises of the son who thus provided for his worthy mother. They were promptly on hand at the time, and the frame went up without mistake or accident. And now came another treat for James. He had had his eye upon a keg of nails for some days, anticipating the highest kind of pleasure from driving them. It was sport for him to drive nails, as it is for boys generally, and he expected to have his fill of the fun.

"Now, Jimmy, you can try your hand at driving nails," said Mr. Treat, addressing the boy-carpenter. "That is pretty work, and won't require quite so much elbow-grease."

"I have a particular liking for driving nails," replied James; "where shall I begin?"

"Right here, where I have put in these two. Lay them just as I have laid these, and it will be right. See if you can 'hit the nail on the head;' some boys never can do it, and so they grow up to be men, and live and die, without ever 'hitting the nail on the head.'" Mr. Treat cast a knowing look at James as he said it, and a smile played over his face, as if curious to see how his figurative expression was taken.

"I can hit that sort of a nail on the head, if I can't any other," answered James, with a smile, understanding the drift of his figure of speech. And hastily he let drive his hammer at a nail, and missed it the first time, much to his chagrin.

"Missed the first blow!" exclaimed the carpenter, with a shout of laughter. "You didn't do that as well as you did the planing and mortising. How is that?"

"Only a blunder," James replied, with evident mortification.

"Well, see if you can strike again without blundering," responded Mr. Treat, laughing. "There's a 'knack' in driving nails as well as in planing boards. Just get the 'knack' of the thing, and it will go."

"Here goes the 'knack,' then," exclaimed James, as his hammer struck the nail squarely on the head. "The 'knack' it is, every time! Nails are made to drive, and I will drive them." And his hammer flew with unerring aim, as nail after nail was driven in, with a will that signified determination and force of character. Missing the first blow just set him on his feet, resolved that a steady aim and square hit should attend every blow that followed. He learned the lesson of carefulness and brave endeavor from his failure, so that he became more expert in the use of the hammer than he would have been otherwise.

Such is the case with all boys who win; a failure arouses their latent skill and energy, and they bid defiance to failures thereafter. In his youth, Curran, who became the famous Irish orator, broke down on his first attempt to speak in a debating society. He was a stammerer, and when he rose in his place his stuttering speech was worse than ever. He floundered at first, stammered out something nobody could understand, and then stood speechless. His companions roared with laughter. One said, in a low voice, "Orator Mum!" Another peal of laughter followed this new title; and it aroused the invincible spirit of the boy.

"You may laugh now," he shouted, finally, "but I will conquer this stammering tongue, and some day you will listen and commend." All of which came to pass exactly as prophesied. The gist of the matter was in him, and the mortifying failure served to bring it out.

"Nothing like being plucky," remarked Mr. Treat, when he witnessed James' success in driving nails. "Pluck wins when luck loses."

"Mother says there is no such thing as *luck*," responded James.

"Your mother is about right, according to my notion," answered Mr. Treat. "Boys that depend on luck for a livelihood go pretty hungry sometimes. I'd rather a boy of mine would have a single ounce of pluck than a whole pound of luck. Luck is like an old United States bank bill, of very uncertain value; but pluck is good as gold all the time."

"Well," said James, jocosely, "you must admit that my first blow was a very *unlucky* one."

"Unlucky! not in the least!" exclaimed Mr. Treat. "It was just what you said it was, 'a blunder,' and a blunder is neither lucky nor unlucky. But you have made amends, so go ahead with your nailing."

And James did go ahead, spending every moment possible in labor upon the new house, and acquiring facility in the use of tools that served him a good turn many years thereafter. To the last day's labor upon the house James rendered all the assistance he could, happy only in the thought that he could make himself useful. Nor was this the best part of the discipline. James received a kind of education when the house was building that proved of great advantage to him through life. Before the house was completed, he conceived the idea of making the carpenter's trade a source of profit. It was on his mind day after day, the last thing he thought of before falling asleep at night, and the first thing when he awoke in the morning. He divulged his purpose to no one, but pondered it for several months in his own heart. The family had removed into the new house, and Thomas had returned to Michigan, and James was manager of the farm-work.

"Mother," he said one day, when he could not keep his purpose a secret any longer, "I have a plan to earn some money."

"What is it?"

"To work at the carpenter's trade."

"I'm afraid that plan won't work."

"Why?"

"You have enough to do on the farm now, and you can't do both."

"I only meant to work at it when I had no work on the farm to do, — a job now and then."

"It will be difficult to find such jobs."

"Perhaps it will, but I can *try*, and you believe in *trying*." James emphasized the words *try* and *trying* because his mother often made the remark to her children, "There is nothing like *trying*."

"Yes, I believe in *trying* always, and you may *try* as hard as you please to find a job."

"I'm going to Mr. Treat; perhaps he may have a job at planing or something of the kind. I want to earn some money for you as well as Thomas. I will go to Michigan when I am old as he is."

"One son in Michigan is enough, I think. Besides, I hope the day will come when you can be more useful than you can be in chopping wood or planing boards."

"I don't know what there is better than such work, to help you."

"There is somebody else in the world to help besides me," replied his mother, earnestly; "and I don't want you to feel that you are always to be bound to this little township and farm."

"I don't expect to be bound to it always," retorted James; "but I am bound to get a job at carpentering this very day, if I can; and I am going over to see Mr. Treat."

Within less than an hour, James entered the carpenter-shop.

"Halloo, Jimmy! that you? How's your mother?" exclaimed Mr. Treat, in a very jolly way, as he was wont to do.

"She is well."

"Not much farming to do just now, I suppose?" continued Mr. T., inquiringly.

"No, not very much; and I came over to see you about some work."

"Ah, that's what brought you here! I see now; what sort of work do you want to do?"

"Your kind of work, of course; carpentering."

"All right, Jimmy! Glad to see there are no lazy oones in you. I hate lazy boys above all things, and I know that you don't belong to that class."

"I hope not," answered James; "I thought I might as well be earning a little something for mother, now Tom's gone, and so I came to see if you could give me a job."

"That's noble, to help your mother. Boys who stick to their mothers don't often make a failure, especially boys with such a mother as you have. You can't think too much of your mother. They are the boys I like to give a job to."

"Can you give me a job?" James interrupted, evidently thinking that Mr. Treat was making a pretty long story over the affair.

"Yes, my boy, I can, and I am right glad to do it, too. There is a pile of boards that I want planed, and I know that you can plane them well. I haven't forgot how you worked on the house."

"How much will you pay me?"

"One cent a board; and that will be pretty good pay."

"When do you want them done?"

"Just as soon as you can; the quicker the better."

"I will come to-morrow and begin."

"All right, sonny; begin to-morrow, and end when you please."

"You wouldn't like to have me keep the job on hand a month, would you?" replied James, pleasantly, thinking about the words "end when you please."

"You won't do that, Jimmy. I know that you will put it through just as soon as possible, and that will suit. When I said 'end it when you please,' I knew that you would please to end it as soon as you could. Your money is ready as soon as the job is done."

"I'll be on hand to-morrow, just as soon as I've done my chores," remarked James, and left.

It was a proud moment for James, and exultation beamed in his eye when he reached home, and reported his good fortune to his mother.

"It will be the first money I ever earned," said James.

"And you are pretty young to earn it," replied his mother. "I'm glad you have the job. I hardly thought you would find one."

"*Trying* brought it," responded James, with a very suggestive expression on his face.

"I guess Mr. Treat made the job on purpose for you; he is a great friend of yours," added Mrs. Garfield. "I know he would be glad to help you to all the jobs possible. When are you going to begin it?"

"To-morrow, early as I can."

"Well, be careful and not overwork. Two hours a day is as much as you ought to work at planing; three hours at most."

"I shall work *six* hours to-morrow, certainly,"

replied James. "I should laugh to see myself work two hours, and then cry 'baby,' and come home; and I guess Mr. Treat would laugh, too."

"I think Mr. Treat will agree with me exactly, that boys must not overwork; and you are so ambitious, James, that you will overwork before you know it, unless somebody warns you." Mrs. Garfield expressed just the opinion that every thoughtful parent would express. James had more energy and ambition than he had discretion, so that he was blind to the value of his mother's counsel.

"If you see me coming home to-morrow in two hours, or three, you may know that I've lost an arm or finished the job," remarked James, very suggestively. And here the conversation closed.

James went to his job the next day with more determination than ever, much as he had shown of this admirable quality before. If his mother looked into his eye, or observed his compressed lips, as he went out of the door, she must have been satisfied that three hours' planing would not satisfy his ambitious desires on that day. Mr. Treat gave him cordial words of welcome, in his jovial way, assuring him that the "early bird catches the worm," at the same time handing him a jack-plane. James stripped off his jacket and vest, leaving only his shirt and jean trousers to encumber him. He was bare-footed, of course, as the luxury of shoes could not be afforded, except in the winter. He was scarcely tall enough to work handily at the bench, but he seemed to straighten himself up one or two inches taller than usual for the occasion. He went to work like a man. Every board was twelve feet long; and by the time he had planed ten of them his mind was fully made up to what nobody knew except himself. They found out, however, at night. All through the day the plane was shoved rapidly, and great beads of sweat stood upon the boy's brow, but no tired look invested his countenance for a moment. Before the sun went down he exclaimed, laying aside the plane, —

"One hundred boards, Mr. Treat, done! count them and see."

"Not a hundred, my boy, you don't mean that, do you?"

"Count them, and see; a hundred boards according to my count."

"A great day's work, if that is the case," said Mr. Treat, as he proceeded to count the boards.

"One hundred it is, surely," remarked Mr. Treat, completing the count. "Too much for a boy of your age and size to do in one day. I wouldn't advise you to do more than half that another day."

"I'm not much tired," said James.

"That is not the thing, my boy; thirty years from now you may feel tired from this day's labor more than you do now."

"If it takes as long as that to get tired, then the tired part is far off," responded James, not appreciating the wise remark of his employer.

"Well, now comes the best part of your day's work, the pay," remarked Mr. Treat. "Let us see; one hundred boards takes one hundred cents to pay for them; that is just one dollar! A great day's work for a boy-carpenter! Now, you count, and I'll count."

And he proceeded to count out one hundred cents, making quite a little pile of coin when the dollar, all in cents, was ready for James' pocket.

Reader, we might as well stop here as to proceed further with the history of that day's labor. It would be quite impossible to describe James' feelings to you, as he pocketed the one hundred cents and started for home. That old jacket never covered just such a breast as it did then. If we could only turn that bosom inside out, and have a full view of the boy's heart, we should learn what no writer can ever describe. It was a man's heart in a boy's breast. There was not room for it under the jacket. It swelled with inexpressible emotions, as ground-swells sometimes lift the ocean higher than usual. "*One hundred cents, all in one day!*" The more he thought of it on his way home the prouder grew the occasion. "Seventy-five days like that would yield him as much as Thomas brought home from Michigan!" The thought was too great for belief. That would not be half so long as Thomas was gone, and away from home, too. And so he thought and pondered, and pondered and thought, on his way home, his boyhood putting on manhood in more than one respect. He was "Great Heart," bare-footed and in jean trousers.

Whether James intended to ape Thomas or not, we cannot say; but, on reaching home, he unloaded the coppers into his mother's lap, saying, —

"Yours, mother."

"All that, James?"

"One hundred cents," was James' reply.

"What! earned a dollar to-day?"

"Yes; I planed a hundred boards."

By this time Mrs. Garfield became as dumb as she was over the seventy-five dollars that Thomas brought to her. There was some trouble in her throat, and the power of speech left her. She could not tell what she thought, nor how she felt. If her eldest son had made her cry with kindness, the youngest one was doing the best he could to imitate his example. The little son could be handled as the big one could not be, and so the dear, good mother folded him to her breast, as the only way to tell her love when the tongue was voiceless.

CHAPTER IX.

BARN-BUILDING.

JAMES' job at Treat's carpenter-shop introduced him into further business in that line. The winter school, however, intervened, and James attended it without the loss of a single day. The day after the school closed, Mr. Treat called.

"I'm after James," said he to Mrs. Garfield. "I have a barn to build for Mr. Boynton, and can give him a job before his farm work begins."

"That will suit him," replied Mrs. Garfield. "I think he likes that kind of work better than farming."

Just then James made his appearance.

"Young man, I'm after you," said Mr. Treat to him.

"For what?" asked James.

"Another job of work."

"Planing boards?"

"No. Better than that."

"What?"

"Building a barn for Mr. Boynton."

"I'd like that," said James; "I want to learn to build a barn myself."

"You can, easily. That's not much of a job."

"When do you want me?"

"Right off, — to-morrow, if you can."

"To-morrow it is, then."

"With other work I have in the shop I can keep you at it until farming begins."

"That will just suit me. Shall I work by the day?"

"Yes, by the day, if you will. I'll give you not less than forty cents a day, nor more than fifty, according as you get along with it."

"I'll be satisfied with that, and will be on hand to-morrow morning," James answered, as Mr. Treat was leaving.

"'Nothing like trying,' mother," said James, after the carpenter was gone, repeating her old, familiar saw. "I shouldn't have got this job if I hadn't tried for one, last fall."

"Very likely not," replied his mother; "and you would not have had this, if you had not done the first one so well. Nothing like doing things well; always remember that."

"It's almost equal to *trying*, isn't it?" added James, roguishly.

"Perhaps it is more than equal to it. They who do their work well, are the ones who get work. People don't want botchers about."

"What are botchers? Blunderers?"

"Those who don't do their work well — they are botchers. Your father used to say, 'What's worth doing at all, is worth doing well,' and he was about right. Another thing he used to say was, 'If you know a thing, know it certainly.'"

"I don't see how a person can really know anything without knowing it certainly," remarked James. "If I know anything, I know it."

"Sometimes you know a lesson better than you do at other times, do you not?" answered his mother.

"That may be; but if I don't know a lesson certainly, I don't know much about it," replied James. "I should be ashamed not to know a lesson certainly."

"I hope you always will be," remarked his mother; "and what is more, I hope you will always be ashamed not to do your work thoroughly."

"I mean to learn how to frame a barn," said James.

"I should think you might learn that easy enough," responded Mrs. Garfield. "It's true I don't know much about it, but it doesn't appear to me to be very difficult to learn to frame a barn."

"I know that I can learn how," added James.

"Mr. Treat will give you a good chance to learn how, I think, if you tell him what you want."

"I shall do that." And James did do it. As soon as he commenced work the next day, he made known his wishes.

"Mr. Treat, I want to learn how to frame a barn," he said. "Can't I learn?"

"Most too much of a youngster for that business," answered Mr. Treat; "but you can have the chance. Just keep your eyes open to see how the work is laid out, and it is easy enough."

"Well, I can do that; my eyes are usually open in the daytime," said James, naïvely.

"And you must see with your brain as well as with

your eyes, if you would learn," added Mr. Treat. "You see how that is, don't you?"

"I see."

"You must have a little idea of the plan to begin with, though;" and Mr. Treat proceeded to exhibit his plan to the boy, explaining it to him as well as he could. James took in the principal idea in the outset, and proceeded to assist in framing the building with increased intelligence. An examination of the plan showed him that it was more necessary for his "brains to see" the why and wherefore than he had supposed. But Mr. Treat was deeply interested in teaching the boy, and so kept him at work directly under his eye. He directed his attention both to the plan and the frame, that he might learn the real use of the former to the carpenter.

"Can't do anything without a plan," remarked Mr. Treat one day, to James.

"How is it about milking?" asked James facetiously.

"It is true in milking, my boy. By *plan* I mean *system*, and you can't milk without system. About such a time, morning and night, you milk the cows, and that systematic way enables you to accomplish other work more successfully. Then, too, the cows, give more milk by milking them systematically."

"I didn't know that," said James, surprised that cows would give more milk by systematic milking.

"It is true, whether you knew it or not," remarked Mr. Treat. "Even the Lord would make a failure in running this world without system. The fact is, Jimmy, you have to run your farm on God's plan, or it won't run at all. If you should plant two kernels of corn where God means that only one shall grow, you would have your labor for your pains. You can raise no corn in that way. You could raise a plenty of stalks, but mighty little corn. Hens would starve to death in such a corn-field. If you should sow two bushels of wheat where there should be only one bushel, on the Lord's plan, your biscuit would be pretty small next winter."

James laughed at this eccentric way of putting things, and, at the same time, he received some very valuable ideas from the sensible carpenter, who continued, very much in the same vein:

"'A place for everything, and everything in its place,' is an old adage, and just as true as Genesis. The men who obey this rule are the men who succeed; and the men who never mind it are the ones who go to smash. I've seen that over and over. There's no use trying to run things on the line of disorder and confusion; they'll get upset, sure. No man can amount to much in this world except on system. Remember that, Jimmy, and you will come out all right."

"You mean a time to study, and a time to work, and a time to play?" inquired James.

"That's it; only I should cut the time to play pretty short," replied Mr. Treat. "Not much time to play in Ohio, when we have all that we can do to make the ends meet. 'All play and no work makes Jack a dull boy,' they say, and I guess 'tis true. But, look here, have we got this right?" (springing up to examine his work). "I have been so busy talking that I didn't stop to think what I was about. All talking and careless work will make a botch of it."

The work was found all right and in a good state of progress. And now in silence the labor went on for an hour or two, James minding his P's and Q's, and the carpenter keeping an eye on his plan and his work.

We must state the upshot of this barn-building in a word, as space is dwindling away. The barn was completed according to the contract, and without a break from the start. Perhaps James could not have framed a barn without assistance when the building was completed, but he learned a great deal about the carpenter's trade while he worked upon it. Evening after evening he studied over it alone. He drew a plan of his own, and studied it hour after hour, in order to learn how to frame a barn. With the same persistent efforts by which he mastered a problem in arithmetic, he studied his plan of framing a building; and although he did not become master of the art, he, nevertheless, approximated to it. When the barn was completed Mr. Treat paid James fifty cents a day, amounting to nearly twenty dollars, saying, —

"You've earned it, every cent of it, James."

During the previous winter, James made great progress in his studies, by improving the long evenings. He had learned about all he could learn in the district school, although he continued to go in the winter time. In some things he was more advanced than his teacher, and often put questions which the teacher could not answer. He mastered Adams' Arithmetic during the winter. Lying flat on the floor, that the light of the fire might shine on his book, he studied arithmetic every evening for weeks, until he had learned all there was to learn in it, and he was really more competent to teach that science than the man who presided over the district school. The scholars said that James actually performed a problem, one day, that had proved too much for their teacher, much to the mortification of the latter.

"I think the answer in the book must be wrong," remarked the teacher, after an ineffectual attempt to solve the problem for a class. "You may try it, Henry, and when you are through, bring me the slate."

Henry Boynton was good in arithmetic, but he could not bring an answer like that in the book, though it differed from the teacher's answer.

"I can't do it," said Henry. "My answer is not like that in the book."

"Bring your slate to me," said the teacher.

Henry carried his slate to the teacher, who examined his work without pointing out an error, but added,

"The answer in the book must be wrong."

Here James interrupted by saying, —

"I did it once."

"And did you get the same answer as the book?"

"Yes, sir, I think so."

"Let me see you do it, and then bring your slate to me."

James went to work in his earnest way, and solved the problem very readily.

"I've done it," said James, carrying his slate to the teacher.

The latter closely examined his solution of the problem, and found it to be correct, agreeing exactly with the text-book.

"It is true, James, you have performed it," said the teacher, with evident mortification, which the larger scholars enjoyed. It was fun for them to have James beat the master. They had an exalted opinion of James' abilities, and now he became their oracle. A boy who was a match for the master was a prodigy in their view. They looked up to him with a kind of reverence, though he was their companion.

We must not forget to mention one book that he read during that winter, "Robinson Crusoe." We know not how it came into his hands, but he obtained it in some way, and read it twice through. Flat on his face before the blazing fire, he read the volume hour after hour, and wondered over it. He was very fond of reading about adventures; but this book surpassed anything of the kind he had ever read.

"I wish this book belonged to me," he said to his mother, one day.

"If you read it much more, its contents will belong to you," his mother replied.

"I wish I *owned* it, then," added James.

"I wish you did, too," responded his mother "What is there about it that interests you so much, my son?"

"It's splendid," was James' answer. "I never read such an interesting book. I could read it ten times over, and not get tired of it. I wonder if there are any more books like it."

"I suppose there are, if we knew where to find them," Mrs. Garfield answered.

"I'd be willing to *hunt* one while for them," said James.

The impression made by that book upon his mind was never effaced. It not only sharpened his appetite yet more for reading, if that were possible, but it set him to inquiring more than ever concerning books which he had never seen.

Some time after this, his cousin, William Boynton, came into possession of a copy of Josephus, and he shared the pleasure of reading it with James. They read it, by the hour, together, and they read it separately, too, over and over. When the winter school opened, the boys asked the teacher for the privilege of reading it in the class, for their reading lesson; and the privilege was granted. All winter they read it in school, in addition to the hours they read it out of school. When James was through with that volume, and ready to take up another, he could repeat pages of it.

The following summer two incidents occurred that illustrate the character of James at that time. The first was a proposition from a companion, whose name we do not know, but whom we will call David, to visit a mutual acquaintance in a distant part of the township, on the Sabbath.

"Not on Sunday," said James.

"Why?"

"Because it is not right."

"If you and I do nothing worse than that, Jim, we shall be pretty good fellows."

"We should not be any better, certainly, for doing that."

"Nor any worse, in my opinion," rejoined David.

"My mother would not consent to it," continued James.

"I don't know whether mine would, and I don't care; I shan't ask her," said David.

"I never should go anywhere against my mother's advice," continued James. "I know what she thinks of the Sabbath, and I respect her feelings. I shan't go on Sunday."

"And you can't go on any other day, because you have so much to do," added David; "so we must give up going at all, for all that I see."

"Rather than go on Sunday, I shall not go at all," was James' emphatic reply. "But it is not certain that we can never go on another day. Wait and see."

"I guess it will be *wait*," answered David, sarcastically, "and keep waiting, and take it out in waiting."

"Well, I shall wait a good while before I shall go on Sunday," added James. "If I had no scruples of my own about it, I could take no comfort, feeling that I went against mother's wishes."

This emphatic refusal ended the matter. It was a fair illustration of the frank and open way that James had of doing things. There was no artifice about him, no double-dealing or deceitfulness. He would not consent to wrong-doing even to please his best friend. He never resorted to subterfuges to excuse himself when tempted to do wrong. He spoke right out plainly and bluntly, as if it were the only way to speak. Not that he seemed to have a higher standard of morality than others, but it was his nature to be frank and honest with every one, and he wanted others to be so towards him. Companions always knew just where to find him at all times. They knew that he could not be counted upon for question able practices at all. He was full of life, and enjoyed a good time as much as any boy in town, ready for a frolic at all suitable times, social, witty, and sharp; but he could not be persuaded or cajoled into wrong-doing. He showed his colors at once.

The other incident illustrates his kindness to animals. The old cat and James were particular friends, and appeared to understand each other perfectly. He was in the garden with James, one day, in whose society he seemed to find real pleasure. The same boy we have spoken of, David, came along, and observing the cat, began pelting him with stones, frightening puss so that he fled to the house. David might as well have pelted James with stones. Stone his cat, and he was stoned.

"That's outrageous," exclaimed James.

"Only a cat," answered David.

"Only *cruelty*, that will stone a cat," responded James.

"I didn't think it was your cat."

"It don't make any difference whose cat it is; a cat is a cat."

"And a rat is a rat," added David, designing to make fun of the affair.

"I can't bear to see an animal abused," continued James.

"I didn't hit him," pleaded David.

"No thanks to you; you meant to hit him. You frightened him half out of his wits."

"He hasn't any wits to be frightened out of," retorted David. "Nothing but a cat."

"And so you might abuse any animal in the world,

and say, 'Nothing but a dog;' 'Nothing but a horse;' 'Nothing but an ox.' I wouldn't abuse any creature so."

"I don't think you would, Jim. You are too tender-hearted for that. A mouse could play on your chin safely, if he only knew you."

"He wouldn't play on yours, Dave, if he knew *you*, that's certain. It would be the most dangerous place he could find."

"Well, Jim, ask pardon of your cat for me, will you! I'm sorry that I offended his majesty. I'll befriend cats forever, now." And David went on his way, leaving James to his reflections.

This was another good trait of James', kindness to animals. He was as kind to them as he was to human beings. He could see no reason for abusing any creature, however insignificant. Abuse was cruelty, in his view.

Still another incident may be rehearsed here as well as any place. James was a boy of spirit, though he was neither pugnacious nor malicious. He wanted to see the rights of the smallest boy respected, and he would contend for it if necessary. In school there was a fatherless boy like himself, and no big brother to take his part. Some of the larger boys were in the habit of teasing him, and James declared that it should stop. James was older than the boy, though not as old as the boys who teased him.

"It's too bad," exclaimed James; "and if you tease him any more you tease me."

"Tease you it is, then," answered one of the boys, with a motion and remark indicating the attempt.

"Just as you like," continued James. "You can operate on me, but you shan't on that little fellow unless you are stronger than I am. Take boys of your size, or none."

"You are mightily taken with that little chap," said another boy; "*I* don't see anything so very interesting about him."

"Well, I do; he has neither father nor big brother, and I'll stand in the place of both to him, in this school."

"Daddy Jim and Brother Jim it is, then," exclaimed a large boy, aiming to make all the fun of it possible.

"Yes, anything you please, so long as you don't run on him," answered James, pleasantly. "I can stand it as long as you can."

And thus he shamed the teasing of the little fellow out of the large boys, exhibiting both courage and principle in the defence of the helpless lad. Taking advantage of the weak, poor, and friendless, appealed to his higher and better nature, as it ever did.

November came, and the harvesting was done. The carpenter came, also, saying,

"Another barn, James. Want another job?"

"Yes, aching for one," James replied.

"All ready for you; can you begin right off?"

"To-morrow, if you want."

"You are a minute-man, I see."

"I s'pose I am, though I don't know what that is."

"Men, in the Revolution, who stood ready to defend their country at a moment's warning, were minute-men."

"Then, I'm a minute-man; I'm ready any minute for building a barn."

"I want to put this one through in a hurry."

"Whose is it?"

"Bernard's, yonder."

"Oh, over there?"

It was further for James to travel than the other barn was; but it was all the same to him.

"It's goin' to be a larger barn."

"Much larger?"

"No; just enough to call it larger, that's all. See you to-morrow morning." And Mr. Treat hastened back, adding, as he turned to go, "same pay as before."

The details must be omitted. The building of this barn provided James with additional facilities for learning how to frame a building; and he improved the opportunity. In many things he was able to go ahead without depending upon his employer, the progress which he made in building the first barn being of great service to him in building the second.

"Not a word of fault to find with you, James," remarked his employer, when the barn was completed. "Work comes easy to you, and you earn your money."

"I mean to know how to frame a barn, yet," answered James.

"Then you don't think you can quite do it, yet?"

"Hardly," said James.

"Pluck and brains will accomplish it, and you have both," added Mr. Treat, intending to pay his young employé a fine compliment.

"I'll give you another chance at it one of these

days," Mr. Treat added. "I owe you fifteen dollars, just." And he counted out the money, and passed it to the happy boy.

"There! the highest price I said, fifty cents a day; and I'm well satisfied, too," Mr. Treat continued.

James had just passed his thirteenth birthday, and he was developing rapidly into a stalwart boy for one of his age. The winter school opened, and he attended as usual, although he had about all there was in the text-books at his tongue's end. He could repeat a good part of his reading-book, and perform the problems in arithmetic with his eyes shut; yet it was excellent discipline to go over them again.

That winter he found somewhere another volume to read, that greatly interested him. It was next to "Robinson Crusoe," in his estimation. The book was "Alonzo and Melissa," well suited to fascinate a boy like him. Once reading did not satisfy him. There were two books now that towered above all the books he ever read, and he wondered if there were any more like them, if so, where? On the whole it was a profitable winter to him; and he began to feel that he could do better for his mother than to run her little farm. Just before the close of school, he said to his mother, "I've been thinking that I can do better for you than to stay on the farm. I could get twelve dollars a month to go out to work."

"Perhaps so," was all his mother said.

"You could keep a cow, hire a man to plant what is necessary, and take care of it; and it wouldn't cost a quarter as much as I can earn," James continued.

"And it would be four times as hard for you" re

sponded Mrs. Garfield. "It's better for a boy like you to go to school while he can, and not labor all the time. Boys should not work too hard."

"I knew what you'd say; I've learned that by heart," replied James. "But I was never hurt by work yet, and I never expect to be."

"Nevertheless, you may be," responded his mother.

"A fellow may as well be earning something when he can; there's need enough of it in this part of the world," added James.

"In this part of the world!" repeated his mother; "you don't seem to have so high an opinion of this part of the country as you might. What's the trouble with it?"

"No trouble as I know, only a fellow has a better chance in some other places."

"Better chance for what?" asked his mother.

"To get a living, or make a man, or most anything," answered James.

"There's a better chance to get an education in some other places, I admit; and I hope you will enjoy it some day," continued Mrs. Garfield.

James knew much about the world, now. All that Morse's Geography could teach him about his own and other countries he knew thoroughly. He had picked up much information, too, about New England and the State of New York; and he understood very well that the opportunities for a boy to earn money, study, and to rise in the world, were greater in many other parts of the country. It was easy to discover the aspirations of a noble spirit in the boy. He was beginning to feel cramped and confined on the little farm. His soul was outgrowing its sphere of childhood, and was waiting to plume its wings for higher flights. The young eagle was getting ready to leave the nest and soar.

His mother did not look with favor upon the boy's suggestions. James must be content to live upon the farm for a while. Providence would open the way out into the broad world at the right time. "Wait for Providence."

So James suppressed ambitious desires, and contented himself to remain at home, running the farm, working out by the day for the farmers, as opportunity offered, as well as working at barn-building. Before he was fifteen years old, Mr. Treat gave him an opportunity to work on three more barns, and one shed, so that he did learn how to frame a barn, and was really a better carpenter, at fifteen years of age, than some of the carpenters in that region who claimed to have learned the trade. Being able to turn his hand to any kind of labor, he found a plenty to do, leaving him but limited time for play.

James was as fond of sports as any other boy; and his genial nature, ready wit, and gentlemanly bearing united to make him popular with pleasure-seekers. Without him they had dull times. His presence added a charm to the social circle.

As already intimated, he had grown into a large, strong boy; as Mr. Treat sometimes said, "as strong as an ox." He could lift as much as the strongest man in the vicinity, although he was not agile. He was too large and heavy to be an expert at jumping or running; but his practical wisdom was as manifest in sports as it was in works. He was such after he had passed his fourteenth birthday, — more advanced and efficient than most youths of that day at eighteen.

We shall close this chapter with a single incident, that occurred in the winter after James' fourteenth birthday.

"Jim, will you go to Cleveland with me, to-morrow?" inquired Edwin Mapes of James, as he called at Mrs. Garfield's in the evening. "I'm going for father."

"I don't know; perhaps I will," replied James, in a hesitating manner, as if it were doubtful.

"Don't know? Who does know, if you don't? Come, go; I want company," pleaded Edwin.

"You'll have a cold ride," suggested James.

"Not very cold if *you* go," responded Edwin. "You and I can keep warm anywhere in Ohio. Say yes, and I'll be off."

"Be off? What's your hurry? Sit down, and I will tell you in the course of half an hour," responded James, teasingly.

Edwin took a seat, whereupon James added, —

"Yes, I'll go, and be glad to; start as early as you please."

"I shan't start very early; no particular need of it. Going over and back, without stopping long," added Edwin.

On the following day, the two boys drove to Cleveland together. Mr. Mapes' horse was a capital roadster, and Edwin understood well how to drive him, and James could ride as fast as Edwin could drive, without raising a serious objection. So their trip was quick, and devoid of monotony.

On their return, a rough, bloated fellow rode up behind them, and shouted, with a volley of oaths, —

"Out of the way, boys, I'm in a hurry;" and suiting his motions to the word, he turned out to drive by them.

"No, you don't," shouted Edwin, as he drew the reins tight, and gave his horse a cut with the whip; and, almost side by side, the two teams flew along the road for half a mile, the whiskey-soaked traveller pouring out oaths at the boys with every blow of his whip.

"Come on," shouted Edwin to the fellow, at the same time beckoning with his hand to him when he had left him ten or fifteen rods in the rear. "Come on! come on!"

They were too far in advance to hear his voice, but they could see the fellow's very expressive gesticulations with his fist. James enjoyed the victory hugely, and shook his sides with laughter.

"He told us to get out of the way, and we have," was about all the remark that James made during the contest.

They drove on at a very good pace three or four miles, when they came up to a little country inn, with which both of them were familiar.

"Let's go in and get warm," proposed James; "my feet are cold as ice."

"Agreed," answered Edwin; and turned the horse into the shed. In less than five minutes they were standing before the landlord's fire. In less than five minutes more, the enraged man who tried to run by them drove up, and entered.

"I've a good will to thrash you boys," he shouted at the top of his voice.

The boys were very much surprised to see him in such a passion.

"What are you going to thrash us for?" answered Edwin.

"Thrash you for, you insulting scamps? I'll let you know," and he shook his fist in the liveliest manner, at the same time belching forth a volley of oaths, that we omit, since they did not embellish his language, though they contributed some force to it.

"Why didn't you let me go by, you young rascals?" he continued.

"You had plenty of room to pass; as much room as we had, and the same right to the road," replied James, coolly.

"But I couldn't," the fellow bellowed; "you good-for-nothing brats."

"That's not our fault," returned James. "Better blame your horse."

The latter sentence had a ring of sarcasm in it, especially as the boys laughed when it was spoken; and the brutal man stormed again, and swore he would thrash them.

"Better thrash *me* first," said James, straightening himself up to his full height, and appearing more like a strong man than a boy of fourteen years. The bully looked at him for a moment, as if querying whether his antagonist was not a man, after all.

"Why take you first?" he said, apparently some what cowed.

"Because you will never want to thrash him afterwards," answered James, in the most thundering voice he could roll out. The bully turned upon his heels jumped into his carriage, and drove on.

James and Edwin were soon on their way home, their conversation being upon the unusual experience of the last hour.

"I was glad that you scared him so," remarked Edwin. "He was a regular coward."

"I knew he was a coward when we were talking with him," James replied. "If I hadn't, I should have kept still. I don't like to get into trouble with anybody."

"I thought you were terribly courageous, for you," remarked Edwin. "You roared at him like thunder. Your big voice is enough to frighten any *coward*."

"I hope that it will never frighten anybody else," was the only reply that James made.

James was in no sense a bully, nor was he given to brag. There was no boy in Orange township more gentlemanly and considerate than he; none more averse to pugilistic contests. At the same time, he would stand up for his rights, and the rights of others. He would defend his companions, too, with great courage, if they were in the right. If they were wrong, he would not defend them at all; and he would frankly state his reason. These facts sufficiently explain his encounter with the bully at the hotel.

CHAPTER X.

A BLACK-SALTER.

THE following colloquy will explain a matter that must not be omitted.

"I have come again for James," said Mr. Smith, entering Mrs. Garfield's cottage. "Can't get along without him, when we weed the peppermint."

"Well, James will be glad to help you if he can, but he is pretty busy now on the farm," answered Mrs. Garfield.

"Perhaps he can squeeze out two or three days now, and that will help me through," continued Mr. Smith. "I shall have twenty boys in the gang."

"I should think that was enough without James," remarked Mrs. Garfield.

"It's altogether too many if I *don't* have him," replied Mr. Smith. "You see, the boys do as well again when James leads them. Somehow he has wonderful influence over them."

"I didn't know that," remarked Mrs. Garfield.

"Well, it's true: and if you should see him leading off, and interesting them by stories, anecdotes, and fun, you'd be surprised. He is a fast worker, and all the boys put in and work as hard as they can to keep up, that they may hear his stories. The boys think the world of him."

"I'm glad to hear such good things of him," remarked Mrs. Garfield. "I'm willing that he should help you if he can."

"I shouldn't mind paying him something extra if he will come," Mr. Smith continued. "I can afford to do that. Each boy does more work, and where there's twenty of them, it's considerable in my pocket."

"Well, you can find James, he is somewhere on the farm; and I'm willing he should go if you can fix it with him," said Mrs. Garfield.

Mr. Smith went in search of James, and found him hard at work in the field. Making known his errand, James could not see how it was possible for him to go, at least for a week. But Mr. Smith soon removed his objections, and arranged for him to come the next day.

This Mr. Smith was a farmer, and his land, on the Chagrin Flats, was adapted to the cultivation of peppermint, which he raised for the market in large quantities. It was necessary to keep it thoroughly weeded, and for this purpose he employed a gang of boys at different times in the season. James had served him more than once in that work, and the shrewd farmer had noticed that the gang would try to keep up with James, so as to hear his stories and interesting conversation. James was a capital storyteller, and all that he ever read or studied was in his head. His remarkable memory served him a good purpose in company, whether in the field of peppermint, or elsewhere. He could recall almost any anecdote that he ever heard, and could relate whatever he had learned about his own or other countries from Morse's Geography. Add to this his jovial nature, his conversational powers, and his singular tact, and we can readily understand how he could "lead the gang."

So James became general of the peppermint brigade for a few days, to accommodate Mr. Smith, and again his precocity and large acquisitions of knowledge enabled him to lead them to victory over the weeds. The weeds melted away before their triumphant march, as the rebels disappeared before the Ohio Forty-second Regiment, sixteen years afterwards.

We said that James assisted Mr. Treat to build a shed, in addition to the several barns. The shed was the last building on which he worked for Mr. Treat, and it was about ten miles from home, near Cleveland. It was an addition to quite a large pot-ashery, the largest in all that region. A pot-ashery was an establishment containing vats for leeching ashes, and large kettles for boiling the lye, reducing it to potash, which, in its crude state, was called "black-salts." The manufacturer of the article was called a "black-salter." The farmers in the region, when they cleared land, drew the logs and branches of trees together into huge piles, and burned them, for the ashes they could collect therefrom, which they sold to the black-salters.

The black-salter for whom Mr. Treat built the shed, took a great fancy to James. It was rather singular that he did; for he was a rough, uncultivated man himself. Yet the politeness, tact, and brightness of James captivated the old man. Before the shed was completed he resolved that he would have that uncommon boy in his employ, if possible. One day he took James aside, and said to him,

"How'd yer like to come and work for me?"

James was just fifteen years old, at that time. The question was unexpected to James, and he hesitated.

"I want jist sich a hand as yer are in my business," the salter, whose name was Barton, continued. "I reckon yer can figger 'nough for me."

"I don't know about it," finally James replied; "it is something I have not thought about. When do you want me?"

"Jist as soon as yer kin; yer kin't come ter quick."

"I couldn't agree to come until I have seen my mother about it, any way," continued James. "Perhaps she will object."

"That's the sorter boy I 'sposed yer was, to mind yer mother. I like yer all the better for that."

"How long will you want me?" inquired James.

"Jist as long as yer'll stay; as long as yer live, maybe."

"How much will you pay me?"

"I'll give yer fourteen dollars a month, and that's two dollars extra pay." By this Barton meant that he would pay him two dollars a month more than he was wont to pay. The offer was proof that he was greatly pleased with James.

"I will consult my mother about it as soon as I go home, and let you know," said James. He would not go home until the shed was completed. He boarded with Barton. But the shed was almost finished; two days more would complete it.

"How shall I know yer'll come?" said Barton, when the shed was done, and James was about returning home.

"If mother is willing I should engage, I will come next Monday. If you don't see me next Monday you may know that I shall not come."

"That's bisniss," Barton replied. "Tell yer mother I kin do the right thing by yer."

It was a rare offer to a boy fifteen years old—fourteen dollars a month. James regarded it in that light. And then, it was constant work as long as he pleased to continue; that was a great consideration. One hundred and sixty-eight dollars a year! The thought of so much pay elated him very much.

"I have a chance to go right to work, mother, and work as many months as I please, at fourteen dollars a month," said James, as soon as he reached home.

"Where," inquired his mother, with an air of surprise.

"For Mr. Barton, the black-salter."

"I don't think it is the right sort of business for you, James," replied his mother.

"It's the right sort of pay, though," James answered. "But why is it not a good business for me, mother?"

"Because a rough class of men carry on the business, and you will be exposed to many evils," his mother said.

"Exposed to evils enough anywhere," remarked James. "But I don't propose to attend to the evils, but to my work."

"I have no doubt of that, my son. Your intentions are good enough; but you may be enticed away, for all that."

"I must be pretty weak, if that's the case."

"We are all weaker than we think we are. 'Let him that thinketh he standeth take heed lest he fall.' We all have reason to adopt that advice."

"Then you won't give your consent for me to go?" James said, inquiringly.

"I don't say that."

"What do you say then?"

"I say that you had better consider the matter well, before you take so important a step."

"Can't think of it a great while, for I have promised to begin work for him next Monday, if I begin at all."

"As soon as that?"

"Yes; and it looks to me as if the time had come for me to give up the farm, that I may earn more for you."

"What did Mr. Treat say about it?"

"He said nothing about it, because he knew nothing about it. I didn't tell him about it."

"I suppose you must go out into the world some time, and perhaps now is the time."

"You told me, once, to wait for Providence to open the door," continued James; "and if Providence didn't open this door, then I shall never know when Providence does open the door."

"The truth was, Mrs. Garfield half thought that Providence would not open the door of a black-salter's establishment to her son; but she did not say so. She smiled at James' application of her teachings about Providence, and remarked:

"Perhaps Providence did open this door. If you go to Mr. Barton's and resist all temptations to evil, and maintain your good character, that will be proof that Providence opened this door. The proof of it depends on yourself."

"Then you give your consent?" said James.

"Yes, I give my consent, and hope it will turn out for the best."

Barton was a happy man on the following Monday, when James presented himself at his door, with all his worldly possessions tied up in a pocket-handkerchief.

"Yer've come," he said. "Yer kin put yer duds in yer sleeping-room;" and he showed him where he would lodge, and then proceeded to the manufactory for work.

The establishment was a dirty place, and the business, or much of it, was dirty. Shovelling ashes, attending to the boilers, and disposing of the black-salts, was not an inviting business. However, James did not have the dirtiest part of the work to do, unless it was occasionally. He kept the books, waited on men who delivered ashes at the establishment, paying their bills, and he waited on customers also, acting as salesman. He did other things when necessary, always improving his time, and looking after the establishment, as if he were Barton's son. He was the first one at the ashery in the morning, and the last one to leave at night. Barton soon learned to trust him with implicit confidence, and a father could not have been kinder to the boy than he was.

One day a man brought a load of ashes, saying, "There are twenty-five bushels." James had not been at the establishment long, before he resolved to measure all ashes purchased as they were unloaded. Mr. Barton usually took them for the number of bushels claimed. James directed the men in the ashery to measure the load in question as it was unloaded, and he kept tally. There were scarcely more than twenty-two bushels.

"Only twenty-two bushels, sir," said James to the owner.

"There were twenty-five bushels according to my measure," said the man.

"And twenty-two according to mine," replied James. "I will pay you for twenty-two bushels — no more."

"I think you made a mistake," remarked the man.

"If there was any mistake, I think you made it," retorted James. "Three heads are better than one, and three of us attended to the measuring. Shall I pay you for twenty-two bushels?"

"Yes, pay away," the man answered, sulkily.

Barton came in just then, when James told him what had happened; and afterwards he told him further, that there was a great deal of cheating practised upon him, and it was quite time for his interests to be looked after more closely. All this served to increase Barton's confidence in James.

The men with whom James had to do about the

establishment were about as his mother had supposed —a rough, wicked class. But James had nothing to do with them except in the business, and they made no impression upon him as to weakening his principles. Most of them were terribly profane, and one day James interrupted one of them, saying:

"Jake, what makes you swear so? You are awful. What good does it do you?"

"I s'pose it gits some of the bad stuff out of me," was Jake's prompt reply.

"If that is the case, all the bad stuff ought to have been out of you long ago; you have sworn enough to empty yourself."

"Nary bisness of yers, any way," the swearer answered.

"I should think that the more bad stuff you let out, the more there was left, Jake," continued James. "I don't want you should empty any more of it about me."

"What is 't to yer, any way?" answered the godless fellow, displeased at the rebuke.

"It is a very bad habit, Jake, as you know," answered James. "It does you no good, and it is very unpleasant to many persons who hear you."

"Stop yer ears, then," said Jake, angrily.

"There is no use being mad over it, Jake. I don't like to hear your profanity; and now suppose you just please me a little, and not spill any more of the stuff near me."

Jake laughed, and turned to his work. He could not be very angry with James, for he thought too much of him. In this frank and honest way, James dealt with the men. There was no danger that he would be enticed away by that class of men. Another danger, however, met him in the house, and for a time it was an unsettled question whether Provideence or Satan opened that door. If his good mother had been cognizant of what was going on, she would have discovered ample reason for her apprehensions.

A book-loving boy like James would not be long in a strange place without finding all the books there were; so books were among the first things that attracted his attention in Barton's house. There were "Marryat's Novels," "Sindbad the Sailor," "The Pirate's Own Book," "Jack Halyard," "Lives of Eminent Criminals," "The Buccaneers of the Caribbean Seas," plundering a Spanish galleon; and perhaps some others of the same character. The adventure and marvelous exploits contained in these volumes were suited to fire his imagination and inflame his heart. He was thus introduced into a new experience altogether, more perilous to him than a regiment of coarse, brutal men. He made books his most intimate companions, and trusted them with entire confidence. He could read deceitful and designing men around him, and bluff them off; but he took the volumes that he read directly to his heart, and communed with them, as friend communes with friend.

Volume after volume of this pernicious reading was devoured, causing Mr. Barton to remark to others of the "great scholar" in his employ. Barton himself did not understand but that the volumes in his house were as safe for a boy to read as the Bible; nor did he care much. His daughter had purchased these books from time to time, and read them, too; and why should he, ignorant man that he was, appreciate the tendency of such reading? His daughter was a young woman grown, possessing considerable native ability, but little culture, though she was the belle of the town. She wrote poetry occasionally for a paper that had been started in Cleveland, a circumstance that gave her some notoriety among the people.

"I see you like reading," she said to James one evening, when he was rapt over one of Marryat's novels.

"There's nothing I like better. I never read books like these before," he answered.

"They are very interesting books, I think," she added.

"You've read them, have you?"

"Yes; I bought them, and I have read them all more than once."

"I think I shall read them more than once. I'm glad I came here to live. These long evenings would be dull for me without books."

"You'd have to go to Damon's with the men, evenings, if you had no books," the young woman suggested. Damon's was the store where the post-office was kept; and there the male portion of the population were wont to congregate in the evening, to talk politics, or nonsense, according to circumstances. It was a motley crowd, whose appearance would have terrified Mrs. Garfield, could she have seen them; and yet her James was in worse company, for him, every evening, poring over those fascinating and corrupting books. He did not know his danger, and so his danger was greater. To the young woman's suggestion, James replied, —

"I couldn't go there."

"Why?" she asked.

"I don't like that sort of company."

"It's not very attractive, I think," she conceded.

"My mother would be frightened to see me in such company."

If James had only known, he might have said, with equal truth, perhaps, that his mother would be frightened to see him in the company of such books. But he had no thoughts in that direction. He had become infatuated over these mute, yet loquacious, companions.

When the family retired at night, James would take his light and book and go to his room, but not to bed. Twelve o'clock often found him reading, almost oblivious to the cold that pinched his flesh and made him shiver. But his young blood seemed to be warmed by the excitement and enthusiasm begotten by his reading.

One night he retired, excited and wakeful. As he lay musing, he said, within himself:

"I will see some of the world yet. I shan't always follow this business."

Then he turned over to invite sleep, but was still wakeful.

"A black-salter!" he continued. "It is not the sort of work for me. Can't see much of the world tied down here."

He turned over again, restless and nervous, but sleep was chary.

"I should like to be a sailor, and see more of the world; go to other countries, and see the great cities; it's splendid," his mind said; and he was not sleepy at all.

"What's the use of staying at home always, and seeing nothing, when the great world is open. I mean to try it some time."

And so he went on discussing the matter within himself, and reasoning away many of the staid and valuable ideas that had kept him a noble boy.

"I wonder what mother will say to it? Women are always afraid, and want to keep their boys at home all the time. I 'spose she will make a terrible fuss about it; but I mean to see more of the world, somehow."

Sleep finally came to his relief, and he dreamed of ships bearing him over the ocean to other lands, where fairy-like cities delighted his vision; and other enrapturing scenes, that exist only in dreams, made him thrice happy. It was quite evident now that Satan was opening the door of the future wide, instead of that providence whose watch and care his good mother had invoked.

He continued a faithful laborer to Mr. Barton, attending to the details of the business with promptness, and securing his love and confidence. Barton watched him with pride, and once he said to him:

"Yer kin read, yer kin write, and yer are death on figgers; so stay with me, keep my 'counts, and tend to the saltery. I'll find yer, and glad to give yer the fourteen dollars a month."

"I want to be a sailor," replied James.

"A sailor!" exclaimed Barton, in amazement. "Yer don't mean it. There's too much of yer for that bisniss. What's put that idee into yer head?"

"I want to see more of the world than I can see in Ohio," answered James. "It will be dull business to make black-salts all my days."

"Well, yer will never go to sea if yer take my advice. Stay here, and some day yer'll have a saltery of yer own."

"I don't want one," replied James. "I'd rather have something else."

"My word for it," continued Barton; "yer are too good a boy to spile on the seas. Stay with me, and some day yer'll have a saltery as big as our'n."

"I wouldn't spend my life in this business for a dozen salteries as big as this," replied James.

Barton was exceedingly afraid that he should lose his excellent employé, and so he endeavored to make his position agreeable as possible. His praise, too, was not stinted at all.

"Yer are a cute boy, good at readin', good at figgers, good at work, good at everything," he would say; "stay with me, and I'll do well by yer."

James continued through the winter, until April opened, when the following incident terminated his career as a salter.

Barton's daughter had a beau, and he came to see her one night, when James was working over some difficult problems in arithmetic. There was but one room below in the farm-house, and that was a very large one, so the young couple occupied a distant corner, James and the "old folks" sitting near the fireplace. James took in the situation well for a boy of his years, and designed to retire as soon as the girl's father and mother did; but he became so absorbed in his arithmetic that he did not notice they had left the room, until the impatient girl startled him by the remark,—

"I should think it was time for *hired servants* to be abed."

James' anger was aroused. He looked at her fiercely for a moment, but said nothing. Then he took his candle and started for his room, his very tread on the floor showing that the invincible spirit within him was thoroughly stirred. The coast was now clear for the matrimonial aspirants, though at quite a loss to the establishment, as the sequel will show.

James could not sleep. The sarcastic girl had knocked sleep out of him.

"'*Hired servant!*" he repeated to himself, over and over. "And that's all I am in this concern,—'a hired servant.' I'll not be a '*servant*' long, let them know." And he tried to compose himself, and forget his trouble by going to sleep, but in vain.

"Hired servant!" It would not down at his bidding. He kept repeating it, in spite of himself; and the more he repeated it, the more his feelings were harrowed.

"'Hired servant!' I can rise above that, I know, and I *will.* I'll not stay in this place another day, let what will happen. I'll leave to-morrow. The trollop shall see whether I'm a '*hired servant,*' or not. *I'll hire* servants yet."

The fact was, that unexpected appellation proved to James just what the kick in the stomach, which the schoolmate gave to Newton, did. The kick made a scholar out of Newton; the girl's remark aroused latent aspirations in James' heart to be somebody. Years afterwards, when James had become a man, and was battling with the stern realities of life, he said, "That girl's cutting remark proved a great blessing to me. I was too much annoyed by it to sleep that night; I lay awake under the rafters of that old farm-house, and vowed, again and again, that I *would* be somebody; that the time should come when that girl would not call me a '*hired servant.*'"

The bad books, however, very nearly turned the aspirations awakened into the way to ruin instead of honor.

James arose early in the morning, dressed himself, and tied up his few possessions in a bundle, and presented himself to Mr. Barton for settlement.

"I'm going to leave to-day," he said.

If he had fired off a pistol at his employer the latter would not have been more astounded.

"Goin' ter leave!" he exclaimed.

"Yes; I'm done working at this business."

"Hi, Jim, yer can't mean it."

"I do mean it," answered James; and he adhered to his purpose against the entreaties and good promises of his employer, and that, too, without saying a word to him about the "hired servant." The upshot was, that Mr. Barton paid him off, and James was at home before noon.

CHAPTER XI.

A WOOD-CHOPPER.

"HOME for good," said James to his mother, on entering the house. "Got enough of saltering."

"I am glad to see you, James; but what's the matter now?" his mother replied.

"Matter enough. I've come home to stay."

"I'm glad of that."

"I can be somebody if I try, instead of a 'hired servant,'" continued James, speaking the last two words contemptuously.

"What now? Have you had any trouble with Mr. Barton?"

"None at all; he is one of the kindest men in the world. I shouldn't want to work for a better man."

"What, then, is to pay?" urged his mother, earnestly.

James rehearsed to her the experience of the previous evening, and his determination to quit the business, together with Mr. Barton's disappointment at his leaving, and his entreaties for him to stay. Mrs. Garfield listened attentively to the recital, which closed by his saying,—

"There are fifty-six dollars for you, mother."

"You are indeed thoughtful of your mother, and the money will add many comforts to our home," replied Mrs. Garfield; "but did you not act rather hastily?"

"Hastily or not, I've acted, and that is the end of it," replied James. "I didn't exactly want to give up the job, on account of the pay, but I have."

"I should think much of Mr. Barton's kindness and his disappointment," suggested his mother.

"And minded nothing about the insulting girl, I s'pose?"

"I shouldn't care for her. I don't suppose she meant any evil by her remark. Besides, it is not dishonorable to be a hired servant, especially if you are a good one," added his mother.

"That is not the thing, mother. I don't think it is dishonorable to be a 'hired servant.' It was the girl's insulting way of saying it, and it stirred me up to want to be somebody in the world, and I mean to be."

"I hope it will all turn out for the best, my son; and I believe that Providence will overrule it for good."

"I must look out for another job, now," remarked James.

"And not stay at home?"

"No; I can earn more for you, away."

"Well, as you think best," said his mother. "I dare say you will have a plenty of chances."

"I would like to go to sea, mother," added James, hesitatingly.

If he had struck his mother in her face, she would not have been more shocked.

"Why, James!" she exclaimed.

"I've been thinking about it," James continued.

"Thinking about it, James! What has got into you? You shock me."

"I don't wish to go against your will, mother," James added.

"You will go against my will, if you ever go to sea, James. Be a salter, or anything else, rather than a sailor."

"Why, mother?"

"You certainly can never be 'somebody,' as you say, by going to sea."

"I can be a commander of a vessel, perhaps, and some day I may own one; who knows?"

"Who knows what you wouldn't be, James, if you should become a sailor? Say no more about such a step, if you want to make your mother happy."

The subject was dropped there, and James proceeded to look about the farm. For several days he busied himself in putting things in order, awaiting work elsewhere. At length he heard that his uncle, living at Newburg, near Cleveland, wanted to hire wood-choppers. His uncle was clearing a large tract of forest near the line of Independence township. After conferring with his mother, and seeking the advice of his uncle, Amos Boynton, he decided to go to Newburg. His mother was quite willing that he should go there, because his sister Mehetabel had married, and was living there; and James could board with her. Three days after, James presented himself at his uncle's door in Newburg, making known his errand.

"Glad to see you, James," was his uncle's cordial

welcome. "How you grow! almost a man, now! Yes, I've work enough to be done at chopping, if men will only do it."

"I like to chop," interrupted James.

"A great many don't," replied his uncle; "and chopping wood is pretty hard work,—about as hard as any work there is."

"I don't think so," remarked James. "I do not get so tired chopping as I have been sometimes planing boards."

"Well, let's see," continued his uncle; "how much of a job at chopping can you undertake? It's coming warm weather, and you don't want to chop wood when it is too hot, do you?"

"Perhaps not; I can chop two months, sure."

"Suppose you take a job of one hundred cords to cut, James; how will that do?"

"I will agree to that. How much will you pay me a cord?"

"I will pay you fifty cents a cord for one hundred cords; and the fifty dollars shall be ready for you as soon as the work is done. How long will you be cutting it?"

"Fifty days," James quickly answered.

"A little longer than that, I reckon, unless you are a mighty smart chopper," suggested his uncle. "There's a great difference in men, and boys, too, in chopping wood."

"I shall cut two cords a day, right along," said James. "I can do it easily."

"That's pretty good chopping—better than the average, by considerable," replied his uncle; "and you are larger and stronger than the average of choppers, I guess."

The bargain was clinched, and James passed on to his sister's, who gave him a warm greeting, and agreed to board him. So James was once more settled, and ready to proceed to business. The next morning he appeared in the rôle of a wood-chopper; not a new occupation to him.

It was unfortunate for James that his work was in full view of Lake Erie, on whose blue bosom he could see a plenty of craft sailing, at any time. The location seemed to conspire with the bad books at Barton's to fan his desire for a sea-faring life into a flame. In the circumstances, it was not strange that James did not forget the books he had read. He often stopped in his work to watch a vessel gliding over the waves like a swan, and sometimes he would seat himself upon a log to count the sails appearing in the distance. It was a rare spectacle to him, and his young heart bounded with delight. He cherished the secret thought that, some day, he would be sailing over that very lake.

There were several choppers near him, one of them a German. He was a clever man, and spoke very broken English. James thought he was a slow chopper, and noticed that his axe did not fly briskly. At the end of a week, however, he found that the German had cut and corded two cords a day, — just the amount he himself had cut.

"I don't understand it," he said to his sister, on going home. "I strike two blows to the German's one, and yet he has cut as many cords as I have."

"Perhaps he strikes heavier blows," suggested his sister.

"I doubt it," replied James; "but I will find out the reason."

James was on the alert to find out the reason of the German's success. Nor was he left long in the dark. Lake Erie had no attractions for the Teutonic chopper, and so he kept steadily at his work, from morning until night, while James frequently stopped to watch the sails in the distance. The German did not strike blows so rapidly as James, nor were his blows more telling, but he was steadily at work from morning until night. James comprehended the whole, and it was a good lesson to him. He took his first lesson of application and perseverance of the German wood-chopper, and reduced it to practice at once. It rather cooled his fiery ardor for the sea. He confessed to his sister that he had wasted some time in watching sails on the lake. At the same time, he owned that he had a longing for the sea.

"You surprise me, James," his sister said. "I never thought that of you. You can't be in earnest, can you?"

"I never was more earnest in my life," answered James, coolly. "The height of my ambition is to command a ship."

"Captain Garfield! That is the title you want to earn, is it?" remarked his sister. "I hope you'll never get it."

"You know that was the title of one of our great ancestors, *Captain* Benjamin Garfield," suggested James.

"But he didn't get his title on a ship, by any means; he got it in the Revolutionary war," retorted his sister. "Anything but a sailor."

"I might be something worse than that," added James.

"Not unless you become a *mean man*," quickly answered his sister.

"You had rather I would get the title by shooting men in war, than bringing goods from foreign ports, had you?" said James, in a sarcastic manner.

"I rather you would be a wood-chopper all your days than to be a sailor," was his sister's prompt reply. "I think mother would say the same. You have too much talent to throw away on the deck of a ship."

James received no encouragement from any quarter to become a sailor; and his aspirations in that direction became somewhat modified. He thought less of a sea-faring life for a time, and devoted himself to wood-chopping with commendable industry. Two cords a day were cut and piled with ease. He could have cut two cords and a half each day without lengthening his days inordinately. But he had fixed the limit when he began, and James was not the boy to change his purpose.

His sister owned a few books, and his uncle more; and, between them both, James was quite well provided with reading. A newspaper, that his uncle took, occupied his attention till each number was read through. Nor were the books objectionable, like those at Barton's. They were healthy and profitable volumes for such a reader as James, who preferred a book to the society of the young men of the town, who might gather at any rendezvous. His reading, too, appeared to offset his growing desire for the sea. Engrossing his attention in the subject-matter of the books, excluded, in a measure, at least for the time, his hankering for a ship. His evenings were wholly given up to reading, some of them extending considerably beyond bed-time. The temptation to lengthen his evenings for reading he could not resist so readily as he could the temptation to lengthen the days for chopping.

James chopped the hundred cords of wood in fifty days, and received his pay, according to the contract. On paying him, his uncle said:—

"I hope you will not always be a wood-chopper, James, although it is a necessary and honorable business. But you are competent to do something of more consequence. The way may open for you to get an education yet: how would you like that?"

"I should like it," answered James, although he would have said, "I want to go to sea," if he had really dared to risk it. But he had good reason to suppose that his uncle would resolutely rebuke any such expression. So he desisted. Nor did he tell a falsehood by saying that he would like to acquire an education, for his taste was strong in that direction; but he could discover no way into that field of clover.

Bidding his uncle and sister good-by, James returned home, and presented his mother with the balance of the fifty dollars, after paying for his board. His mother was rejoiced to see her boy, wondering all the while if his desire for a sea-faring life survived. She thought it not best, however, to open a subject that was so unpleasant to her, for fear it might prove agreeable to him. Nothing was said about the sea.

It was the last week in June, and James would like a job for the summer. His uncle Amos told him of a farmer, five or six miles away, who wanted to hire a man through haying and harvesting, about four months. James went immediately to see him, bargained to work for him from July to November, four months, and accordingly took up his abode with the man on the first day of July.

A stout, muscular fellow like James was supposed to be an efficient hand in the hay-field. His employer liked his appearance, and expected much of him. Nor was he disappointed. His strength enabled him to swing a scythe and pitch hay with power, though he was a boy in age. Then he possessed a boy's pride in his strength, and delighted to astonish his employer by an exhibition of it. Boy-like, he found great pleasure in keeping squarely up with his employer in the mowing field, sometimes cutting his corners. His power of endurance was remarkable; and he never appeared to tire, or "play out," as the boys say.

James found no books here, or none worth mentioning. The people cared little about reading, though they were people of character. But farming was their business, and they worked early and late. When the day's work was done, they went to bed, and, at four o'clock in the morning, they were up and ready for another day's work. Thus it was through the whole busy season of the year. James kept abreast of them. "If I can't do what other folks can, I'll quit," he said to himself, more than once.

Nothing unusual occurred during the four months, excepting only two incidents, which we will narrate.

James was digging potatoes in October, and putting them into the cellar. On going to the house with a load one day, he found a neighbor discussing the subject of baptism with his employer's daughter.

"Sprinkling is baptism," James heard him say, "Immersion is no more. A drop of water is as good as a fountain."

"Sprinkling is not baptism, according to Alexander Campbell," replied the young woman; "and I don't see how it can be."

"I said, according to the Bible. I don't care a fig for Alexander Campbell," the neighbor rejoined.

"That makes your position harder to support," interrupted James, with the design of affording relief to the farmer's daughter, whom he very much respected.

"What do you know about it?" exclaimed the neighbor, somewhat annoyed at the boy's interruption. "You know more about potatoes than the Scriptures, according to my idea."

"You can't prove that sprinkling is baptism, from the Bible," added James.

"That's all you know about it," retorted the man.

"See here," continued James, thinking he would surprise the disputant by his familiarity with the

Scriptures; "how do you get along with this?" And he proceeded to quote from Hebrews: "Let us draw near with a true heart, in full assurance of faith, having our hearts sprinkled from an evil conscience."

"There, you see it says 'sprinkled,'" interrupted the neighbor, quite elated.

"But, hold on!" replied James; "wait, and hear the rest of it. You are in too big a hurry." And James repeated the remainder of the text: "and our bodies *washed* with pure water." He laid stress on the word "washed," adding: —

"Now tell me, if you can, how can you *wash* your body in a drop of water."

Without waiting for a reply, he hurried away to the potato-patch.

The other incident relates to his desire to go to sea. He concluded to sound his employer one day, and he said: —

"What do you think about my going to sea?"

"Going to *see* what?" answered the farmer.

"To ship, and be a sailor," answered James.

"Likely story that you would undertake that business."

"I'm thinking of it."

"I guess you'll take it out in thinking."

"Honest, though, I'm not joking. I want to command a ship."

"Well, if you were my boy," retorted the farmer, "I should *command* you to *shut up*. It's the last place for you to go. Better dig potatoes all your days."

"I will shut up," repeated James, quite amused at the farmer's decided way of opposing a sea-faring life. He did not mention the subject again.

James completed his four months' labor with the farmer, for which he received twelve dollars a month, — forty-eight dollars in all, — with the farmer's laconic endorsement:

"You've done well."

CHAPTER XII

A CANAL BOY.

AMES was restive and dissatisfied when he returned home. His mother saw that he was uneasy, and she feared that he was thinking about the sea. Nor was she mistaken in her apprehensions, although she remained silent on the subject. Thus matters continued through the winter, James attending school, and looking after the place. In the spring, he worked at odd jobs in the town, until the farm demanded his attention. It was evident, however, that his heart was not in his work. His thoughts were on the sea. At last he seemed to reach a point where he could restrain his desires no longer. It was about the first of July. He said to his mother:

"Mother, you don't know how I long for the sea. Why cannot I look after a place on a ship?"

"Where do you want to ship to, James?" his mother replied.

This answer was unexpected. James anticipated a direct refusal, but the answer indicated a change of feeling in his mother, he thought; and it encouraged him to proceed. There was really no change in his mother's feelings, but she was a sagacious woman, and there was a change in her tactics.

"I'm not particular where; I want to see something of the world," was James' answer.

"It's rather queer for a boy of your ability not to know where he wants to go," said his mother. "If I wanted to go somewhere, I would find out *where* in the first place. You don't care whether you go to Europe, Asia, or Africa!"

"Not exactly that," replied James; "I would like to cross the Atlantic."

"And be sick enough of it before you got half across," remarked Mrs. Garfield. "Boys don't know what they want."

"*I* know what *I* want," retorted James; "and that is what I am trying to tell you. I want to try life on the ocean. If I don't like it, I'll give it up."

"That's not so easy. You get out to the Mediterranean, or to China, and it will not be very easy to give it up and come home. You will wish that you had taken your mother's advice." His mother said this with much feeling.

"I shall never know till I try," James continued. "But I will never go to sea, or anywhere else, unless you consent."

"Suppose you try a trip in a schooner on Lake Erie first, and see how you like it," suggested his mother. "Perhaps you won't like it. You will not be far from home, then."

"Are you willing that I should do that?" inquired James, brightening up at the prospect.

"I'd much rather you would do that than to cross

the Atlantic, and I would give my consent to that," his mother answered, with reluctance.

"It is settled, then," replied James. "I shall start for Lake Erie as soon as I can get ready."

Mrs. Garfield's tactics prevailed. She had given much thought to the subject, and had reluctantly concluded that, if worst came to worst, she would compromise with the boy, and allow him to ship on Lake Erie. She feared that his desire to become a sailor would prove uncontrollable, and that he would eventually go to sea, any way. Perhaps allowing him to try life on shipboard, in a smaller way, and so near home as the familiar lake, would result in his abandoning the idea of a "life on the ocean wave," altogether.

James prepared for his departure as soon as possible; and taking what money was necessary, with his inevitable bundle, he returned his mother's kiss, but not her tears, and started for Cleveland, where he expected to ship. He walked the whole distance, seventeen miles, and was in sight of the tempting sails at twelve o'clock, noon.

He proceeded directly to the wharf, and boarded the first schooner he found.

"Chance for another hand on board?" he inquired of one of the crew.

The sailor addressed answered, "The captain will soon come up from the hold."

So James waited, expecting soon to stand in the presence of a stout, gentlemanly, noble-looking man, just such a captain as he had read of in books. He did not wait long before the sailor, whom he had addressed, remarked:

"The captain is coming."

James heard a tremendous noise below, as if there was trouble of some kind; and then he heard a human voice belching out most horrible oaths at somebody, or something, as if the captain of the infernal regions was approaching. He scarcely knew what to make of it. But, while he stood wondering, the captain appeared, — a drunken, beastly, angry fellow, — a whiskey-barrel on legs, his mouth its bung-hole, pouring out the vilest stuff possible. James had seen some hard customers before, but if the pit could send up a more horrible sample of humanity from its "hold," he did not wish to meet him. James looked at the creature a moment, and the disgusting creature looked at him, when he ventured to approach him, saying, in a gentlemanly way:

"Captain?"

"Yes; what do you want?"

"Do you want to hire another hand for your schooner?"

"What if I do, you green land-lubber?" exclaimed the captain, with another torrent of oaths. "Get off this schooner in double-quick, or I'll throw you into the dock."

James attempted to excuse himself in a polite way, but the infuriated wretch only cursed and raved the more, swinging his fists in the most threatening manner.

"Get out, I say, or I'll be the death of you. 'Spose I'd hire such a lubber and greenhorn to run my schooner!" And the blackest oaths continued to roll out of his mouth.

The last sound of that terrible voice that lingered on James' ear, as he hurried from the craft, was that of profanity. Such a repulse he never dreamed of. He scarcely thought such a scene possible anywhere. He had read of sailors and captains, but he had never read of such a captain as that. He began to think that books are not always reliable. It was the first time he had ever stopped to think that men are not always what they are represented to be in books. The experience was a damper to his seafaring propensity. In this respect it was a good thing for the boy. As it turned out, the drunken captain prevented him from becoming a sailor. It was a rather rough way of being turned aside from a purpose, but the roughest usage sometimes leads to the best results.

James sat down on a pile of wood to muse on the ways of the world, and to eat a lunch which he put into his pocket on leaving home. He could not understand the philosophy of such a course as the captain pursued. He did nothing to provoke him. "He," he thought, "was provoked before I saw him, for I heard his fearful oaths." He concluded, finally, that he did appear rather green and rough to the captain, for his clothes were countrified and worn; and perhaps he did not know exactly how to present himself to a sea captain, salter, wood-chopper, and farmer as he was. The more he pondered the more he found an excuse for the captain, and the less disposed he was to relinquish his purpose to be a sailor.

He ceased to muse, and walked along the wharf, perhaps not exactly satisfied what to do next. He was soon startled, however, by a voice:

"Jim! Jim!"

James turned about; the voice came from a canal boat.

"Halloo, Jim! How came you here?"

It was Amos Letcher, his cousin, who called to him rom the canal boat.

"You here, Amos?" exclaimed James; and he was on board the boat in a hurry, shaking hands with his old friend and relative.

"How came you here?" inquired Amos. "The last knew of you, you were chopping wood."

"I came over to see if I could find a chance to ship on the Lake," replied James.

"What luck?"

"Not much, yet?"

"Seen anybody?"

Finally James rehearsed his experience on the chooner, to which Amos listened with a kind of omical interest.

"Hot reception," remarked Amos, after listening to he recital. "Some of the captains are hard cusomers, I tell you."

"Hard!" repeated James; "that is no name for that ellow. I 'spose he is human; he looks like a man, out he is more of a demon."

"You wouldn't like to ship with such a brute, would ou?" Amos inquired.

"No; I'd rather chop wood."

"How would you like a canal boat?"

"I don't know; would it help me to get a place on a hip?"

"It might, some."

"Another hand wanted on this boat?" James asked.

"Yes, we want another driver."

"Where's the captain?"

"*I* am captain."

"You captain, Amos?" replied James, with much surprise.

"Yes, I am captain; and I should be right glad to hire you."

"Driver! that is, I drive the horses?" added James, inquiringly.

"That is just it; not so hard as chopping wood."

"Where do you go to?"

"To Pittsburg."

"What do you carry?"

"Copper ore."

"I think I will engage, Captain Letcher," continued James, repeating the title of his cousin, to see how it sounded. "How much will you pay me?"

"Twelve dollars a month; that is what we pay drivers."

"I'll take the position, Captain Letcher, and do the best I can."

"And I shan't ask you to do any better than that," said Amos, as facetiously as James had repeated his title.

"We start to-morrow morning," added the captain. "You will not lose much time."

"So much the better," answered James, thinking himself quite fortunate on the whole.

The canal at that time was a great thoroughfare between Lake Erie and the Ohio River. Copper mining was carried on extensively on Lake Superior, and the ore was brought down to Cleveland in schooners, and from thence was taken to Pittsburg by canal. The name of the canal boat commanded by Captain Letcher was "Evening Star," and its capacity was seventy tons. It was manned with two steersmen, two drivers, a bowman, and a cook, besides the captain, —seven men in all. The bowman's business was to make the locks ready, and to stop the boat as it entered the lock, by throwing the bowline, that was attached to the bow of the boat, around the snubbing post. The drivers were furnished with two mules each, which were driven one before the other; one driver with his mules serving a given number of hours, then giving place to the other, and going on board with his mules.

Boatmen, as a class, were rough fellows, then. "Profane, coarse, vulgar, whiskey-drinkers," describes them exactly. Rum and tobacco were among their necessaries of life, about as much so as bread or meat. They cared nothing for morals and religion, and often made them the butt of ridicule. The best fellow was the one who could drink the most whiskey, and sing the worst songs. Of course such fellows were no company for James. The contrast between him and one of this class was very marked. It was a new and hard school for him.

At sunrise, on the following morning, James took his turn at mule-driving, the captain starting him off well by some instructions. The boat was to pass through the first lock before James hitched on. This done, and James stepped directly into the rank of mule-driver. It was going to sea on a small scale, and so there was some fascination about it. And yet he was on the tow-path instead of the water, except when he tumbled in. Within an hour James heard the captain, —

"Hi, Jim! Boat coming. Steady."

James knew it as well as the captain, and designed to pass the boat with signal success. But somehow, he could scarcely tell how, the two drivers got their lines tangled, interrupting the progress of the mules. The lines were soon separated, but the impetus of Captain Letcher's boat, in the delay, pushed it up square with the mules, when the steersman called out, "Hurrah, Jim, whip up that team, or your line will catch on the bridge." There was a waste-way just ahead.

"Ay!" James answered, as he whipped the mules into a trot.

"Steady, steady!" called the captain, fearing that James was rushing into trouble by too much speed. The caution was too late, however. Just as the team reached the middle of the bridge the lines tightened, and jerked driver and mules into the canal.

"Quick! help!" shouted the captain, and every man ran to their rescue.

"Hold on, Jim!" cried the bowman, meaning that James should understand deliverance was at hand. James was holding on as well as he could, with two stupid mules to manage in the water. For some minutes it was difficult to tell how the affair would terminate, for there was serious danger that mules and driver would go to the bottom together. But it had always been James' good fortune to come to the top. So he did here; and he was soon astride the leading mule, urging him out of the difficulty. A few minutes only elapsed before all were rescued, with no injury except a good ducking.

During the process of rescuing the unfortunate victims of the accident, there was no jesting or light remarks, but one serious, earnest effort to save the mules, and to rescue James. But no sooner were the sufferers safe on the tow-path than a general laughter and merry time over the mishap ensued.

"Yer a good Baptist now, Jim," exclaimed one of the steersmen, terminating his explosive laughter.

"Yer see how we 'nitiate greenhorns into canal bisniss," said another of the men.

"I kind o' thought yer was a goner at first," added a third.

Finally, the captain said, jocosely, "Jim, what were you doing down there in the canal?"

"Taking my morning bath," answered James. "Refreshing."

"Washin' the mules, I reckoned," chimed in one of the men.

"All ready, now!" shouted the captain; "Jim has washed himself, and is now ready to proceed to business. All aboard!" And they were off in a jiffy.

The bantering did not cease with that day. Many a hearty laugh was enjoyed over it for several days, and James was the subject of many jocose remarks; all of which served to keep the crew in good humor. James enjoyed it as well as the rest of them.

At "Eleven Mile Lock," the captain ordered a change of teams. James went on board with his mules, and the other driver took the tow-path with his fresh mules.

"Goin' to take the mules into yer bunk with yer, as yer did in a-swimmin'?" remarked one of the hands.

"Put up your team, Jim, and then come on deck," said the captain, addressing James; "I want to see you."

James took good care of his mules, and went on deck.

"Jim, I hear there is some come-out to you, and if you have no objections I would like to make up my own mind in regard to it. It is a long ways to Pancake Lock, and this will be a good time; so I should like to ask you a few questions."

"Proceed," answered James; "but be sure and not ask too hard ones."

"You see, I've kept school some in the backwoods of Steuben County, Indiana," added the captain.

"Schoolmaster and captain," repeated James. "Honor enough for one family. What did you teach?"

"Reading, writing, spelling, geography, arithmetic, and grammar."

"Go ahead, then," continued James, "and examine me in these branches. I'll answer the best I know."

The captain proceeded with his questions, first in arithmetic, then in geography and grammar, and James answered every question promptly.

"You are a trump, Jim; I've heard a good deal about your talents, and I wanted to see whether it was so, or not. You'll not shame your relations; I'll own you for cousin," remarked the captain, discontinuing his questions.

"Now, s'pose I put a few questions to you," said ames; "it's a poor rule that won't work both ays."

"As many as you choose," answered the captain.

The captain could not answer the first question that ames put, nor the second, nor third; nor, indeed, any f them. James had studied all the branches named ar more thoroughly than the captain, so that "hard uestions" were at his command. He intended to onfound the captain, and he did.

"If you'll let me alone, I'll let you alone," remarked he captain, after several ineffectual attempts to answer ames's questions.

The captain did not know so much as he thought he lid. Because he had taught school in Indiana, and tudied arithmetic, grammar, and geography, he hought he was superior even to James, of whom he iad heard large stories. A few years ago he spoke of he matter to a friend, and said, "I was just green nough in those days to think that I knew it all. You see, I had been teacher for three years in the ackwoods of Steuben County, Indiana." That over-stimate of himself put him into an awkward position efore James. At the close of the interview, the cap-ain said, seriously:

"Jim, you've too good a head on you to be a wood-hopper, or a canal driver."

"Do you really think so?" asked James.

"Yes, I do, honest."

"What would you have me do?"

"Teach school. Go to school one or two terms, and then you will be qualified to teach a common school; and after that you can make anything you have a mind to out of yourself."

"That is more easily said than done," answered James. "What do you think of my going to sea."

"I don't think much of it, to tell you the truth, Jim. It's a terrible hard, rough life, and it's a pity to throw away your talents on the deck of a ship. Never do any such thing, Jim. That's my advice."

"But I don't intend to *serve* all my days, if I become a sailor," said James; "I intend to *command*."

"Command or serve, it will be all the same to you, Jim. You will be greater than the business, any way, and that's unfortunate for any one. It won't help the matter any to be called Captain Garfield."

"You don't know what a longing I have for life on the ocean," added James. "For ever so long I have been thinking of the matter; but mother never gave her consent till lately, and then, only to ship on Lake Erie."

"There's where your mother is right. She knows your abilities, and wants you should follow what your abilities fit you to become. I shouldn't think she would ever consent to such a wild project as your going to sea. To be a sailor, when you might be a teacher or governor, is the most foolish thing in the world."

"Now, captain," replied James, as if doubting his sincerity, "do you really think that my talents promise any such result as that?"

"Certainly I do; I shouldn't say it if I didn't think so. I would go to school in the autumn, and teach school next winter, if I were in your place. You'll earn money enough this summer, nearly, to pay your way."

The conversation ceased; but James's thoughts ran on. He began to wonder whether he was such a fool as would appear from the captain's remarks. It was quite evident that Captain Letcher had set him to thinking in the right direction. If he did possess talents for some high position, he was a fool, surely, to throw them away for nothing. He began to see it in that light. What his cousin had said tallied very well with what several other people had told him, and he began to think that all of them could not be wrong. "In the mouth of two or three witnesses, every word shall be established."

CHAPTER XIII.

TRIUMPHS ON THE TOW-PATH.

HE boat was nearing the twenty-one locks of Akron.

"Make the first lock ready," cried the captain to his bowman. It was ten o'clock at night.

"Ay!" answered the bowman, promptly.

As the bowman approached the lock, a voice came through the darkness from the bowman of another boat, —

"Don't turn this lock; our boat is just around the bend, ready to enter."

"I *will* turn it; we got here first," answered the bowman of the "Evening Star," with an oath that seemed blacker in the absence of the sun.

"You won't turn it unless you are stronger than we are," shouted bowman number one, adding sufficient profanity to match the vocabulary of the other.

A fight was imminent, as all hands on board saw, and they rallied for the fracas. Such scenes were common on the canal. The boat whose bowman reached the lock first was entitled to enter first, but when two bowmen reached the lock about the same time a dispute was almost sure to arise, the result of which was a hand-to-hand fight between the two crews. The boat's crew that came to the top of the pile won the lock. Captains were usually powerless to prevent these contests, however well disposed they might be.

Captain Letcher's bowman commenced turning the gate just as the two boats came up so near that their head-lights shed the brightness of day on the exciting scene.

"Say, bowman," called Captain Letcher, motioning with his hand for attention. His bowman looked up in response.

"Were you here first?" Evidently the captain questioned his right to the lock.

"It's hard to tell," replied the bowman; "but we're goin' to have the lock, anyhow;" and the ring of his voice showed determination and fight.

"All right; just as you say," answered the captain, supposing that no interference of his could prevent an encounter.

The men stood panting for the fray, like war-horses. They seemed to be in just the right mood for a contest. It was a new scene to James, and he stood wondering, with the loud oaths bandied falling on his ear. After having restrained himself as long as he could, he tapped the captain on his shoulder, saying, —

"See here, captain, does that lock belong to us?"

"I really suppose, according to law, it does not; but we'll have it, anyhow," was the captain's reply.

"No, we will not," answered James, with a good deal of determination.

"Why not?" asked the captain, very much surprised at the boy's interference.

"Because it does not belong to us."

"That's so," the captain replied, seeing at once that James was right.

Probably the captain had never stopped to think whether the custom of fighting for a lock was right or not. But the suggestion of James seemed to act as an inspiration on him, and he called out to his bowman,—

"Hold on! hold on, boys!"

The men looked up in surprise, as if wondering what had happened. One minute more, and some hard knocks would have been given.

"Hold on!" repeated the captain, in the loudest tone of authority that he could command. "Let them have the lock."

The order was obeyed; the free fight was prevented; the other boat entered the lock; "peace reigned in Warsaw." James commanded the situation. His principles prevailed.

The boat was all night getting through the twenty-one locks, but at sunrise was on Lake Summit, moving forward under as bright a day-dawning as ever silvered the waters. The mules were moving on a slow trot, under the crack of the driver's whip, and everything was hopeful. Breakfast was called. George Lee, the steersman, came out and sat down to the table, and the first word he spoke was,—

"Jim, what's the matter with ye?"

"Nothing; I never felt better in my life," replied James.

"What did you give up the lock for last night?"

"Because it didn't belong to us."

"Jim," continued Lee, in a tone of bitterness, accompanied with his usual profanity, "yer are a coward; yer aint fit to be a boatman. Yer may do to chop wood or milk cows, but a man or a boy isn't fit for a boat who won't fight for his rights."

James only smiled at his fellow-boatman, and went on with his breakfast, making no reply. The captain heard the remarks, and admired the more the courage, coolness, and principle of his boy-driver. He saw that there was a magnanimous soul under that dirty shirt, and he enjoyed the evidence of its reign.

The boat reached Beaver, and a steamer was about to tow her up to Pittsburg, when the following incident occurred, just as the captain describes it.

James was standing on deck, with the setting-pole against his shoulders, and several feet away stood Murphy, one of the boat-hands, a big, burly fellow of thirty-five, when the steamboat threw the line, and, owing to a sudden lurch of the boat, it whirled over the boy's shoulders, and flew in the direction of the boatman.

"Look out, Murphy!" shouted James; but the rope had anticipated him, and knocked Murphy's hat off into the river.

"It was an accident, Murphy," exclaimed James, by way of excuse, "I'm very sorry."

"I'll make yer sorry," bellowed Murphy, thoroughly mad, and like a reckless bull he plunged at James, with his head down, thinking to knock him over, perhaps, into the water, where his hat had gone;

out James stepped nimbly aside, and dealt him a heavy blow behind the ear, tumbling him to the bottom of the boat, among the copper ore. Thinking to bring hostilities to a sudden close, he leaped upon Murphy, and held him down.

"Pound the fool, Jim," cried the captain. But James had him fast in his grip, so that the fellow could not harm him, and he refused to strike. He only said, —

"I have him, now."

"If he has no more sense than to get mad at accidents, give it to him. Why don't you strike?"

"Because he's down, and in my power," answered the noble boy. He never would have it said that he struck a man save in self-defence; and it is not self-defence to strike a man when he can be restrained without striking.

"Got enough, Murphy? You can get up when you have," said James to his conquered antagonist.

"Yis, 'nuff," answered Murphy. James rose, and allowed his assailant to rise also; then, extending his hand, in the magnanimous spirit of a victor, he said, —

"Murphy, give us your hand."

And they shook hands, and were fast friends thereafter. From that time James moved among the crew not as a greenhorn and coward, but as a boy-man, — a boy in age, but a man in action; a boy in physical appearance, but a man in convictions and generous spirit.

Among the boatmen was one Harry Brown, a good-hearted, rough, dissipated fellow, who had a strong liking for James, and would do almost anything for him. Harry was impetuous, and whiskey often increased his impetuosity, so that he was frequently in trouble.

"Look here, Harry, it's a little rough for you to be in rows so often; let whiskey alone, and you'll not be in trouble half so much," said James to him, in a kind way. If any one else on board had said that, Harry would have resented it and told him to "mind his own business." But he pleasantly said to James, —

"That's so, Jim; I'd giv a pile to be like yer."

"You can be, if you have a mind to," replied James. "Whiskey is the last stuff I should think of drinking, Harry; sooner drink the dirty water in this canal."

"Yer are a trump, Jim."

"I'm just what I am," replied James, "and you don't begin to be what you might be, Harry. Your generous soul could make sunshine all about you, only break your bottle."

This compliment tickled Harry in the right place, and he concluded that James was rehearsing more truth than poetry. James saw that he held the key to the rough boatman's heart, and he proceeded:

"I don't see why boatmen can't be as decent as other people, but they are not. They are about the hardest set I ever saw—drinking, swearing, bragging, fighting. Isn't it so, Harry?"

"Yer about right, Jim," Harry answered, with a comical shrug of his shoulders.

"If I was captain of a boat, I would have a new

order of things, or fling up my commission," James continued.

"I'll bet yer, Jim; we'd all behave well to please yer," interrupted Harry, acquiescing in the supposition.

"Well, now, Harry, don't you think yourself that it would be a great improvement, on canal boats, to give whiskey a wide berth?"

"True as preachin', Jim."

"And yet you continue to make yourself a disgrace to your sex, and are in hot water half your time. Isn't it so, Harry?"

Harry shook his sides over James' plainness of speech, and admitted that the boy was right.

"I hate this beastly way of living," continued James, "and I don't see why a fellow should act like a brute, when he is a man. I don't believe that you respect yourself, Harry."

"Right agin!" shouted Harry. "Yer see, if I did 'spect myself, I shouldn't do as I do. That's the trouble,—I have no 'spect for myself." And the poor, weak fellow never spoke a plainer truth in his life. Proper self-respect will lead such devotees of vice to reform, and be men.

"Yer see, Jim," added Harry, "I couldn't be like yer, if I tried."

"That's bosh," replied James. "Just as if a man can't be decent when he tries! You can't make that go, Harry. Throw whisky and tobacco overboard, as Murphy's hat went, and the thing is done."

"So you'd take all a feller's comforts away, Jim, t'backer and all," interposed Harry.

"Yes; and this awful profanity that I hear, also," retorted James. "I would make a clean sweep of the whole thing. What good does it all do?"

"What good! humph!" exclaimed Harry. "Yer are not fool 'nough to think we 'spect to do good in this way!" And Harry laughed again heartily, admitting the truth of James' position, without proposing to defend himself.

"What *do* you do it for, then?"

"Do it *for!* don't do it for nothin', Jim," responded Harry. "Nary good or evil we are after."

"You're a bigger fool than I thought you were," added James. "Making a brute of yourself for *nothing*. If that isn't being a fool, then I don't know what a fool is."

Harry laughed more loudly than ever, as he turned away, accepting the advice of James in the same spirit in which it was tendered. That he was not at all offended is evident from the fact that he was heard to say to Murphy afterwards, —

"Jim is a great feller. I've an orful itchin' to see what sort of a man he'll make. The way he rakes me down on whiskey, t'backer, and swearin', is a caution; and he don't say a word that ain't true; that's the trouble. And he says it in sich a way, that yer knows he means it. Jist think, Murphy; a boy on this old canal as don't drink rum, or smoke, or chew, or swear, or fight, — would yer believe it, if yer didn't see it?"

Murphy acknowledged that it was an anomaly on the Ohio and Pennsylvania canal, and hinted that he should like to know where the "feller" came from.

"I like him, though, Murphy," Harry continued. "I allers liked a man to show his colors. I like to know where a feller is, if he be agin me. And Jim is so cute; he'll beat the whole crowd on us tellin' stories, only they are not nasty, like the rest on us tell. Isn't he a deep one? He knows more'n all the crew put together, and two or three more boat-loads added, into the bargain."

James had fairly established himself in the respect and confidence, not only of the sober and intelligent captain, but of the drunken, ignorant crew, as well. On the whole, they were proud of him. Said the steersman to the bowman of another boat, "We've got a feller in our crew just the biggest trump yer ever see. Nary drinks whiskey, smokes, chews, swears, or fights, — d'ye believe it, old feller?" and he slapped the bowman on the back as he said it.

"Where'd he cum from?" the bowman inquired.

"That's what we'd like ter know, yer see: where he cum from, and how he happen'd to cum," responded the steersman. "But he's a jolly good fellow, strong as a lion, could lick any on us if he's a mind to; and he's a peeler for work, too; ain't afraid to dirty his self; and buckles right down to bisness, he does, jist like any on us. I never seed jest such a boy."

That the captain was won by the amount and quality of James' work, as well as by the reliability of his character, is evident from the fact that he promoted him to bowman at the end of his first trip. We mistrust that, in addition to the captain's confidence in his ability for the position, he exercised military tactics in the appointment, and concluded that it would put an end to brutal fights for the possession of locks.

By the confession of captain and crew, most of whom are still alive, James was a successful peacemaker on the canal boat, and his influence elevated the rough boatmen to some extent. He did it, too without making an enemy, but real friends of all. His forte lay in that direction.

The testimony of the captain is, that James did everything thoroughly as well as promptly; that he was as conscientious as he was resolute, declining to participate in any project that he considered wrong; that he possessed remarkable tact in his business as well as in dealing with men; and that he was a model boy in every respect, — "not talkative, but very intelligent; and when drawn into conversation, he surprised us by the depth of his knowledge on the topics of the day."

On the canal boat James had no books to read; and this was a serious privation. Occasionally, the captain had an opportunity to purchase newspapers, and these James read through and through. The captain thinks, however, that the absence of reading-matter was fully made up to him by the opportunity and demand for the exercise of his *observation*. He studied men and business, and asked a multitude of questions. Patrick Henry once said that he owed his success to "studying men more than books." Garfield studied men more than books, and the captain aided him materially by answering his questions. Perhaps it was an advantage for him, in the circumstances, to be where no books could be had for love or money.

James appeared to possess a singular affinity for the water. He fell into the water fourteen times during the two or three months he served on the canal boat. It was not because he was so clumsy that he could not keep right side up, nor because he did not understand the business; rather, we think, it arose from his thorough devotion to his work. He gave more attention to the labor in hand than he did to his own safety. He was one who never thought of himself when he was serving another. He thought only of what he had in hand to do. His application was intense, and his perseverance royal.

The last time he fell into the water he came near losing his life. It was on one very rainy night, when he was called up to take his turn at the bow. The boat was just leaving one of those long reaches of slack-water which abound in the Ohio and Pennsylvania Canal. James was awakened out of a very sound sleep, and he responded with his eyes half open, scarcely comprehending as yet the situation, and took his stand upon the platform below the bow-deck. He began to uncoil a rope to steady the boat through a lock it was approaching. The rope caught somehow on the edge of the deck, and resisted several pulls that he made to extricate it. At last it yielded, but, in the rebound, sent him headlong over the bow into the water. It was a very dark night, and he went down into the water, which was blacker than the night. In the mean while the boat was sweeping on, and no mortal knew of his mishap, and not a helping hand was near. Death seemed inevitable. Fortunately his hand seized the rope in the darkness, by accident, men will say, but by providential guidance really, and he drew himself, hand over hand, upon deck. He saw that he had been saved as by a miracle. The rope would have been of no service to him, only it caught in a crevice on the edge of the deck and held fast. He stood there dripping in his wet clothes, his thoughts running thus :

"What saved me that time? It must have been God. I could not have saved myself. Just a kink in the rope catching in that crevice saved me, nothing else. That was almost miraculous, and God does miraculous things. He thinks my life is worth saving, and I ought not to throw it away on a sea-faring life, and I won't. I will renounce all such ideas and get an education."

During the time that he was thus reflecting he was trying to throw the rope so that it would catch in the crevice. Again and again he coiled the rope and threw it; but it would neither kink nor catch. Repeated trials satisfied him that supernatural causes put the kinked rope into his hand, and saved his life.

That accident made a very deep impression upon his mind. His thoughts more than ever turned to his home and praying mother. He knew that every-day his dear mother remembered him at the throne of grace. He had no more doubt of it than he had of his existence. "Was it her prayers?" He could not evade the inquiry. He thought of all her anxieties and wise counsels, and her undying love. "Such a mother!" The thought would force itself uppermost in spite of himself. He felt rebuked, although he had been a good, obedient son. He had not been tender enough of his mother's feelings; he would be in future. He would quit the canal boat forever.

It was but a few weeks after the last immersion when James was quite severely attacked by ague, a disease that prevailed somewhat in that region. It prostrated him to such a degree that he was unfitted for labor; and this offered a favorable opportunity for him to carry out the resolution of that night of disaster.

"I must go home, captain," said James.

"It's a wise conclusion, Jim. You are too unwell for work, and there's no place like home for sick folks. I don't want to part with you, and the men will be sorry to have you go; but I think you'd better go."

"I regret to leave your service, captain, for I've enjoyed it; but I've been thinking of your advice, and I guess I shall put it in practice."

"You can't do a wiser thing, Jim; and I wouldn't lose a day about it. As soon as you are able, I'd go to studying, if I was in your place."

The captain settled with James, paying him at the rate of twelve dollars a month while he was driver, and eighteen dollars a month while he was bowman; and James started for home.

James was never so melancholy in his life as he was on the way home. The ague had taken his strength away, and made him almost as limp as a child. Then, he was thinking more of his duties, and his good mother. He had not written to her in his absence, between two and three months, and he rather rebuked himself for the neglect. "True," he thought, "I have been on the wing all the time, and there has been little opportunity for writing;" and so he partially excused himself for the neglect. His mother supposed that he was serving on a schooner somewhere on Lake Erie. He ought to have informed her of his whereabouts. So his thoughts were busy during his lonely journey home. It was nearly dark when he left the boat, so that he did not reach home until eleven o'clock at night.

As he drew near the house, he could see the light of the fire through the window. His heart beat quick and strong; he knew that it would be a glad surprise to his mother. Looking in at the window, he beheld her kneeling in the corner, with a book open in the chair before her. Was she reading? He looked again: her eyes were turned heavenward; she was praying. He listened, and he distinctly heard, "Oh, turn unto me, and have mercy upon me! Give Thy strength unto Thy servant, and save the son of Thine handmaid!" That was enough; he waited to hear no more. Mother and son were united again in loving embrace; and the tears that were shed were tears of joy.

CHAPTER XIV.

THE TURNING-POINT.

"WHY, James!" exclaimed his mother, when the excitement of their meeting was over, "you look sick."

"I am sick; and that's the reason I came home. It's been a very hard walk for me, I am so weak."

"How long have you been sick?" inquired his mother, with much anxiety.

"Not long. I've got the ague; had it a week or more."

"The ague!" answered his mother, astonished; "I didn't know that they ever had the ague on a ship."

"I have not been on a ship, but on the canal."

"On the canal!" rejoined his mother, still more surprised. "I thought you were on the lake all this time. How did it happen that you were on the canal?"

James rehearsed his experience on the schooner that he boarded, especially narrating his encounter with the captain, and his haste to escape from such a demon; how he met his cousin, Amos Letcher, of the canal-boat "Evening Star," and bargained with him for the position of driver, not omitting his hair-breadth escapes on the boat; concluding by a description of the exposures of the business, in consequence of which he was attacked by the ague.

His mother listened to the narration, which was more interesting to her than a novel, remarking at the close of it, —

"God has wonderfully preserved you, and brought you back, in answer to my prayers."

James was too full to make much reply. He managed, however, to say, "Nobody saved me from drowning, that dark night, but God." This brief remark sent a thrill of pleasure through his mother's heart. With all his obedience and excellence of character, James had not given before so much evidence as this that he recognized his personal obligations to God. His mother construed it into genuine religious conviction, and she was rejoiced beyond measure by the revelation.

"You must say no more to-night; you must go to bed, and get some rest," added his mother. "In the morning I will see how you are, and what can be done for you."

Both retired; his mother to a restless bed, being too full of joy and grateful thoughts to sleep. She lived over her whole life again, during that night, with all its checkered scenes; and she penetrated the future, in imagination, and beheld her dear boy dignifying his manhood by an honorable and useful career. "If he could only become a preacher!" The thought grew upon her in the "night watches." It became a source of real delight to her; and she thanked God, again and again, for his goodness. She found more enjoyment in wakefulness, and her thoughts, on that night, than she could have had in the sweetest sleep. It was the silent communing of a truly Christian heart.

Very early in the morning Mrs. Garfield was at the bedside of her son, anxious to learn how he was. He was in a sound sleep. She waited until the sunlight was bathing his brow, when she entered his room again. Her presence awoke him.

"You've had a sweet sleep, James," she said, inquiringly.

"The best sleep I've had for a week," James answered. "I was dreadful tired last night. I feel better this morning."

The ague is a fitful disease, and attacks its victims periodically, leaving them comparatively comfortable and strong on some days. James was really very comfortable on that morning,—there was no visible appearance of the ague upon him,—and he proposed to get up, dress himself, and look about the home that seemed more pleasant to him than ever. Returning to the kitchen, Mrs. Garfield prepared some simple remedy for him, such as pioneers were wont to administer to ague-patients. Pioneers were more or less familiar with the disease, and understood somewhat how to manage it. In severe cases a physician was called in to administer calomel—that was considered a specific at that time—until salivation was produced.

James was not comfortable long. On the following day a violent attack of the disease prostrated him completely.

"There's a hard bunch on my left side, and pain," said James to his mother.

"That's the ague-cake," replied his mother, on examining the spot. "That always appears in severe cases." The name was given by pioneers to the hardness; perhaps physicians called it by some other name.

"You are pretty sick, my son," continued Mrs. Garfield, "and I think you must have the doctor. Don't you think you better have the doctor?"

"Perhaps so; just as you think about it," was James' reply.

The physician of a neighboring village was sent for; and he put the patient through the usual calomel treatment, salivating him, and really causing him to suffer more by the remedy than by the disease. For weeks the big, strong boy lay almost as weak and helpless as a child. It was a new and rough experience for James. It was the first sickness he ever had; and to lie in bed and toss with fever, and shake with ague, by turns, was harder for him than chopping wood or planing boards. But for the wise management and tender care of his mother his experience would have been much more trying yet.

"How fortunate it was, James, that you came home when you did," remarked his mother.

"It was so, though I should have come home before long, if I had been well," replied James.

"Then you thought of giving up work on the canal?" continued Mrs. Garfield.

"Yes; I got about enough of it. Amos told me that I was a fool to follow such business when I am capable of something better," replied James, dropping just a word concerning his interview with Captain Letcher.

"I should agree with Amos on that," remarked his mother, smiling. "You knew that before."

"If God saved my life on that night, I didn't know but he saved it for something," added James; another indication of higher aspirations, that gratified his mother very much.

"If God did not save your life, it would be hard telling who did," responded Mrs. Garfield. "None of us should be blind to the lessons of His Providence. It's my opinion that the Lord didn't mean you should go to sea, and so he headed you off by that monster of a captain."

"Perhaps so," James answered, in a tone that might indicate either indifference or weakness.

"If God answers my prayers, James, you'll get an education, and be a teacher or preacher. My cup will run over when I see you in such a position."

"What if I should be a lawyer," remarked James.

"Well, I shall not object to that, if you are a good man. A wicked lawyer is almost as bad as a sailor. Above all things, I want you should feel that the Lord has the *first* claim upon your love and service. Don't you ever think, James, that you ought to give your heart to Him, and try for a more useful life?"

This question was unexpected to James, at the time, although such interrogations had often been put to him formerly. Indeed, the inquiry that Mrs. Garfield put was unexpected to herself, for she did not intend to put such a question when the conversation began. She expected to come to it sometime, however. She was feeling her way along, and leading her boy as best she could; yet, James answered, —

"I've thought more about it, lately."

"I hope you will continue to think about it, my son. It is the greatest thing you can think about. If you will only consecrate your powers to God, I know that you will make the best possible use of them; and you won't make such use of them unless you do that."

Mrs. Garfield was very discreet, and thought it not best to press the matter too persistently, but leave James to his own reflections. She was confident that the Lord had taken him in hand, and was leading him in a way the son knew not. She was greatly encouraged, and her prayers were more earnest than ever for his conversion to Christ.

The weeks dragged heavily along, and winter set in. James was still sick, but convalescent. A few weeks more, according to his improved symptoms, and he would be well enough for business, or school.

The winter school near Mrs. Garfield's began the first week in December, and it was taught by a young man by the name of Samuel D. Bates. He was a person of ability, a very earnest Christian, looking forward to the ministry in connection with the Disciples' Church. He was, also, an energetic, working young man, possessing large common sense, and intensely interested in benefiting the young people, intellectually and spiritually. From the commencement of the school he was very popular, too.

Mrs. Garfield made his acquaintance, and at once

concluded that he was just the person to influence James to aspire to an education. She could not help him herself, but her faith that God would open the way for him to go to school was unfaltering. She improved the first opportunity to tell Mr. Bates about James, — his sickness, frame of mind, and aspirations. She frankly announced to him that she wanted he should bring all his influence upon James to induce him to strive for an education. The teacher readily consented, for that was a kind of business in which he delighted, to help young men onward and upward. His first call upon James was immediate, though he did not announce the real object he had in view, thinking it would not be wise.

"Mr. Bates is a very interesting man, James," remarked Mrs. Garfield, after the teacher left. "I don't wonder the scholars like him."

"I like him very much," replied James. "I hope he will come in here often. I wish I was able to go to school to him."

"I wish you could; but Providence orders otherwise, and it will be all for the best, I have no doubt. Mr. Bates is working his way into the ministry. He teaches school in order to earn money to pay his bills. That is what you could do. If you could go to school a few months, you could teach school next winter, and, in that way, earn money for further schooling."

"I don't know as I should be contented in that occupation," responded James. "Once in a while, mother, I have a strong desire to go to sea again. There is something about the water that fascinates me. The sight of a ship fills my eye; indeed, the *thought* of a ship awakens a strong desire within, to tread its deck and handle its ropes."

"But you are not disposed to return to the canal, or to follow a sea-faring life?" inquired his mother, surprised at his frank avowal. She had begun to think that he had abandoned all thoughts of the sea.

"I should like it, if I thought it was best," he answered.

"It is not best, James; I can see that plainly."

"Since I have got better, my desire for the sea has returned, in a measure," added James, "causing me to ask myself if I shall not be disappointed if I abandon the purpose altogether."

"Not at all," responded Mrs. Garfield. "When you once get engaged in study you will like it far better than you can the sea, I am sure; and teaching school is a business that will bring you both money and respect. I think we can manage to scrape together money enough for you to start with."

"I will think it over," added James; "I shan't decide in a hurry."

"If you work on the canal, or become a sailor on the lake, you will have work only part of the year," continued his mother. "You will find little to do in the winter. How much better it will be for you to go to school, and qualify yourself for a teacher! Then you can sail in the summer, and teach school in the winter."

Mrs. Garfield feared that a total abandonment of the idea of going to sea would be quite impossible for James at present; and so her policy was to lure him into the way of knowledge by degrees. She suggested sailing in summer, and teaching in winter, hoping, that when he had qualified himself to teach, he would be so much in love with books as to banish all thoughts of a ship.

There was a sort of mystery, in James' strong desire for a sea-faring life, to his mother. And yet there was no mystery about it. Many are born with an adventurous, daring spirit, which the reading of a book may set strongly in a given direction. There is no doubt that the books James read at the black-salter's were the spark that kindled his adventurous spirit into a flame. We have seen a sailor who enjoys life on the ocean with the keenest relish, and his attention was first turned in that direction by a book presented to him by his uncle.

It is related of a traveller, that he sought lodgings one night at a farm-house in Vermont. He found an aged couple, well-to-do in this world's goods, living there alone. In the course of the evening he learned that they had three sons following the sea. It was an inexplicable affair to them, that their sons, living far away from the sea, should have so strong a desire to be sailors, from boyhood. One after the other, when they attained the age of twelve or fifteen, an almost uncontrollable desire for the sea had taken possession of them. In each case, too, the parents gave their consent to entering upon a sea-faring life not until they feared the sons would go without it. While the father was rehearsing the story of their lives, the traveller was observing a painting on the ceiling, over the mantel-piece. It was an ocean scene, — a ship sailing over a tranquil sea, — painted after the manner of the olden times. When the father ceased his remarks, the traveller said, pointing to the painting,—

"There is the cause of your sons' sailor-life. From infancy they have had that painting before their eyes, and it has educated them for the sea. In the earliest years, when their hearts were most impressible, that ocean scene set them in that direction; and finally their hearts were made to burn with unconquerable desire."

This explanation was perfectly satisfactory to the aged couple, and, no doubt, it was the correct one. The fact shows that there is no mystery about such a love for the ocean as James possessed. Such a fervent nature as his would readily be ignited by a random spark from a glowing book or a glowing speech. Nor did he ever outgrow this delight in the sea. After more than thirty years had elapsed since his conflict with the ague, he said, in reference to this feeling: "The sight of a ship fills me with a strange fascination. When upon the water, and my fellow-men are suffering sea-sickness, I am as tranquil as when walking the land in serenest weather. The spell of 'Jack Halyard' has not yet worn off."

Mr. Bates continued his calls at the Garfields', always aiming to draw out James in respect to his religious convictions, and his plans for the future. All these interviews were very profitable to James. His mother saw clearly, that in the skilful hands of the teacher he was being moulded, and her heart rejoiced. She was satisfied that he was making progress in religious purpose. He was frank to confess his need of Divine grace, and renewing, and to express a purpose to become a Christian. At the last interview which we have space to notice, Mr. Bates brought him to a final decision.

"Look here, young man," he said; "the difference between a scholar and sailor is the difference between somebody and nobody." And he rung the changes on the words SCHOLAR and SAILOR, until the latter appeared almost beneath notice.

"Go to school with me at Chester on the first week in March," said Mr. Bates. "Settle that first, that you will go with me to school at that time. That will be the first step, and the most important."

"I will go," answered James, unexpectedly at that moment to his mother. He said it with emphasis, indicating that the matter was settled.

"That's business," continued Mr. Bates. "I have no concern about the details, as to how you will raise money to pay your way, or whether you will have to relinquish the attempt to acquire an education after you have begun your studies. All these things will come right at the time, and the way will be provided. You have said, '*I will go*,' and that commits you to the great purpose of your life. It is the *turning point* of your career. You have set your face towards 'Geauga Seminary,' and I have no idea that you will look back, or hanker for a ship, or do any other unmanly thing. I consider that the turning point of *my* life was when I finally decided to be educated for the ministry; and from that moment I have felt it was the great decision of my life."

These words exerted a profound influence upon James, and that influence deepened from year to year as he grew older. Years afterwards, as we have seen, when addressing an audience of young men, he bore strongly upon this point, and said, "It is a great point gained when a young man makes up his mind to devote several years to the accomplishment of a definite work."

A mother's prayers and love had triumphed. Was she not a happy woman?

"I have a little money, and I know where I can get a little more, and that will be enough to start on," his mother remarked.

"I can find work to do out of school, and on Saturdays, when school don't keep, and so earn money to pay my way," responded James.

"Yes, I've no doubt of it. You know that Mr. Bates said all these things would come around right when you had decided to go," remarked Mrs. Garfield.

"I mean to see if William and Henry will not go, too; we can room together," continued James. These were his two cousins, who lived close by, sons of his uncle, Amos Boynton. They were members of his Spelling Club a few years before, when, together, they mastered Noah Webster's Spelling Book.

"That will be a good idea, James; and I think they will go," responded his mother, encouragingly. "There is no reason why they should not go."

It was only three weeks before the school at Chester would begin. James announced to his cousins that he had resolved to attend Geauga Seminary, and wanted they should go, too. The subject was discussed in the family for a week; Mr. Bates was consulted, and was glad to influence two other boys to take so wise a step; and finally it was settled that William and Henry should go with James.

While matters were progressing thus favorably, James heard that Dr. J. P. Robinson, of Bedford, was coming into the neighborhood on a professional visit, and, without consulting any one, he resolved to consult him concerning the practicability of his decision to acquire an education. It was not because he was wavering at all, but it was more of a curiosity on his part. So he called upon the doctor after his arrival at the neighbor's, and the interview, as narrated by Dr. Robinson to a writer, recently, was as follows:

"He was rather shabbily clad, in coarse satinet trousers, far out-grown, and reaching only half-way down the tops of his cowhide boots; a waistcoat much too short, and a threadbare coat whose sleeves went only a little below the elbows. Surmounting the whole was a coarse slouched hat, much the worse for wear; and as the lad removed it, in making his obeisance to the physician, he displayed a heavy shock of unkempt yellow hair that fell half-way down his shoulders.

"'He was wonderfully awkward,' says the good doctor, 'but had a sort of independent, go-as-you-please manner, that impressed me favorably.'

"'Who are you?' was his somewhat gruff salutation.

"'My name is James Garfield, from Orange,' replied the latter.

"'Oh, I know your mother, and knew you when you were a babe in arms; but you have outgrown my knowledge. I am glad to see you.'

"'I want to see you alone,' said young Garfield.

"The doctor led the way to a secluded spot in the neighborhood of the house, and there, sitting down on a log, the youth, after a little hesitation, opened his business.

"'You are a physician,' he said, 'and know the fibre that is in men. Examine me, and tell me with the utmost frankness whether I had better take a course of liberal study. I am contemplating doing so; my desire is in that direction. But if I am to make a failure of it, or practically so, I do not desire to begin. If you advise me not to do so I shall feel content.'

"In speaking of this incident, the doctor has remarked, recently: 'I felt that I was on my sacred honor, and the young man looked as though he felt himself on trial. I had had considerable experience as a physician, but here was a case much different from any other I had ever had. I felt that it must be handled with great care. I examined his head, and saw that there was a magnificent brain there. I sounded his lungs, and found that they were strong, and capable of making good blood. I felt his pulse, and saw that there was an engine capable of sending the blood up to the head to feed the brain. I had seen many strong physical systems with warm feet, but cold, sluggish brain; and those who possessed such systems would simply sit around and doze. Therefore I was anxious to know about the kind of an engine to run that delicate machine, the brain. At the end of a fifteen minutes' careful examination of this kind, we rose, and I said, "Go on, follow the leadings of your ambition, and ever after I am your friend. You have the brain of a Webster, and you have the physical proportions that will back you in the most herculean efforts. All you need do is to work. Work hard, do not be afraid of overworking, and you will make your mark." ' "

"I wish you had a better suit of clothes, James," remarked his mother, "but we shall have to make these do, I guess." It was the same suit he had on when he called upon Dr. Robinson. Indeed, he possessed no other suit. The trousers were nearly out at the knees, but under the skilful hand of his mother, they were made almost as good as new.

"Good enough, any way," said James, in reply to his mother's wish. It was fortunate that he was not the victim of a false pride: if he had been, he would not have consented to attend a "seminary" in that plight.

It was settled that the boys should board themselves, each one carrying his own outfit in utensils and provisions, doing it as a matter of economy.

When Mrs. Garfield had scraped together all the money she could for James, the amount was only about eleven dollars.

"That will do to begin with," he remarked. "I can earn more."

CHAPTER XV.

GEAUGA SEMINARY.

ON the fifth day of March, the day before the school opened, James and his cousins travelled to Chester, on foot, quite heavily loaded with cooking utensils and provisions. The distance was ten miles, over roads that were poor, indeed, at that season of the year. They carried dippers, plates, a knife and fork each, a fry-pan, kettle, and other things to match, with a quantity of ham, or "bacon," as the settlers called it. James was arrayed in the suit of clothes in which he appeared before Dr. Robinson, and the other boys were clad about ditto. No one would have charged them with pride, on their way to the "Seminary." At this day, some faithful constable would arrest such a troop for tramps, who had robbed a farmer's kitchen and were taking "leg bail." Nevertheless, they were three as jolly boys as Cuyahoga County could boast. Their errand was nobler and grander than that of any aspirant who was fishing for an office in the State of Ohio. Why should they not be jolly?

They proceeded directly to the house of the principal, Mr. Daniel Branch, an eccentric man, though a very respectable scholar in some departments.

"We've come to attend your school," said James, addressing himself to Mr. Branch. "We came from Orange."

"What's your name?" inquired the principal.

"*My* name is James A. Garfield; and these are my cousins [turning to the boys]; their names are William and Henry Boynton."

"Well, I'm glad to see you, boys; you might be engaged in much worse business than this. I suppose you are no richer than most of the scholars we have here."

The last remark of Mr. Branch is good evidence that he had surveyed the new-comers from head to foot, and that the remark was prompted by their poor apparel.

"No, sir," answered James, dryly; "we are not loaded down with gold or silver, but with pots, and kettles, and provisions for housekeeping."

"Going to board yourselves, then," replied the teacher, by way of inquiry.

"Yes, sir; can you tell us where we can find a room?" answered James.

"Yes; near by," answered Mr. Branch; "a good deal of that business is done here. Scores of our boys and girls would never stay here if they could not board themselves. "Look here," and stepping out from the door-way he pointed to an old, unpainted house, twenty or thirty rods away. "You see that old house there, do you?" he said. James assented. "I think you will find a room there: an old lady, as poor as you are, lives in one part of it. You will go to her to inquire."

"Thank you, sir, thank you," repeated the boys, politely, as they started for the antique habitation. They found the old lady, and hired a room, for a pittance, in which there were a fireplace, three old chairs, that corresponded with the building, and two beds on the floor, or what the good woman of the house was bold enough to call beds. Here they unpacked their goods, and set up housekeeping by cooking their first meal.

The "Geauga Seminary" was a Free-will Baptist institution, in quite a flourishing condition, having a hundred students, of both sexes, drawn thither from the towns in that region. The town in which it was located, Chester, was small, but pleasant, the academy furnishing the only attraction of the place.

School opened, and James devoted himself to grammar, natural philosophy, arithmetic, and algebra. He had never seen but one algebra before he purchased the one he used. The principal advised him to take this course of study.

It was a new scene for James, a school of one hundred pupils, male and female, most of them better clad than himself. He was awkward and bashful, especially in the presence of young ladies, whom he regarded as far superior to young men of the same age and attainments. Still he broke into the routine of the school readily, and soon was under full headway, like a new vessel with every sail set.

Singularly enough, he encountered an unexpected difficulty in the grammar-class within a very few days.

James said, "*but* is a conjunction."

"Not so; *but* is a *verb*, and means *be out*," replied the teacher.

"A *verb! but* a *verb?*" exclaimed James, in reply, without scarcely thinking that he was calling the teacher's opinion in question. He had Kirkman's grammar at his command, even to its preface, which he could glibly repeat, word by word; and he knew that *but* was a conjunction, according to Kirkman, and all the teachers whose pupil he had been. Could his teacher be joking, or did he make a blunder?

"Yes; *but* is a verb, no matter what the books say, young man; whose grammar have you studied?" the teacher answered.

"Kirkman's," replied James.

"Kirkman! and he is just like all the rest of them, wrong from beginning to end," said Mr. Branch. "That's not the grammar you will learn in this school, I can tell you, by any means. I teach a grammar of my own, the grammar of common sense."

James thought it was the grammar of nonsense, though he did not say so. At that time he did not know that Mr. Branch was at war with all the grammarians, and had introduced a system of instruction in that study peculiarly his own.

"Besides Kirkman, all the teachers I ever had have called *but* a conjunction," added James, directly implying that he did not accept Branch's grammar.

"You don't believe it, I clearly see, young man; but you *will* long before you have spent twelve weeks in this school," remarked Mr. Branch. "You will have sense to see that I am right, and the old grammarians wrong."

"If *but* is a verb, I don't see why *and* is not a verb

also," remarked James, being quite inclined to array Kirkman against Branch.

"It is a verb, James; *and* is a verb, I want you to understand, in the imperative mood, and means *add*; that is all there is to it," was the emphatic answer of Mr. Branch.

James looked at the boys, and smiled in his knowing way. The teacher saw the unbelief which pervaded that look, and he continued,

"See here, young man; *and* does something more than connect two things; it *adds*. I want to speak of you and Henry, two of you together, and I say, James and Henry; that is, *add* Henry to James: don't you see it now? It is clear as daylight."

There was no daylight in it to James, and he so expressed himself. Each day brought discussions in the class between the principal and James. The former's system of grammar was all of a piece with *and* and *but*, so that the hour for the grammar class was an hour of contention, very spicy to the members of the class, but rather annoying to the teacher. The latter was not long in discovering that he had a remarkable scholar in James,—one who would not receive anything on trust, or without the most substantial reason or proof. His respect for James' talents somewhat reconciled him to his annoying contradictions.

The boys had much sport over Branch's grammar; we mean James and his cousins.

"If *but* is a verb, then but*ter* must be an *ad*verb, since it only *adds* three more letters and one more syllable," said James.

"You ought to have told him so," replied Henry; "it's a good point: it is carrying out his system exactly."

"Not much system about it, any way," responded James, "but a good deal of egotism and stubbornness."

"You can be as stubborn as he is," remarked Henry. "He don't hardly know how to get along with Kirkman; it's tough for him.

We will not follow the grammar class. It should be said, however, that James never adopted Branch's grammar. He contended against it so long as he continued in the class; and it is our private opinion that the author of Branch's Grammar was well pleased when James exchanged it for another study.

The boys succeeded tolerably well at housekeeping, though they did not extract quite so much fun from it as they expected. After a short time, they hired the old lady in the house to cook some of their food. She did their washing, also. It was only a very small amount they paid her weekly. Still, buying his books, and incurring some other unavoidable expenses, James saw his eleven dollars dwindling away quite rapidly.

"I must look up work, or I shall become bankrupt soon," remarked James. "I can see the bottom of my purse now, almost."

"What sort of work do you expect to find in this little place?" inquired William.

"Carpenter work, I guess," answered James. "I've had my eye on that carpenter's shop yonder [pointing] for some time. They seem to be busy there. I never lived anywhere yet that I couldn't find work enough. I shall try them to-morrow."

"What is that carpenter's name," inquired William.

"Woodworth — Heman Woodworth. I have had my eye on him for some time."

Before school, on the following morning, James applied to Mr. Woodworth for work.

"What do you know about this business?" Mr Woodworth inquired.

"I have worked for Mr. Treat, of Orange," James replied.

"I know him; what can you do?" said Mr. Woodworth.

"I can build a barn, if you want I should," answered James, laughingly. "I have helped in building five or six barns. I can plane for you."

"You look as if you might be a good, strong fellow for planing," continued Mr. Woodworth. "You pay your own way at school?"

"Yes, sir; I had only eleven dollars to begin with, and that won't last long."

"Not long, I should think, as board is here."

"I board myself," added James, by way of enlightening the carpenter.

"Board yourself? That is rather tough, though many do it."

"Many things are tougher than that," remarked James.

"Perhaps so; but that is tough enough. You may come over after school, and I'll see what I can do for you."

"And what you can do for yourself," quickly responded James. "If I can't work so as to make it an object for you to hire me, then I don't wish to work for you. I don't ask you to let me have work as a matter of charity."

Mr. Woodworth admired the pluck of the boy, and he repeated, "Come over after school, and I will see what I can do for you."

"I can work two or three hours a day, and all day on Saturdays; and you needn't put a price on my work until you see what I can do," added James, as he turned away.

The result was that Mr. Woodworth hired James, who worked at the shop before school in the morning, and then hurried to it at the close of school, at four o'clock; and on Saturdays, he made a long day's labor. He continued this method through the term, denying himself the games and sports enjoyed by the scholars, excepting only an occasional hour. No boy loved a pastime better than he, but to pay his bills was more important than sport. At the close of the term he had money enough to pay all his bills, and between two and three dollars to carry home with him.

One of the chief attractions of the seminary to James was its library, although it was small. It contained only one hundred and fifty volumes; but to James that number was a spectacle to behold. He was not long in ascertaining what books it contained; not that he read a great many of them, for he had not time; but he examined the library and found it destitute of books of the "Jack Halyard" style; nor was he sorry. He found a class of books just suited to aid students like himself in their studies, and he was well satisfied. He made as much use of them as possible in the circumstances, and often read far into the night. It was a luxury to him, rather than a self-denial, to extend his studies into the night, in order to be perfect in his lessons, and secure a little time for reading.

The regulations of the school made it necessary for James to write a composition twice a month, sometimes upon a subject announced by the principal, and sometimes upon a topic of his own selection. Occasionally, the authors of the essays were required to read them to the whole school, from the platform. The first time that James read an essay, he trembled more than he did before rebel cannon twelve or fourteen years thereafter.

"Lucky for me," said James to his room-mates, "that there was a curtain in front of my legs," alluding to a narrow curtain on the edge of the platform.

"How so?" inquired William.

"No one could see my legs shake; you would have thought they had the shaking palsy."

"I never would have thought that of you?" added William.

"It's true, whether you thought it of me or not. I never trembled so in my life."

"Then you were scared?" remarked William.

"I guess that was the name of it," replied James.

"Your essay wasn't scared, Jim; it was capital," continued William. "I should be willing to shake a trifle, if I could write such an essay. Some of them were astonished that such a suit of clothes as yours should hide such a production."

"Much obliged," answered James; "you seem to praise my essay at the expense of my clothes. I can afford an essay better than a suit of clothes. It costs only thought and labor to produce the essay, but it costs money to get the clothes."

James had taken from the library the "Life of Henry C. Wright," and had become deeply interested in its perusal. He learned of the privations and denials of Mr. Wright, as well as his methods in acquiring an education; and he was captivated by the spirit of the man.

"We can live cheaper than we do," he remarked to his cousins. "Another term we must adopt Mr. Wright's diet."

"What was that?" inquired Henry.

"Milk."

"Nothing but milk?"

"Bread and milk; a milk diet wholly."

"How long?"

"Right through his course of study."

"Was it cheaper than we are living — thirty-five cents a week, apiece."

"Yes, but better than that, it was healthier."

"How did he know that?"

"Because he was better than ever before, and had a clearer head for study."

"It may not suit us, though," remarked William, who had been listening to the conversation.

"We shan't know till we try," answered James.

"I propose to try it, next term. We are a little too extravagant in our living, now; we must cut down our expenses. I have had the last cent that I shall take from my friends. I shall pay my own way, hereafter."

"You can't do it," said Henry.

"Then I will quit study. I know I can do it. My mother needs all the money she can get without helping me."

"I admire your pluck," added Henry; "but I think you will find yourself mistaken."

"As I am earning money now, I can pay my way," continued James; "and on a milk diet I can scrimp a little more."

"And if you should conclude not to eat anything, you could live at very small expense," retorted Henry, by way of making fun of his milk diet.

"Laugh at it as much as you please," replied James; "meat is not necessary to health; I am satisfied of that. There is more nourishment in good bread and milk than there is in roast-beef."

"Well, I should take the roast-beef if I could get it," interrupted William. "Milk for babes; and I am not a baby."

"Milk for scholars," responded James; "I actually believe that a better scholar can be made of milk than of beef."

"If you will say 'bacon' instead of beef, perhaps I shall agree with you," said William, playfully. "I don't think that bacon can produce high scholarship."

"Jim's essay was made out of it chiefly," remarked

Henry; "that was scholarly. Bacon has contributed too much to my comfort for me to berate it now."

And so the boys treated with some levity a subject over which James became an enthusiast. He was thoroughly taken with Mr. Wright's mode of living, and thoroughly resolved to adopt it the next term.

The Debating Society, also, interested James very much; it was the first one he had ever become acquainted with. The principal recommended it highly as a means of self-culture, and James accepted his recommendation as sound and pertinent. He engaged in debate hesitatingly at first, as if he had grave doubts of his ability in that direction; but he soon learned to value the Society above many of his academical privileges. The trial of his powers in debate disclosed a faculty within him that he had not dreamed of. He possessed a ready command of language, could easily express his thoughts upon any question under discussion, and was really eloquent for one so ungainly in personal appearance. He studied each question before the club as he would study a lesson in algebra, determined to master it. He could usually find books in the library that afforded him essential aid in preparing for debates, so that he appeared before the school always well posted upon the subject in hand. His familiarity with them often evoked remarks of surprise from both scholars and teachers. It was here, probably, that he laid the foundation for that remarkable ability in debate for which he was distinguished during his Congressional career. He began by preparing himself thoroughly for every discussion, and that practice was maintained by him to the end. It made him one of the most prompt, brilliant, and eloquent disputants in the national legislature.

It was not strange that James won enviable notoriety in the Debating Society of the Geauga Academy. The debates became important and attractive to the whole school because he was a disputant. Scholars hung upon his lips, as afterwards listening crowds were charmed by his eloquence. Teachers and pupils began very soon to predict for him a brilliant future as a public speaker. In their surprise and admiration of the young orator they forgot the jean trousers, that were too short for his limbs by four inches.

Henry Wilson discovered his ability to express his thoughts, before an audience in the village Debating Society of Natick, Mass., in early manhood. Here he subjected himself to a discipline that insured his eminence as a debater in Congress. The celebrated English philanthropist Buxton had no thought of becoming an orator or a statesman, until he learned, in the debating society of the school which he attended, that he possessed an undeveloped ability for the forum. The distinguished English statesman, Canning, declared that he qualified himself for his public career in the school of his youth, where the boys organized and supported a mock parliament, conducting the debates, appointing committees, enforcing rules, and pitting one party against the other, precisely as was done by Parliament. In like manner, the hero of this volume really began his distinguished public career in the lyceum of Geauga Seminary.

CHAPTER XVI.

AFTER VACATION.

VACATION of two months in the summer gave James ample opportunity for manual labor. Thomas was at home, and he decided to build a frame barn for his mother. He could have the assistance of James, who really knew more about barn-building than Thomas did.

"I s'pose you can frame it, Jim," said Thomas.

"I suppose that I can, if algebra and philosophy have not driven out all I learned of the business."

"You can try your hand at it, then. I should think that algebra and philosophy would help rather than hinder barn-building," added Thomas.

"Precious little they have to do with barns, I tell you," responded James. "They are taking studies, though."

"It won't take you long to find out what you can do," continued Thomas; "it spoils some boys to go to school too much."

Thomas had prepared sufficient lumber when he was at home, at different times, for the barn. It was all ready to be worked into the building; and the brothers proceeded to the task resolutely, James leading off in framing it. No outside help was called in, Thomas and James considering themselves equal to the task.

We need not delay to record the details of the job. It will answer our purpose to add, simply, that the barn was built by the brothers, and thus one more convenience was added for the comfort of their mother. The day of log buildings was now over for the Garfield family. Times had wonderfully changed since Mr. Garfield died, and the population of the township had increased, so that "the wilderness and solitary place" had disappeared.

As soon as the barn was completed, James sought work elsewhere among the farmers. He must earn some money before returning to Chester, for a portion of his doctor's bill remained unpaid, and then, a new suit of clothes, shirts, and other things, would require quite an outlay.

He found a farmer behind time in getting his hay.

"Yes, I want you," the farmer said; "and I wish you had been here two weeks ago: it seems as if haying would hold out all summer."

"You are rather behind time, I judge," replied James. "Better late than never, though."

"I don't know about that, James. I rather have it read, *better never late*," remarked the sensible man.

"That is my rule," answered James. "At school we are obliged to be on time. Tardiness is not allowable."

"It never should be allowed anywhere. It seems as if we can never catch up when we once get behind," continued the farmer; "and then there is no comfort in it. It keeps one in torment all the while, to feel that he is behindhand : I don't like it."

"Neither do I," answered James. "It is worse to be behindhand in school than it is on a farm, much worse, I think. A scholar behind his class is an ob ject of pity."

The farmwork did not continue behindhand long, however. The remainder of the haying was accomplished in a week, and James had opportunity for other jobs. He found work clear up to the close of his vacation, not having even a day for pastime. Thus he was able to pay off his doctor's bill, provide a better outfit for another school term than he had the first term, and to aid his mother also.

James was not idle during the evenings of his vacation. Algebra occupied a portion of his time; and two or three reading books, which he brought from the Chester library, beguiled many of his evening hours. If he had any leisure hours during his vacation, they were not idle hours. Every hour told upon the new purpose of his life. He had ceased to talk about going to sea, or even coasting on Lake Erie, in his enthusiasm for an education. His mother, of course, never reverted to the subject, and she was rejoiced to find that James was aspiring to something higher and nobler. He was too much absorbed in his course of study to talk about a sea-faring life, or even to think about it.

"I wish you had some money to take back with you James," remarked his mother, the day before he left for the seminary.

"I don't know as I care for more," answered

James. "I have a *ninepence* [showing the bit, and laughing], and that will go as far as it is possible for a ninepence to go. I have it all arranged to work for Mr. Woodworth, out of school, and I can easily pay my way."

"That may be true; but a few dollars to begin the term with would be very convenient," replied Mrs. Garfield.

"Better begin with nothing and end with something, than to begin with something and end with nothing," added James.

"I suppose, then, that you expect to end the term with more money than you begin it with?" said his mother, inquiringly.

"Yes, I do; for I shall want a little change in my pocket in the winter, if I teach school," replied James.

"Then you really expect to be qualified to teach school next winter, do you?"

"I design to; perhaps I shall be disappointed, though."

"I hope not," continued his mother. "By teaching school in the winter you can get together money enough to pay your school bills the rest of the year; and that will make it easy for you. I want to see you able to earn enough in winter to pay all your school bills, so that you will not be obliged to work before and after school to earn money."

"I don't expect to see that time, mother. I am content to work my way along as I have done," was James' brave reply. "Nobody can be healthier than I am; so that it don't wear upon me much."

James returned to Geauga Seminary at the opening

of the fall term, with the solitary ninepence in his pocket. He playfully suggested to Henry that "the bit must be very lonesome," and thought he might provide a "companion" for it ere long. The circumstances remind us of the experience of the late Horace Mann, of Massachusetts. Born in poverty, though not so poor as James, he had little hope of gratifying his strong desire for an education. Providence, however, opened the way for him to prepare for college, which he did in six months, not knowing whether he would be able to enter or not. By dint of perseverance, he scraped together money enough to get him into college, although he could not tell where the money was coming from to keep him there. After a few weeks he wrote to his sister, "My last two ninepences parted company some days ago, and there is no prospect of their ever meeting again." That is, he had a solitary ninepence in his pocket.

On the Sabbath after James' return to the seminary he was at public worship, when the contribution-box was passed through the audience. Whether James' sympathy for the lonely bit in his pocket got the better of his judgment, or whether it was the generosity of his soul (we suspect it was the latter), he dropped the ninepence into the box, thereby creating as great an emptiness as possible in his pocket. He was now upon an equality with the widow of the Scriptures, who cast her two mites (all she had) into the treasury of the Lord.

James and his cousins boarded themselves during the fall term, adopting Wright's milk diet at first, thereby reducing their expenses a very little, though not much.

"Just thirty-one cents each, per week," remarked James, after the trial of that method of living four weeks. He had kept a careful account, and now found the result to be as indicated.

"I feel as if it had not cost us more than that," answered Henry. "My physical constitution is reduced quite as much as our expenses, I think." He said this humorously in part, although he was not much captivated by their mode of living.

"That which costs the least is not always the cheapest," remarked William, whose opinions coincided with those of his brother. "*I* feel as if we were having pretty *cheap* living;" and he emphasized the word "cheap" in his peculiar way.

"Well, I feel as if I had been living on the fat of the land," responded James. "I think I could handle you both," he added, laughingly.

"There's no doubt of it," replied Henry; "you would grow fat on sawdust pudding, only have enough of it; but this sticking to one article of diet right along don't suit me."

"You are one of the philosophers who maintain that 'variety is the spice of life,' in eating as well as in pleasure, I suppose," answered James. "For my part, one thing at a time will do for me, if it is only *good* enough."

"I don't know of one thing alone that is good enough for me," remarked Henry. "I go for increasing our expenses a little. We can go up to fifty cents a week without damaging anybody."

"That's what I think," added William. "I think I can be pretty well satisfied with that."

"Just as you choose, boys; I can make way with nineteen cents' worth of luxuries more, in case of necessity," replied James. "Sawdust pudding or plum pudding is all the same to me; I can thrive on either."

"Now, Jim," said Henry, very philosophically, "I believe, after all, that you are as anxious as we are for better living, only you don't want to own it, and back down. You are the last fellow to back out of anything." Henry was about right in his remark. James was not at all unwilling to adopt a more expensive fare, although his iron will would carry him through his work with almost any sort of diet. His health was so robust, and his power of endurance so great, that he could eat much or little, apparently, and thrive.

The upshot of this interview was, that James assented to the increase of expenses to fifty cents per week, each. Milk was continued chiefly as their diet, but other things were added for variety. The last half of the term their board cost them fifty cents per week.

James had never spoken with the principal about becoming a teacher, although he was intending to do it. But Mr. Branch opened the subject about the middle of the term. He well knew the poverty of James, and took additional interest in him for that reason. He felt that a youth of his talents ought to acquire an education; and he could see no better way of accomplishing it than by teaching school in the winter.

"How would you like to try your hand at school-keeping, James?" inquired Mr. Branch.

"I *intend* to try my hand at it next winter, if I can get a school," answered James. "My mother has always said that I could get an education if I would qualify myself to teach school."

"A good plan, James; I agree with your mother, exactly. Glad to see that you mind your mother, for such boys usually come out all right." Mr. Branch was in a happy frame of mind when he said this, and his real kindness to James appeared in every word.

"Then," he continued, "what is better than all, you can do a good deal of good by teaching school You will not only find it the best way to help your self, but you will find it the best way to help others; and that is the highest of all considerations. We don't live for ourselves in this world, or *ought not* to live for ourselves alone. That is too selfish and contemptible to be tolerated."

"Do you think I can obtain a school, without any doubt?" inquired James.

"Unquestionably," answered Mr. Branch. "Teachers are more numerous than they were ten years ago, and so it is with schools. More than that, I think you will succeed in the business. Every one will not be successful in the calling."

"Why do you think I shall succeed?" asked James, who was curious to understand what particular qualities would win in the school-house.

"You will be well qualified; that is one thing. You possess ability to express your thoughts readily; that is very important for a teacher. Your mind is discriminating and sharp, to analyze and see the reason of things; that is also an indispensable qualification for a successful teacher. You will govern a school well, I think, without much trouble. A young man who is popular with associates in study usually makes a good teacher." This was the honest reply of the principal to the last inquiry of James; all of which was a substantial encouragement to the latter. He began to look forward to the new occupation with much pleasure.

One incident occurred at this term of school, relating to its discipline, in which James played a conspicuous part. At that time there were about as many rogues in a school of one hundred pupils as there are to-day. Human nature averaged about as it does now among pupils. There was the same need of wise government and watchfulness, on the part of the principal, to maintain order. In this respect, the principal was well qualified for his position; and roguish pupils could not rebel against his government with impunity. This was quite well understood; and still there were occasional scrapes, in which a class of pupils engaged, as the best way, in their estimation, to dispose of a surplus fund of animal spirits.

A youth of considerable pertness insulted one of the town's people, and it came to the ear of the principal. Indeed, the citizen entered a complaint against the pupil, rehearsing the facts to Mr. Branch. The credit of the school, and the credit of the principal himself, demanded that he should take notice of the matter, rebuke the act, and lecture the whole school, that there might not be a repetition of the act.

As often happens in large schools, the pupils took

sides with the author of the naughty deed. The sympathies of young people, especially in school, unite them together as by strong cords. Without regard to the merits of the case, they decide for the accused party, and sustain him.

"If Bell goes, I go," exclaimed one of the boys, meaning that if the principal expelled Bell, he would be one to leave the school, also. The fact shows that feeling played a more prominent part in the affair than judgment.

"And I'll be another to go," answered a smart young fellow; that is, smart in his own estimation.

"Will you take me along with you?" asked a third, who was more disposed to show humor than passion. "I'll add one to the company."

"Me, too!" exclaimed a fourth. "Put me down for that scrape. A great many folks think that school-boys have no rights."

In this way the subject was discussed among a class of the boys, and even some girls signified a willingness to express their indignation in some such way as that proposed. It was claimed that as many as "twenty" pupils would quit school if Bell was expelled. But when, at last, they came around to James with their proposition, they met with a serious embarrassment.

"Why should I leave the school, because another fellow is sent away?" answered James. "Can you tell me?"

Of course they could not give a reason why he should. One boy did venture to reply, —

"We want to show our indignation."

"Indignation about what?" asked James.

"At sending Bell away."

"But he is not sent away, yet; and he may not be."

"Well, I don't believe in treating a fellow so."

"How?" persisted James.

"Why, call a fellow up, and make such a touse over his way of speaking to a man."

"How did he speak?"

"The citizen claims that he insulted him. But that's not the thing for us boys to look at; we ought to stand by our fellows."

"Stand by them, right or wrong?" inquired James.

"Yes, if necessary."

"Well, I shall not," answered James, emphatically. "If one of our fellows gets into a scrape, I will not help him out, unless it can be done honorably; you can depend on that."

"I think it is mean," continued the boy, "for a citizen to complain of a scholar just because he did not use his tongue quite right."

"I don't agree with you," answered James; "Bell ought to use his tongue as well as he does his hands, for all that I can see; and if he gets into trouble, he has no one to blame but himself."

"That may all be true," added Bell's persistent friend; "but if he gets into trouble thoughtlessly, I am willing to help him out."

"So am I," quickly responded James; "provided he is sorry, and is willing to be helped out of it in a proper way."

"I suppose, by that, you have not a good opinion of our method of helping him?"

"No, I have not. If Bell will apologize to the citizen, and signify to Mr. Branch that he is sorry, and will not repeat the insult, I will be among the first to intercede for him, but he must help himself, before I am willing to help him."

This ended the proposed rebellion in school. Bell did make all suitable amends for his misconduct, and remained in the school. The incident illustrates a prominent trait of character in James, running through his life. He had an opinion of his own, and maintained it, in his youth, as he did in later life. He would not knowingly defend even a school-companion in wrong-doing. He repudiated the so-called "code of honor" in schools, requiring boys to support each other, whether right or wrong.

The fall term was a very profitable one to James. His scholarship became fully established. He led the school in talents and progress. He paid all his bills, also, by his daily labor in the carpenter's shop, and had several dollars left for pocket-money at the close of the term.

CHAPTER XVII.

KEEPING SCHOOL.

HE next day after James reached home, at the close of the term, he started out to find a situation as teacher.

"When will you return?" inquired his mother.

"When I get a school. Somehow I feel as if it would be a hard matter to get a school."

"I hope not, my son," answered his mother, rejoicing in her heart that James was going to be a teacher, and not a sailor.

"*I* hope not," responded James; "but I don't seem to feel as elated over the prospect as I did once. I shall do my best, however, and I may be gone several days."

James took the most favorable route, on foot, and made his first application about ten miles from home.

"You are too young," replied the committee to his application; "we don't want a *boy* to teach our school."

"I have a recommendation from Mr. Branch, Principal of the Geauga Seminary;" and he proceeded to exhibit his testimonials.

"No matter about that," replied the committee-man. "No doubt you know enough, but you can't make yourself any older than you are; that's the trouble. We've had boys enough keep our school."

This was quite a damper upon the ardor of James; and he left the man, and continued his journey, reflecting upon the value of age to pedagogues.

The next school district that he reached had engaged a teacher.

"If you had come a week ago, I'd hired yer," the man said.

It was encouraging to James that he had found a district where age was not an absolute requirement. He thought better of youth, now.

"Possibly in the Norton District they've not a teacher yet," the man added.

"Where's that?" inquired James.

"About three miles north of here," pointing with his finger. "Go to Mr. Nelson; he's the man you want ter see. He'll hire yer, if he's no teacher."

James posted away to the Norton District, and found Mr. Nelson, just about dark.

"Just found a teacher, young man, and hired him," Mr. Nelson said. "Can't very well hire another."

"Of course not," answered James; "and perhaps the one you hired needs the chance as much as I do."

"Perhaps so; he's trying to get an education."

"So am I," responded James.

"Where?"

"At Geauga Seminary."

"Ah! we had a teacher from that seminary, two years ago, and he was as good a teacher as we ever had."

"That is fortunate for me," remarked James, pleasantly. "If he had not proved a good teacher you would not want another from that institution."

"Very like," replied Mr. Nelson. "But come, you can't look after any more schools to-night; it is getting dark. Come in, and stop over night with us."

James accepted the cordial invitation, stopped with the family over night, and, on the following day, continued his school-hunting trip. But he did not find a school. He met with one committee-man who declined to hire him because "We had one feller from Gaga Seminary, and he made sich a botch of it that we don't want another."

After two days of hard work in the vain search for a school, James reached home more thoroughly discouraged than his mother ever knew him to be before.

"It is impossible to find a school; most of them have teachers engaged," said James. And he gave a full account of his travels and disappointments.

"Perhaps the Lord has something better for you in store, James," answered his mother. "It is not best for you to be discouraged, after you have overcome so many obstacles."

James did not tell his mother that if the Lord had anything better in store for him he would be obliged if he would make it known; but he thought so.

"You are tired enough to go to bed," added his mother; "and to-morrow you can talk with your Uncle Amos about it."

Uncle Amos was their counsellor in all times of trial; and James accepted the suggestion as a kind of solace, and retired.

The next morning, before he was up, he heard a man call to his mother, from the road.

"Widow Garfield!"

She responded by going to the door.

"Where's your boy, Jim?"

"He is at home. He is not up, yet," Mrs. Garfield replied, a little curious to know what he wanted of James so early in the morning.

"I wonder if he'd like to keep our school at the Ledge, this winter," the man continued.

James bounded out of bed at the sound of the word *school*, beginning to think that Providence had sent an angel, in the shape of a man, to bring the "something better," which his mother told about. He stood face to face with the man in an incredibly brief period. The caller was a well-known neighbor, living only a mile away, and the school for which he wanted a teacher was not much further than that.

"How is it, Jim; will you keep our school at the Ledge, this winter?" he inquired.

"I want a school," was James' indirect reply. He knew the character of the school,—that it was rough and boisterous, — and he hesitated.

"Reg'lar set of barbarians, you know, Jim, down there," the man continued.

"Yes; I know it is a hard school to teach. Do you think I can manage it? All the scholars know me." This reply of James showed what thoughts were passing through his mind. The committee-man replied:

"They all know you, of course; and they know that you can whip the whole of them without any trouble, if you set about it; and you are just the chap to run the school. The boys have driven out the master for two winters, now; and I want somebody to control the school this winter, if he don't do a thing but stand over them with a cane. A thrashing all round would do them an immense amount of good. Now, what do you say? Give you twelve dollars a month and board."

This portrayal of the character of the school rather discouraged James than otherwise; but his mother spoke, by way of helping him out of the difficulty:

"This is an unexpected call to James, and he had better consider it to-day, and let you know his decision to-night."

"I will do that," said James.

"That will answer; but I hope you won't fail me," the man responded, and drove off.

"Go over and consult your uncle Amos, after breakfast," advised his mother. "It is a very difficult school to undertake for the first one."

"I should prefer to teach among strangers, at least my first school," responded James. "Do you think this is the 'something better' Providence had in store for me?"

"Perhaps so. If you should be successful in this school, your reputation as a teacher would be established; you would have no more trouble in finding schools to keep."

"I see that; and still, if I had a chance to take a school among strangers, I should decline this one," said James.

"Perhaps that is the very reason you did not find a school. Providence means you shall take this one. I really think, James, that this is the correct view of the case."

James could not suppress a laugh over this turn of affairs; nor could he fail to respect his mother's moral philosophy. He really began to think that Providence was forcing him to take this school, and he mentally decided to take it before he saw Uncle Amos.

"Tough school," remarked Uncle Amos, when James sought his advice. "Those rough fellows have had their way so long in school that it will be a hard matter to bring them into subjection. How do you feel about it yourself?"

"I would prefer to teach where the scholars are not acquainted with me," replied James.

"That might make a difference with some teachers, James; but the boys have nothing against you. Perhaps they will behave better because they know you so well. I think they respect you, and that will be a great help."

"Then you think I had better teach the school?" remarked James, understanding the drift of his uncle's remarks to mean that.

"On the whole, I am inclined to think you had better teach the school."

"If I had an opportunity to teach a better school, you would not advise me to take the one at the Ledge: I understand you to mean this."

"About that," his uncle answered. Pausing a few moments, as if to reflect upon the matter, he continued:

"It is just here, James; you will begin that school as 'Jim Garfield;' now, if you can leave it, at the close of the term, as 'Mr. Garfield,' your reputation as a teacher will be established, and you will do more good than you can in any other school in Ohio."

Uncle Amos was a very wise man, and James knew it. His opinion upon all subjects was a kind of rule to be followed in the Garfield family. In this case, his counsel was wise as possible; its wisdom appeared in every word.

"I shall take the school," said James, decidedly, as he rose to go.

"I think it will prove the best decision," added his uncle.

The committee-man was notified according to agreement, and within two days it was noised over the district that "Jim Garfield" would teach the winter school. At first, remarks were freely bandied about, pro and con, and the boys and girls, too, expressed themselves very decidedly upon the subject, one way or the other. Before school commenced, however, the general opinion of the district, parents and pupils, was about as one of the large boys expressed it:

"I like Jim: he's a good feller, and he knows more'n all the teachers we ever had. I guess we better mind. He can lick us easy 'nuf, if we don't; and he'll do it."

This hopeful school-boy understood that the committee-man had instructed James to keep order and command obedience, "if he had to lick every scholar in school a dozen times over."

It was under these circumstances that James entered upon his new vocation. He dreaded the undertaking far more than he confessed; and when he left home, on the morning his school began, he remarked to his mother:

"Perhaps I shall be back before noon, through with school-keeping," signifying that the boys might run over him at the outset.

"I expect that you will succeed, and be the most popular teacher in town," was his mother's encouraging reply. She saw that James needed some bracing up in the trying circumstances.

James had determined in his own mind to run the school without resorting to the use of rod or ferule, if possible. He meant that his government should be firm, but kind and considerate. He was wise enough to open his labor on the first morning without laying down a string of rigid rules. He simply assured the pupils he was there to aid them in their studies, that they might make rapid progress; that all of them were old enough to appreciate the purpose and advantages of the school, and he should expect their cordial coöperation. He should do the best that he could to have an excellent school, and if the scholars would do the same, both teacher and pupils would have a good time, and the best school in town.

Many older heads than he have displayed less wisdom in taking charge of a difficult school. His method appeared to be exactly adapted to the circumstances under which he assumed charge. He was on good terms with the larger boys before, but now those harmonious relations were confirmed.

We must use space only to sum up the work of the winter. The bad boys voluntarily yielded to the teacher's authority, and behaved creditably to themselves and satisfactorily to their teacher. There was no attempt to override the government of the school, and former rowdyism, that had been the bane of the school, disappeared. The pupils bent their energies to study, as if for the first time they understood what going to school meant. James interested the larger scholars in spelling-matches, in which all found much enjoyment as well as profit. He joined in the games and sports of the boys at noon, his presence proving a restraint upon the disposition of some to be vulgar and profane. He was perfectly familiar with his scholars, and yet he was so correct and dignified in his ways, that the wildest boys could but respect him.

James "boarded around," as was the universal custom; and this brought him into every family, in the course of the winter. Here he enjoyed an additional opportunity to influence his pupils. He took special pains to aid them in their studies, and to make the evenings entertaining to the members of the families. He read aloud to them, rehearsed history, told stories, availing himself of his quite extensive reading to furnish material. In this way he gained a firm hold both of the parents and their children.

His Sabbaths were spent at home with his mother, during the winter. The Disciples' meeting had become a fixed institution, so that he attended divine worship every Sabbath. A preacher was officiating at the time, in whom James became particularly interested. He was a very earnest preacher, a devout Christian, and a man of strong native abilities. He possessed a tact for "putting things," as men call it, and made his points sharply and forcibly. He was just suited to interest a youth like James, and his preaching made a deep impression upon him. From week to week that impression deepened, until he resolved to become a Christian at once; and he did. Before the close of his school he gave good evidence that he had become a true child of God. And now his mother's cup of joy was overflowing. She saw distinctly the way in which God had led him, and her gratitude was unbounded. James saw, too, how it was that his mother's prophecy was fulfilled: "Providence has something better in store for you."

The verdict of parents and pupils, at the close of the term, was, "THE BEST TEACHER WE EVER HAD." So James parted with his scholars, sharing their confidence and esteem; and his uncle Amos was satisfied, because he left the school as MR. GARFIELD.

He returned to Geauga Seminary, not to board himself, but to board with Mr. Woodworth, the carpenter, according to previous arrangement. Mr. Woodworth boarded him for $1.06 per week, including his washing, and took his pay in labor. It was an excellent opportunity for James, as well as for the carpenter. His chief labor in the shop was planing boards. On the first Saturday after his return he planed fifty-one boards, at two cents apiece; thus earning, on that day, one dollar and two cents, nearly enough to pay a week's board.

We shall pass over the details of his schooling, that year, to his school-keeping at Warrensville, the following winter, where he was paid sixteen dollars a month and board. It was a larger and more advanced school than the one of the previous winter, in a pleasanter neighborhood, and a more convenient school-house. We shall stop to relate but two incidents connected with his winter's work, except to say that his success was complete.

One of the more advanced scholars wanted to study geometry, and James had given no attention to it. He did not wish to let the scholar know that he had never studied it, for he knew full well that he could keep in advance of his pupil, and teach him as he desired. So he purchased a text-book, studied geometry at night, sometimes extending his studies far into the night, and carried his pupil through, without the latter dreaming that his teacher was not an expert in the science. James considered this as clear gain; for he would not have mastered geometry that winter, but for this necessity laid upon him. It left him more time in school for other studies.

This fact is a good illustration of what James once said after he was in public life, viz.: "A young man should be equal to more than the task before him; he should possess reserved power." He had not pursued geometry, but he was equal to it in the emergency. His reserved force carried him triumphantly over a hard place.

One day he fell, when engaged in out door sports with his big boys, the result of which was a large rent in his pantaloons. They were well-worn, and so thin that it did not require much of a pressure to push one of his knees through them. He pinned up the rent as well as he could, and went to his boarding-place, after school, with a countenance looking almost as forlorn as his trousers. He was boarding with a Mrs. Stiles, at the time, a motherly kind of a woman. possessing considerable sharpness of intellect.

"See what a plight I am in, Mrs. Stiles," showing the rent in his pants.

"I see; how did you do that?" said Mrs. Stiles.

"Blundering about, as usual," James replied. "I hardly know what I shall do."

"What! so scared at a rent?" the good lady exclaimed; "that's nothing."

"It is a good deal, when it is all the pantaloons a fellow has," answered James. "This is all the suit I possess in the world, poor as it is."

"It is good enough, and there's enough of it as long as it lasts," replied the good woman; "make the best of things."

"I think I could make the best of an extra suit," responded James; "but this making the best of a single suit, and a flimsy one at that, is asking too much." He said this humorously.

"Well," continued Mrs. Stiles, "I can darn that rent so that it will be just as good as new, if not better. That's easy enough done."

"On me?" asked James, in his innocence.

"Mercy, no! When you go to bed, one of the boys will bring down your trousers, and I'll mend them. In the morning, no one will know that you met with such an accident. You mustn't let such small matters trouble you. You'll forget all about them, when you become President."

James's wardrobe was not much more elaborate at this time than it was when he began attending school at Chester. He had no overcoat nor underclothing preferring to expose his body to the cold rather than rob his mind of knowledge.

At the close of his school in Warrensville, James returned home, where an unexpected change in his programme awaited him.

CHAPTER XVIII.

THIRD YEAR AT SCHOOL.

JAMES spent three years at Geauga Seminary, including school-keeping in winter. It was during his last term there that he met a young man who was a graduate of a New England college. James had never thought of extending his education so far as a college course. He scarcely thought it was possible, in his extreme poverty, to do it.

"You can do it," said the graduate. "Several students did it, when I was in college. I did it, in part, myself."

"How could I do it?" inquired James.

"In the first place," answered the graduate, "there is a fund in most of the New England colleges, perhaps in all of them, the income of which goes to aid indigent students. It is small, to be sure, but then, every little helps, when one is in a tight place. Then there is a great call for school-teachers in the winter, and college students are sought after."

"How much is the annual expense, to an economical student?" asked James.

"It varies somewhat in different colleges, though

two hundred dollars a year, not including apparel, could be made to cover the running yearly expenses, I think. A young man would be obliged to be very saving in order to do it."

"I am used to that," added James. "They say that 'necessity is the mother of invention,' and I have invented a good many ways of living cheaply."

"I have known students to obtain jobs of work in term time, — those who know how to do certain work," continued the graduate. "I knew a student who took care of a man's garden two summers, for which he received liberal pay. I knew one who taught a gentleman's son in the place, an hour or so every day, for which he was paid well. The boy was in delicate health, not able to enter a school for hard study. I have known students to get jobs of the faculty, about the college buildings. I knew one student who sawed wood for his fellow-students, in the fall and winter terms, and he was one of the best scholars in his class. He was very popular, too, and was honored for his perseverance in acquiring an education. I think that he must have paid half of his bills by sawing wood."

James began to see further than he did. In his imagination, he began to picture a college building at the end of his career. It was further off than he had intended to go in the way of study, but the way before him seemed to open up to it. What he supposed was impossible, now appeared among possibilities.

"What is the shortest time that it would require me to prepare for and get through college?" James asked further.

"The necessary time is four years in preparation,

and four years in college," the graduate answered. "Some students shorten the preparatory course, and enter college one year in advance."

"*I* should have to *lengthen* it in order to earn the money to pay my way," responded James. "I would be willing to undertake it, if I could get through in twelve years, and pay all my bills."

"You can get through in less time than that, I know. I forgot to tell you that students sometimes enter college with money enough to carry them through the first two years; then they stay out a year, and teach an academy or high school, for which they receive sufficient remuneration to carry them through the remainder of the course. It is a better plan, I think, than to teach a district school each winter; it don't interfere so much with the studies of the college, and it is easier for the student. Then I have known several students who borrowed the money of friends to pay their bills, relying upon teaching, after getting through college, to liquidate the debt. By waiting until their college course was completed, they obtained more eligible situations, at a higher salary, than would have been possible before."

"Well, I have no friends having money to loan," remarked James. "I shall have to content myself with working my own way by earning all my money as I go along; and I am willing to do it. I had never thought it possible for me to go to college; but now I believe that I shall try it."

"I hope you will," answered the graduate, who had learned of James' ability, and who had seen enough of him to form a high opinion of his talents

"You will never regret the step, I am sure. You get something in a college education that you can never lose, and it will always be a passport into the best society."

From that time James was fully decided to take a college course, or, at least, to try for it; and he immediately added Latin and Greek to his studies.

During the last year of his connection with Geauga Seminary, James united with the Disciples' church in Orange. He took the step after much reflection, and he took it for greater usefulness. At once he became an active, working Christian, in Chester. He spoke and prayed in meeting; he urged the subject of religion upon the attention of his companions, privately as well as publicly; he seconded the religious efforts of the principal, and assisted him essentially in the conduct of religious meetings. In short, the same earnest spirit pervaded his Christian life that had distinguished his secular career.

In religious meetings, his simple, earnest appeals, eloquently expressed, attracted universal attention. There was a naturalness and fervor in his addresses that held an audience remarkably. Many attended meetings to hear him speak, and for no other reason. His power as a public speaker began to show itself unmistakably at that time. No doubt his youthful appearance lent a charm to his words.

"He is a born preacher," remarked Mr. Branch to one of the faculty, "and he will make his mark in that profession."

"One secret of his power is, that he is wholly unconscious of it," answered the member of the faculty addressed. "It seems to me, he is the most eminent example of that I ever knew. He appears to lose all thought of himself in the subject before him. He is not a bold young man at all; he is modest as any student in the academy, and yet, in speaking, he seems to be so absorbed in his theme that fear is banished. He will make a power in the pulpit, if present appearances foreshadow the future."

"It cannot be otherwise," responded Mr. Branch, "if cause and effect follow each other. He develops very rapidly, indeed. I wish it were possible for him to have a college education."

All seemed to take it for granted that James would be a preacher, although he had not signified to any one that he intended to be. He had given no thought to that particular subject. He was too much absorbed in his studies, too much in love with them, to settle that question. But his interest in religious things, and his ability as a speaker, alone led them to this conclusion. The same feeling existed among the pupils.

"Jim will be a minister, now," remarked one of his companions to Henry.

"Perhaps so," was Henry's only reply.

"He will make a good one, sure," chimed in a third. "By the time he gets into the pulpit, he will astonish the natives."

"That will be ten years from now," said the first speaker.

"Not so long as that," rejoined Henry. "Five or six years is long enough."

"He won't wear trousers of Kentucky jean, then," added the second speaker, in a jocose manner.

"He won't care whether he does or not," remarked Henry. "He would wear Kentucky jean just as quick as broadcloth; such things are wholly unimportant in his estimation."

So the matter of his becoming a preacher was discussed, all appearing to think that he was destined to become a pulpit orator. Doubtless some thought it was the only profession he would be qualified to fill.

During the summer vacation of his last year at Geauga Seminary, in connection with a schoolmate, he sought work among the farmers in the vicinity. He found no difficulty in securing jobs to suit his most sanguine expectations. An amusing incident occurred with one of the farmers to whom he applied for work.

"What do you know about work?" inquired the farmer, surveying them from head to foot, and seeming to question their fitness for his farm.

"We have worked at farming," answered James, modestly.

"Can you mow?"

"Yes, sir."

"Can you mow *well?*" emphasizing the last word.

"You can tell by trying us," answered James, not wishing to praise his own ability at labor.

"What wages do you want?"

"Just what you think is right."

"Well, that is fair; where did you come from?"

James enlightened him on this subject, and informed him, also, that they were trying to get an education.

"You are plucky boys," the farmer added; "I think you may go to work."

He conducted them to the hay-field, where they were provided with scythes, remarking to the three men already mowing, "Here are two boys, who will help you."

James exchanged glances with his companion, and the initiated might have discovered in their mutual smiles an inkling of what was coming. Their glances at each other said, as plainly as words, "Let us beat these fellows, though we are *boys*." James thought that the farmer emphasized the word *boys* more than was justifiable.

The boys had mowed an hour, the farmer being an interested witness, when the latter cried out to the three men:

"See here, you lubbers; those *boys* are beating you all holler. Their swaths are wider, and they mow better than you do. You ought to be ashamed of yourselves."

The men made no reply, but bent their energies to work more resolutely. The boys, too, were silent, although they enjoyed the praise of their employer very much. They comprehended the situation fully, and their labors were pushed accordingly. One day, while at work with the men, one of them said to James:

"Yer are school-boys, I understand."

"Yes, we are," answered James.

"Where'd yer larn to farm it?"

"At home, and all about. We've had to earn our living," was the reply of James.

"Yer are no worse for that; it won't damage your larnin'."

"I expect not; I should say good-bye to the scythe, if I thought so," replied James. "If there had been no work, there would have been no education for me."

"What yer goin' to make — a preacher?"

"That is an unsolved problem," answered James, in a playful way. "I have undertaken to make a man of myself, first. If I succeed, I may make something else afterwards; if I don't succeed, I shall not be fit for much, any way."

"Yer in a fair way to succeed, I guess," responded the laborer, who seemed to have the idea, in common with other people, that James was aiming to be a minister.

When the day of settlement with the boys came, the farmer said:

"Now, boys, what must I pay you?"

"What you think is right," replied James, at the same time thinking that the farmer's emphasis of the word *boys* indicated boys' pay.

"I s'pose you don't expect men's wages; you are only boys."

"If boys do men's work, what the difference?"

"Well, you see, boys never have so much as men: there's a price for boys, and there's a price for men. Some boys will do more work than others, but the best of them only have boys' pay."

"But you told the men that we mowed wider swaths, and mowed better than they, and beat them. Now, admit that we are boys, if we have done men's work, why should we not have their pay? I told you at first to pay us what was right, and I say so now; and if we have worked as well as your men, or better, is it not *right* that we should have their pay?"

James' plea was a strong one, and the farmer felt its force. There was but one honorable course out of the difficulty, and that was to pay the boys just what he did the men.

"Well, boys, I can't in justice deny that you did as much work as the men," he said, "and so I'll pay you men's wages; but you are the first boys I ever paid such wages to."

"I hope we are not the last ones," added James, who was never in a strait for a reply.

The farmer paid them full wages, and parted with them in good feeling, wishing them success in their struggles for an education, and saying to James:

"If, one of these days, you preach as well as you mow, I shall want to hear you."

When they left the farmer, James remarked to his companion:

"Everybody seems to think that I am going to be a preacher; why is it?" He was so unconscious of his abilities for that profession that he was actually puzzled to know why it was.

"I suppose it is because they think you are better qualified for that than any other calling," his companion replied. "I never heard you say what profession you should choose."

"No, I don't think you have; nor any one else. When the time comes, I shall choose for the best. I should like to be a preacher, and I should like to be a teacher. I don't know but I should like to be a lawyer. I shouldn't want to be a doctor."

James stated the matter here just about as it was at that time. He was going to make the most of himself possible, in the first place, — a very sensible idea for a youth, — and then devote himself to the manifest line of duty.

At this time the anti-slavery contest ran high throughout the country. In Ohio, its friends were as zealous and fearless as they were anywhere in the country. The question of the abolition of slavery was discussed, not only in pulpits and on public rostrums, but in village and school lyceums. It was discussed in the Debating Society of the Seminary. "OUGHT SLAVERY TO BE ABOLISHED IN THIS REPUBLIC?" This was a question that drew out James in one of his best efforts. From the time his attention was drawn to the subject, he was a thorough hater of slavery. It was such a monstrous wrong that he had no patience with it.

"A disgrace to the nation," he said. "People fighting to be free, and then reducing others to a worse slavery than that which they fought! It is a burning shame!"

"The founders of the government didn't think so," answered the schoolmate addressed. "If they had thought so, they would have made no provision for it.

"So much more the shame," replied James. "The very men who fought to break the British yoke of bondage legalized a worse bondage to others! That is what makes my blood boil. I can't understand how men of intelligence and honor could do what is so inconsistent and inhuman."

"Slavery wouldn't stand much of a show where you are, I judge," added his schoolmate. "You would sweep it away without discussing the question whether *immediate* emancipation is safe or not."

"Safe!" exclaimed James, in a tone of supreme contempt; "it is always *safe* to do right, and it is never safe to do wrong; especially to perpetrate such a monstrous wrong as to buy and sell men."

It was this inborn and inbred hostility to human bondage that James carried into the discussion of the question named, in their school lyceum. He prepared himself for the debate with more than usual carefulness. He read whatever he could find upon the subject, and he taxed his active brain to the utmost in forging arguments against the crime.

Companions and friends had been surprised and interested before, by his ability in debate; but on this occasion he discussed his favorite theme with larger freedom and more eloquence than ever. There was a manly and exhaustive treatment of the question, such as he had not evinced before. It enlisted his sympathies and honest convictions as no previous question had done; so that his fervor and energy were greater than ever, holding the audience in wrapped and delighted attention.

Commenting upon this effort afterwards, one of his schoolmates said to a number of his companions present:

"We'll send Jim to Congress, one of these days."

James was present, and the remark was intended both for sport and praise.

"I don't want you to send me until I have graduated at Geauga Academy," retorted James, disposed to treat the matter playfully."

"We'll let you do that; but we can begin the campaign now, and set the wires for pulling by and by," replied the first speaker. "I'll stump the District for you, Jim, and charge only my expenses."

"And whom will you charge your expenses to?" inquired James.

"To the candidate, of course, Hon. James A. Garfield," the schoolmate answered, with a laugh, in which the whole company joined, not excepting James. The incident illustrates the place that James held in the opinions of his school-fellows. Not the immature opinions of partial friends, but the well-considered and honest estimate of faculty and pupils.

In the fall term of that year there came to the school a young lady by the name of Lucretia Rudolph, a modest, unpretentious, talented girl. James soon discovered that she was a young lady of unusual worth and intellectual ability. He was not much inclined to the company of school-girls; he was too bashful to make much of a display in that line. He was not very companionable in their society, for he was not at home there. But he was unconsciously drawn to this new and pretty pupil, Miss Lucretia Rudolph. First, her modest, lady-like demeanor attracted his attention. There was a grace in her movements, and evidence of intellectual strength in her conversation. Her recitations were perfect, showing industry and scholarship

These things impressed James sensibly. No female student had attracted his attention at all, before. Nor was there any such thing as falling in love with her on his part. He regarded her with more favor than he had ever regarded a young lady in school; and it was her worth and scholarship that drew him. They were intimate, mutually polite, helpers of each other in study, real friends in all the relations of school-mates. Further than that, neither of them had thoughts about each other. They associated together, and parted at the close of the term with no expectation, perhaps, of renewing their acquaintance again. We speak of the matter here, because the two will meet again elsewhere.

James made rapid progress in Latin after he decided to go to college. It was the study that occupied his odd moments especially. Every spare hour that he could snatch was devoted to this. The following winter he taught school, and Latin received much of his attention in evening hours. He enjoyed the study of it, and, at the same time, was stimulated by the consideration that it was required in a college course of study.

Late in the autumn, James met with a young man who was connected with the Eclectic Institute, a new institution just established in Hiram, Portage County, Ohio. James knew that such an institution had been opened, and that was all; of its scope and character he was ignorant.

"You can fit for college there," he said to James; "there is no better place in the country for that business The school opened with over one hundred scholars, and the number is rapidly increasing."

"Any fitting for college there, now?" James inquired

"Yes, several; I am one of them."

"How far along are you?"

"Only just begun. I have to work my own way, so that it will be slow."

"That is the case with me. So far, I have had but eleven dollars from my friends, and I have more than returned that amount to them."

"A fellow can do it, if he only has grit enough."

"How expensive is the school?" continued James.

"Not more expensive than Geauga Seminary. It is designed to give a chance to the poorest boy or girl to get an academical education. Besides, it is conducted under the auspices of the Disciples, and the teachers belong to that sect."

"I belong to the Disciples' church," said James.

"So do I. That would not take me there, however, if it was not a good school. I think it is one of the best schools to be found."

"The teachers are well qualified, are they?"

"They are the very best of teachers; no better in any school"

"I am glad that you have called my attention to the school," added James; "I think I shall go there next year."

Here was the second casual meeting with a person, in a single term, that had much to do with the future career of James. His mother would have called it providential: so did James, afterwards. Meeting with one of them led to his decision to go to college; meeting with the other carried him to the Hiram Eclectic Institute.

James closed his connection with the Geauga Seminary at the expiration of the fall term, leaving it with a reputation for scholarship and character of which the institution was justly proud. As we have said, he taught school during the following winter. It was at Warrensville, where he had taught before. He received eighteen dollars a month, and board, with the esteem and gratitude of his patrons.

We should not pass over the oration that James delivered at the annual exhibition of Geauga Seminary, in November, 1850. It was his last task performed at the institution, and the *first* oration of his literary life. The part assigned to him was honorary; and he spent all the time he could spare, amid other pressing duties, upon the production. He was to quit the institution, and he would not conceal his desire to close his course of study there with his best effort. He kept a diary at the time, and his diary discloses the anxiety with which he undertook the preparation of that oration, and the thorough application with which he accomplished his purpose. Neither ambition nor vanity can be discovered, in the least degree, in his diary, that was written for no eyes but his own. His performance proved the attraction of the hour. It carried the audience like a surprise, although they expected a noble effort from the ablest student in the academy. It exceeded their expectations, and was a fitting close of his honorable connection with the school.

Returning home, he found his mother making preparations to visit relatives in Muskingum County, eighteen miles from Zanesville.

"You must go, James; I have made all my arrangements for you to go with me," said his mother.

"How long will you be gone?"

"All the spring, and into the summer, perhaps."

"I had concluded to go to the Eclectic Institute, at Hiram, when the spring term opens."

"You have? Why do you go there?"

"To prepare for college."

"Do you expect you can work your way through college?"

"I expect I can, or I should not undertake it." And James then rehearsed the circumstances under which he decided to go to college, if possible, and to take a preparatory course at Hiram.

"I shall be glad, James, to have you accomplish your purpose," remarked his mother, after listening to his rehearsal, in which she was deeply interested. "I think, however, that you had better go with me, and enter the Eclectic Institute at the opening of the fall term."

"It will be wasting a good deal of time, it seems to me," said James.

"I don't mean that you shall go there to idle away your time. Take your books along with you. You can find *work* there, too, I have no doubt. Perhaps you can find a school there to teach."

"Well, if I can be earning something to help me along, perhaps I had better go. It will give me an opportunity to see more of the world—"

"And some of your relations, also," interrupted his mother.

It was settled that James should accompany his

mother on her visit; and they started as soon as they could get ready. The journey took them to Cleveland first, where James was sensibly reminded of his encounter with the drunken captain, and his providential connection with the canal boat. The Cleveland and Columbus railroad had just been opened, and James and his mother took their first ride in the cars on that day. James had not seen a railroad before, and it was one of the new things under the sun, that proved a real stimulus to his thoughts. He beheld in it a signal triumph of skill and enterprise.

The state capitol had been erected at Columbus, and the legislature was in session. It was a grand spectacle to James. He had scarcely formed an idea of the building, so that the view of it surprised him. He visited the legislature in session, and received his first impressions of the law-making power. It was a great treat to him, and the impressions of that day were never obliterated.

From Columbus they proceeded by stage to Zanesville. On their way, James remarked,—

"I never should have made an objection to this trip, if I had expected to see the capitol, or the legislature in session. That alone is equal to a month's schooling to me. It has given me an idea about public affairs, that I never had before."

"It is fortunate that you came," replied Mrs. Garfield. "It does boys who *think* much good to see things which set them to *thinking*."

"I guess that is so," replied James, with a roguish smile, as if he thought his mother had exerted herself to compliment him. "*Thinking* is needed in this world about as much as anything."

"*Right* thinking," suggested his mother.

"Mr. Branch says a young man better think erroneously than not to think at all," responded James.

"I don't think I should agree with Mr. Branch. It is safer not to think than to think wrong," said Mrs. Garfield.

"I suppose that Mr. Branch meant to rebuke dull scholars, who never think for themselves, and take every assertion of the books as correct, without asking *why*," added James.

James and his mother thus discussed the scenes and the times on their way to Zanesville, enjoying the change and the scenery very much. From the latter place they floated down the Muskingum river, in a skiff, to their destination, eighteen miles distant. Here they found their relatives the more rejoiced to see them because their visit was unexpected.

As soon as they were fairly settled among their relations, within four or five days after their arrival, James began to cast about for something to do.

"Perhaps you can get a school to keep over in Harrison, four miles from here," said his aunt. "I heard they were looking after a teacher."

"Whom shall I go to there to find out?" inquired James.

"I can't tell you, but your uncle can, when he gets home."

James learned to whom application should be made, and posted away immediately, and secured the school, at twelve dollars a month, for three months.

"You are fortunate," said his mother, on hearing his report. "You will be contented to stay now until

I get ready to go home. What kind of a school-house have they?"

"A log-house; not much of an affair."

"How large is the school?"

"About thirty; enough to crowd the building full."

"When do you begin?"

"Next Monday."

"Board round, I suppose?"

"Yes; and some of the families are between two and three miles away."

James commenced his school under favorable auspices, so far as his relations to the pupils were concerned. The conveniences for a school were meagre, and the parents were indifferent to the real wants of their children. Most of them failed to appreciate schooling. It was quite cold weather when the school opened, and there was no fuel provided. Near by the school-house, however, there was coal, in a bank, and James proposed to his pupils to dig fuel therefrom; and, in this way, their fire was run until it became so warm that fire was not needed.

The pupils were not so far advanced as the pupils at Warrensville, but not so rough as those at the Ledge. The neighborhood was not so far advanced in the arts of civilization as the region with which James had been familiar. Yet, he enjoyed school-keeping there; and his connection with the families was pleasant. At the close of the term he received many expressions of affection and confidence from the pupils, and separated from them with the best of feeling.

Mrs. Garfield was ready to return to Orange at the

close of the school: nor was James sorry to start on the journey home. After an absence of over three months, James found himself at the homestead with more money than he had when he left.

CHAPTER XIX.

THE ECLECTIC INSTITUTE.

EVERAL weeks would intervene before the commencement of the term at Hiram; and James looked about for work that he might add to his funds for an education. He was planning now to lay up money to assist himself through college. He found jobs to occupy his time fully until he should leave to enter the Eclectic Institute.

It was the last of August, 1851, when James reached Hiram. The board of trustees was in session. Proceeding directly to the institution, he accosted the janitor.

"I want to see the principal of the institute," he said.

"He is engaged with the board of trustees, who are in session now," replied the janitor.

"Can I see him, or them?"

"Probably; I will see." And the janitor went directly to the room of the trustees, and announced, "A young man at the door, who is desirous to see the board at once."

"Let him come in," answered the chairman.

James presented himself politely, though, perhaps, awkwardly.

"Gentlemen," he said, "I am anxious to get an education, and have come here to see what I can do."

"Well, this is a good place to obtain an education,' answered the chairman, without waiting for James to proceed further. "Where are you from?"

"From Orange. My name is James Abram Garfield. I have no father; he died when I was an infant. My mother is widow Eliza Garfield."

"And you want what education this institution can furnish?"

"Yes, sir; provided I can work my way."

"Then you are poor?"

"Yes, sir; but I can work my way. I thought, perhaps, that I could have the chance to ring the bell and sweep the floors, to pay part of my bills."

"How much have you been to school?"

"I have attended Geauga Seminary three years, teaching school in the winter."

"Ah! then you are quite advanced?"

"No, not very far advanced. I have commenced Latin and Greek."

"Then you think of going to college?"

"That is what I am trying for."

"I think we had better try this young man," said one of the trustees, addressing the chairman. He was much impressed by the earnestness and intelligence of the applicant, and was in favor of rendering him all the aid possible.

"Yes," answered the chairman; "he has started

out upon a noble work, and we must help him all we can."

"How do you know that you can do the sweeping and bell-ringing to suit us?" inquired another trustee of James.

"Try me—try me two weeks, and if it is not done to your entire satisfaction I will retire without a word." James' honest reply settled the matter.

James was nineteen years old at this time; he became twenty in the following November. So he was duly installed bell-ringer and sweeper-general.

Hiram was a small, out-of-the-way town, twelve miles from the railroad, the "centre" being at a cross-road, with two churches and half a dozen other buildings. The institution was located there to accommodate the sons and daughters of the Western-Reserve farmers. President Hinsdale, who now presides over the college (it was elevated to a college, twelve or fifteen years ago), says: "The Institute building, a plain but substantially built brick structure, was put on the top of a windy hill, in the middle of a corn-field. One of the cannon that General Scott's soldiers dragged to the city of Mexico in 1847, planted on the roof of the new structure, would not have commanded a score of farm-houses. Here the school opened, at the time Garfield was closing his studies at Chester. It had been in operation two terms when he offered himself for enrolment. Hiram furnished a location, the board of trustees a building and the first teachers, the surrounding country students, but the spiritual Hiram made itself. Everything was new. Society, traditions, the genius of the school, had to be evolved from the forces of the teachers and pupils, limited by the general and local environment. Let no one be surprised when I say that such a school as this was the best of all places for young Garfield. There was freedom, opportunity, a large society of rapidly and eagerly opening young minds, instructors who were learned enough to instruct him, and abundant scope for ability and force of character, of which he had a superabundance.

"Few of the students who came to Hiram in that day had more than a district school education, though some had attended the high schools and academies scattered over the country; so that Garfield, although he had made but slight progress in the classics and the higher mathematics previous to his arrival, ranked well up with the first scholars. In ability, all acknowledged that he was the peer of any; soon his superiority to all others was generally conceded."

James sought an early opportunity to confer with the principal.

"I want your advice as to my course of study," he said. "My purpose is to enter college, and I want to pursue the best way there."

"You want to make thorough work of it, as you go along?" the principal answered, by way of inquiry.

"Yes, sir, as thorough as possible. What I know, I want to know *certainly*."

"That is a good idea; better take time, and master everything as you go along. Many students fail because they are satisfied with a smattering of knowledge. Be a scholar, or don't undertake it."

"I agree with you perfectly, and I am ready to

accept your advice; and will regulate my course accordingly."

"Our regular preparatory course of study cannot be improved, I think," continued the principal. "You can pursue higher studies here, and enter college in advance, if you choose. But that can be determined hereafter. At present, you can go on with the branches undertaken, and time will indicate improvement and changes necessary."

"It will be necessary for me to labor some out of school hours, in order to pay all my bills," added James. "Then I would like to be earning something more, to help me through college."

"What do you propose to do?"

"I can work on a farm, or in a carpenter's shop, or do odd jobs at almost anything that offers. I have already seen the carpenter here."

"Well, what prospect for work?"

"After a few days he will have work for me, mostly planing; and that I have done more than anything in the carpenter's line."

"You are fortunate to find work at once."

"I never have failed to find work, since I have been dependent upon my own exertions."

"I hope you always will find work, that you may realize the accomplishment of your object. I shall do everything in my power to assist you, and do it with all my heart."

"Thank you," responded James, grateful for the deep interest the principal appeared to manifest in his welfare.

He secured quarters in a room with four other

students, rather thick for the highest comfort, but "necessity multiplies bedfellows." Here he set about his literary work with a zeal and devotion that attracted attention. The office of bell-ringer obliged him to rise very early; for the first bell was rung at five o'clock. The office of sweeper compelled him to be on the alert at an early hour, also. Promptness was the leading requirement of the youth who rang the bell. It must be rung on the mark. A single minute too early, or too late, spoiled the promptness. *On the mark precisely*, was the rule. Nor was it any cross to James. Promptness, as we have seen, was one of his born qualities. It was all the same to him whether he arose at four or five o'clock in the morning, or whether he must ring the bell three, or a dozen times a day. He adapted himself to circumstances with perfect ease. Instead of bending to circumstances, circumstances bent to him. He made a good bell-ringer and sweeper, simply because it was a rule with him to do everything well. One of his room-mates said to him:

"Jim, I don't see but you sweep just as well as you recite."

"Why shouldn't I?" James responded, promptly.

"Many people do important things best," replied his schoolmate, "and a lesson is more important than sweeping."

"You are heretical," exclaimed James. "If your views upon other matters are not sounder than that, you will not make a very safe leader. Sweeping, in its place, is just as important as a lesson in Greek is, in its place, and, therefore, according to your own rule, should be done as well."

"You are right, Jim; I yield my heresy, like the honest boy that I am."

"I think that the boy who would not sweep well, would not study well," continued James. "There may be *exceptions* to the rule; but the rule is a correct one."

"I guess you are about right, Jim; but my opinion is that few persons carry out the rule. There are certain things about which most people are superficial, however thorough they may be in others."

"That may be true; I shall not dispute you there," rejoined James; "and that is one reason why so many persons fail of success. They have no settled purpose to be thorough. Not long ago I read, in the life of Franklin, that he claimed, 'thoroughness must be a principle of action.'"

"And that is why you sweep as well as you study?" interrupted the room-mate, in a complimentary tone.

"Yes, of course. And there is no reason why a person should not be as thorough in one thing as in another. I don't think it is any harder to do work well than it is to half do it. I know that it is much harder to recite a lesson poorly than to recite it perfectly."

"I found that out some time ago, to my mortification," rejoined the room-mate, in a playful manner. "There is some fun in a perfect lesson, I confess, and a great amount of misery in a poor one."

"It is precisely so with sweeping," added James. "The sight of a half-swept floor would be an eye-sore to me, all the time. It would be all of a piece with a poor lesson."

"I could go the half-swept floor best," remarked the room-mate.

"I can go neither best," retorted James, "since there is no need of it."

James had told the trustees to try him at bell-ringing and sweeping two weeks. They did; and the trial was perfectly satisfactory. He was permanently installed in the position.

A person, now an esteemed clergyman, who acted in the same capacity six or eight years after James did, writes, "When I did janitor work, I had to ring a bell at five o'clock in the morning, and another at nine o'clock in the evening, and I think this had been an immemorial custom during school sessions. The work was quite laborious, and much depended upon the promptness and efficiency of the person who handled the bell-rope, as the morning had to be divided into equal portions, after a large slice had been taken out of it for the chapel exercises, which were always protracted to uncertain lengths. It was annoying, tedious work."

A lady now living in the State of Illinois was a member of the school when James was inaugurated bell-ringer, and she writes: "When he first entered the institute, he paid for his schooling by doing janitor's work,—sweeping the floor and ringing the bell. I can see him even now standing, in the morning, with his hand on the bell-rope, ready to give the signal calling teachers and scholars to engage in the duties of the day. As we passed by, entering the schoolroom, he had a cheerful word for every one. He was the most popular person in the institute. He was always good natured, fond of conversation, and very entertaining. He was witty, and quick at repartee, but his jokes, though brilliant and striking, were always harmless, and he never would willingly hurt another's feelings."

The young reader should ponder the words, "most popular person in the institute,"—and yet bell-ringer and sweeper! Doing the most menial work there was to do with the same cheerfulness and thoroughness that he would solve a problem in algebra! There is an important lesson in this fact for the young. They can afford to study it. The youth who becomes the most "popular" student in the institution, notwithstanding he rings the bell and sweeps the floors, must possess unusual qualities. Doubtless he made the office of bell-ringer and sweeper very respectable. We dare say that some of the students were willing to serve in that capacity thereafter who were not willing to serve before. Any necessary and useful employment is respectable; but many youths have not found it out. The students discovered the fact in the Eclectic Institute. They learned it of James. He dignified the humble offices that he filled. He did it by putting *character* into his work.

There were nearly two thousand volumes in the library belonging to the school. From this treasury of knowledge James drew largely. Every spare moment of his time was occupied with books therefrom. He began to be an enthusiastic reader of poetry at Geauga Seminary. "Young's Night Thoughts," which he found there, was the volume that particularly impressed his mind, just before he became a Christian under the preaching of the Disciples minister at Orange. His tenacious memory retained much that he read, both of poetry and prose. Here he had a wider field to explore, more books to occupy his attention, though not more time to read. He began to read topically and systematically.

"What are you doing with that book?" inquired a room-mate; "transcribing it?"

"Not exactly, though I am making it mine as much as possible," James replied. "Taking notes."

"I should think that would be slow work."

"Not at all, the way I do."

"What way are you doing?"

"I note the important topics on which the book treats, with the pages, that I may turn to any topic of which it treats, should I have occasion hereafter. I mean to do the same with every book I read, and preserve the notes for future use."

"A good plan, if you have the patience. I want to dash through a book at double-quick; I couldn't stop for such business," added the room-mate.

"I spend no more time over a book than you do, I think," answered James. "I catch the drift, and appropriate the strong points, and let all the rest slide. But taking notes serves to impress the contents upon my memory. Then, hereafter, when I speak or write upon a given topic, my notes will direct me to necessary material."

"Your ammunition will be ready; all you will have to do will be to load and fire," suggested his room-mate. "That is not bad. I think the plan is a good one."

It will save much time, in the long run. Instead of being obliged to hunt for information on topics, I can turn to it at once." James remarked thus with an assurance that showed his purpose was well matured. Years afterwards he testified that the method proved one of the most helpful and important rules of his life. Many scholars have pursued a similar course, and their verdict respecting the usefulness of the plan is unanimous. It is an excellent method for the young of both sexes, whether they are contemplating a thorough education or not; for it will promote their intelligence, and increase their general information. This result is desirable in the humblest as well as in the highest position. An intelligent, well-informed citizen adorns his place. That honored and lifted into respectability the office of bell-ringer and sweeper at Hiram Institute, as we have seen.

When James had completed his collegiate course, and became Principal of Hiram Institute, he wrote to a youth whom he desired should undertake a liberal course of education:

"Tell me, Burke, do you not feel a spirit stirring within you that longs *to know, to do, and to dare*, to hold converse with the great world of thought, and holds before you some high and noble object to which the vigor of your mind and the strength of your arm may be given? Do you not have longings like these, which you breathe to no one, and which you feel must be heeded, or you will pass through life unsatisfied and regretful? I am sure you have them, and they will forever cling round your heart till you obey their mandate. They are the voice of that nature which God has given you, and which, when obeyed, will bless you and your fellow-men."

Whether Burke felt this "spirit stirring within him" or not, it is certain that it moved James, as some mysterious power, when he entered this new field, and long before, impelled him onward and upward in a career that could not have been denied him without inflicting an everlasting wound upon his soul.

In the spring after James became connected with the school, the principal proposed that the pupils should bring trees from the forest, and set them out on the Campus, to adorn the grounds, and provide a lovely shade for those who would gather there twenty and thirty years thereafter.

"A capital idea!" exclaimed James to Baker, with whom he was conferring upon the subject. "If each male student will put out one tree for himself, and one for a female student, we can cover the Campus with trees, and the streets near by as well; and do it next Saturday, too."

"That is real gallantry, Jim," answered Baker "The girls, of course, can't set out trees."

"And the boys will take pride in setting them out for them," interrupted James.

"And calling them by their names," added Baker.

"A bright idea is that, to name the trees after those for whom they are set out," responded James. "You are an original genius, George; I should not have thought of that. It must be because you think more of girls than I do."

"But the plan to plant a tree for each girl is yours, Jim. I can't claim the patent for that."

"I am not ashamed to own it. It is worthy of the boys of the Western Reserve. We can have a rich time in carrying out the plan, better than a ride or party."

"I think so," said Baker.

"The satisfaction of knowing we are doing something that will be a great blessing thirty years from now, adding beauty and comfort to the Institute and town, is stimulus enough," continued James.

This enterprise was nobly prosecuted, and the trees were planted and named as above. James enjoyed it hugely. He was a great admirer of nature, and a tree or a flower afforded him genuine pleasure. To plant trees about his favorite institution, that would furnish shady walks in future days, was to him a privilege that he would not willingly miss.

During his first year's connection with the school, a female student of considerable brightness and scholarship violated some rule of the institution, for which the principal thought she should be publicly rebuked. The rebuke would be administered after the chapel exercises on the following morning. The affair caused much discussion among the pupils. Their sympathies were wholly enlisted for the girl, as she was deservedly quite popular.

"It is almost too bad," remarked James to a lady student. "It will well-nigh kill her; I pity her."

"I think it is a shame to make a small affair like that so public," replied the young lady. "If it was one of the boys it would not be half so bad."

"You think boys are used to it, or are of less consequence than girls?" retorted James, in a vein of humor.

"Not exactly that. I think the worst way of rebuking a young lady should not be selected."

"I agree with you exactly; but I suppose there is no help for it now."

"Unless we get up a petition asking that the rebuke be privately administered."

"I will sign it," said James; "but it must be done immediately."

"I will see some of the girls at once." And, so saying, the young lady hastened away.

In many groups the matter was discussed on that day, and much excitement prevailed; but the movement for a petition failed, and the following morning dawned with the assurance that the rebuke would be administered before the whole school. The scholars assembled with hearts full of pity for the unfortunate girl. No one felt more keenly for her than James. He expected to see her overcome and crushed.

The principal called upon her to rise, and the rebuke was administered, while all the scholars dropped their heads in pity for her. She survived the ordeal. She neither wept nor fainted. On retiring from the chapel, with the crowd of scholars, she remarked to James, in the hearing of many, —

"It seems to me that Uncle Sutherland was rather personal."

The jocose remark created a laugh all around, and none laughed more heartily than James, who concluded that their profound sympathies had been sadly wasted.

James had not been at Hiram long before the students discovered one prominent trait of his character, viz., a keen sense of justice. He was fond of ball-playing, and he wanted everybody to enjoy it. One day he took up the bat to enjoy a game, when he observed several of the smaller boys looking on wistfully, seeming to say in their hearts, "We wish we could play."

"Are not those boys in the game?" he asked.

"What! those little chaps? Of course not; they would spoil the game."

"But they want to play just as much as we do. Let them come in!"

"No; we don't want the game spoiled. They can't play."

"Neither shall I, if they cannot," added James decidedly. And he threw down his bat.

"Well, let them come, then," shouted one of the players, who wanted the game to go on. "Spoil it, if you will."

"We shall make it livelier," responded James, taking up his bat and calling upon the little boys to fall in. "We may not have quite so scientific a game, but then all hands will have the fun of it; and that is what the game is for."

CHAPTER XX.

STUDENT AND TEACHER.

JAMES ceased to be a janitor at the close of his first year at Hiram, and was promoted to assistant teacher of the English department and ancient languages. His rapid advancement is set forth by Dr. Hinsdale, who is now president of the institution:

"His mind was now reaching out in all directions; and all the more widely because the elastic course of study, and the absence of traditionary trammels, gave him room. He was a vast elemental force, and nothing was so essential as space and opportunity. Hiram was now forming her future teachers, as well as creating her own culture. Naturally, then, when he had been only one year in the school, he was given a place in the corps of teachers. In the catalogue of 1853–'54, his name appears both with the pupils and teachers: 'James A. Garfield, Cuyahoga County,' and 'J. A. Garfield, Teacher in the English Department, and of the Ancient Languages.' His admission to the faculty page may be an index to a certain rawness in the school; but it gave to his talents and ambition the play that an older school, with higher standards, could not have afforded him.

Now he was filling three important positions, student, teacher and carpenter. He had become nearly as indispensable to the carpenter's business as to that of the Institute. The sound of his hammer, before and after school, was familiar to the students and the citizens.

"See there!" exclaimed Clark, pointing to James on the roof of a house, building near the academy. "Jim has taken that roof to shingle."

"Alone?" inquired Jones.

"Yes, alone; and it won't take him long, either, if he keeps his hammer going as it does now. Jim's a brick."

"Very little brick about him, I should say; more brain than brick."

"With steam enough on all the while to keep his brain running. Did you ever see such a worker?"

"Never. Work seems as necessary to him as air and food. If he was not compelled to work, in order to pay his way, his brain would shatter his body all to pieces in a year. He is about the only student I ever thought was fortunate in being poor as a stray cat."

"I declare, I never thought of that. Poverty is a blessing sometimes. I had thought it was a curse to a student always."

"It is Jim's salvation," added Jones. "I have thought of it many times. I suppose that his carpentering business is better exercise for him than our ball-playing, or pitching quoits."

"Minus the *fun*," added Clark, quickly; really believing that James was depriving himself of all first-class sport. "Have you not observed how he enjoys a game of ball or quoits when he joins us?"

"Of course; but he does not seem to me to enjoy these games any more than he enjoys study, reading, and manual labor. He studies just as he plays ball, exactly, with all his might; and I suppose that is the way we all ought to do."

"That is what Father Bentley said in his sermon on, 'Whatsoever thy hand findeth to do, do it with thy might.' You remember it?"

"Certainly; and who knows but Father Bentley has engaged Jim to illustrate his doctrine? He preaches and Jim practices. Nobody in the Eclectic Institute will dispute such a sermon while Jim's about; you can count on that." The remark was made jocosely, and, at the same time, a compliment was intended for James.

This conversation discloses the facts about James' manual labor while connected with the Institute. We have not space for the details of his work with the plane and hammer during the whole period. We can only say, here, once for all, that he continued to add to his money by manual labor to the end of his three years at Hiram. He planed all the siding of the new house that he was shingling when the foregoing conversation took place. His labor was expended upon other buildings, also, in the place, during that period. Several jobs of farming, also, were undertaken at different times. He was laying up money to assist himself in college, in addition to paying his way at the Institute.

When James entered the school his attention was

attracted to a class of three in geometry. As he listened to the recitation in this study, which was animated and sharp, he became particularly impressed. Since that time he said, "I regarded teacher and class with reverential awe." The three persons in the class were William B. Hazen, who became one of our most distinguished major-generals in the late rebellion, and who is now in the public service; Geo. A. Baker, now a prominent citizen of Cleveland, Ohio; and Miss Almeda A. Booth, a very talented lady of nearly thirty years, who was teaching in the school, and at the same time pursuing her studies in the higher mathematics and classics. As this Miss Booth exerted a more powerful influence upon James than any other teacher, except Dr. Mark Hopkins, of Williams College, we shall speak of her particularly, and her estimate of our hero. She was the daughter of a Methodist preacher, whose circuit extended a thousand miles on the Reserve; a man of marked mental strength, and of great tact and energy. The daughter inherited her father's intellectual power and force of character, so that, when the young man to whom she was betrothed died, she resolved to consecrate herself to higher intellectual culture, that her usefulness might be augmented. This resolution brought her to the Eclectic Institute. She died in 1875, and afterwards General Garfield said of her talents, "When she was twelve years of age she used to puzzle her teachers with questions, and distress them by correcting their mistakes. One of these, a male teacher, who was too proud to acknowledge the corrections of a child, called upon the most learned man in town for help and advice in regard to a point of dispute between them. He was told that he was in error, and that he must acknowledge his mistake. The teacher was manly enough to follow this wise advice, and thereafter made this little girl his friend and helper. It was like her to help him quietly, and without boasting. During her whole life, none of her friends ever heard an intimation from her that she had ever achieved an intellectual triumph over anybody in the world."

It was fortunate for James that this accomplished lady became deeply interested in his progress and welfare.

"The most remarkable young man I ever met," she said to the principal. "There must be a grand future before him."

"True, if he does not fall out of the way," answered the principal.

"I scarcely thought that was possible when I spoke. His Christian purpose is one of the remarkable things about him. His talents, work, everything, appear to be subject to this Christian aim. I feel that he will make a power in the world."

"I agree with you: such are my feelings in regard to him, notwithstanding the prevalence of temptations that lure and destroy so many of our hopeful young men." The principal had seen more of the world than Miss Booth, so he spoke with less confidence.

James had been connected with the school but a few months before his studies were the same as those of Miss Booth, and they were in the same classes. "I was far behind Miss Booth in mathematics and the physical sciences," he said, since, "but we were nearly in the same place in Greek and Latin." She could render him essential aid in his studies, and she delighted to do it. Their studies were nearly the same until he ceased to be a member of the school. The librarian kept text-books for sale, and the following are his memoranda of sales to them:

"January, 1852. Latin Grammar and Cæsar.
March, 1852. Greek Grammar.
April, 1852. French Grammar.
August, 1852. German Grammar and Reader.
November, 1852. Xenophon's Memorabilia and Greek Testament."

All this in a single year.

"August, 1853. Sophocles and Herodotus.
November, 1853. Homer's Iliad."

During the fall term of 1853, Miss Booth and James read about one hundred pages of Herodotus and one hundred of Livy. They met two of the professors, also, on two evenings of each week, to make a joint translation of the book of Romans. His diary has this record for December 15, 1853: "Translation society sat three hours at Miss Booth's room, and agreed upon the translation of nine verses." The record shows that these studies were pursued critically, and therefore slowly.

Miss Booth was more or less familiar with the standard authors of English literature, both prose and poetry; and she aided James greatly in the selection of books, many of which they read together, discussing their merits and making notes. In a tribute to her memory, a few years since, General Garfield said: "The few spare hours which schoolwork left us, were devoted to such pursuits as each preferred, but much study was done in common. I can name twenty or thirty books, which will be doubly precious to me because they were read and discussed in company with her. I can still read between the lines the memories of her first impressions of the page, and her judgment of its merits. She was always ready to aid any friend with her best efforts."

James was appointed to prepare a thesis for an exhibition day. One evening he repaired to the room of Miss Booth.

"I want your help, Miss Booth," he said. "I am afraid that I shall make a botch of it, without your assistance."

"I will risk you," Miss Booth replied; "but I will render you all the assistance in my power."

"That will be all I shall need," remarked James, facetiously; "and I hardly see how I can get along with less. I like to talk over subjects before I write: it is a great help to me."

"It is an essential help to everybody," answered Miss Booth. "Two heads may be better than one in canvassing any subject. Discussion awakens thought, sharper and more original; and it often directs the inquirer to new and fresher sources of information. I am at leisure to discuss your thesis at length."

So James opened the subject by stating some of his difficulties, and making inquiries. Both were soon absorbed in the subject before them, so thoroughly absorbed as to take no note of time, nor dream that the night was gliding away, until surprised by the morning light coming in at the window.

In 1853, Miss Booth proposed that twelve of the advanced pupils — James and herself among the number — should organize a literary society for the purpose of spending the approaching vacation of four weeks in a more thorough study of the classics. The society was formed, and the services of one of the professors were secured, to whom they recited statedly. During that vacation they read "the Pastorals of Virgil, the first six books of the Iliad, accompanied by a thorough drill in the Latin and Greek grammars at each recitation." It proved a very profitable vacation to James, a season to which he always looked back with pride and pleasure. He regarded Miss Booth as the moving and controlling spirit of that society, increasing his sense of obligation to her.

Perhaps the chief reason of Miss Booth's confidence in the Christian purpose of James, as expressed to the principal, was found in his consistent Christian life. From the time he became a member of the Institute he took an active part in the religious meetings, identifying himself with the people of God in the village. His exhortations and appeals were examples of earnestness and eloquence, to which the students and citizens listened in rapt attention. No student of so much power in religious meetings had been connected with the school. Indeed, it was the universal testimony that no such speaker, of his age, had ever been heard.

Father Bentley, pastor of the Disciples' Church in Hiram, was wonderfully drawn to James. After a few months, he felt that James' presence was almost indis pensable to the success of a meeting. He invited him specially to address the audience. Often he urged him to take a seat upon the platform, that he might address the assembly to better advantage. In his absence he invited James to take charge of the meeting. The last year of his stay at Hiram, Father Bentley persuaded him several times to occupy his pulpit on the Sabbath, and preach, which he did to the gratification of the audience.

His gift at public speaking was so remarkable, that a demand was frequently made upon him for a speech on social and public occasions. It is related, that, at a weekly prayer-meeting, he was on the platform with Father Bentley, waiting to perform his accustomed part, when a messenger came for him to address a political meeting, where speakers had failed them. Father Bentley scarcely noticed what was going on, until James was half-way down the aisle, when he called out:

"James, don't go!" then quickly, as if thinking his request might be unreasonable, he said to the congregation, "Never mind, let him go; that boy will yet be President of the United States."

"I remember his vigorous exhortations, now," remarked a Christian woman recently, who was connected with the Institute at that time; "they were different from anything I was accustomed to hear in conference meetings."

"How were they different?" she was asked.

"They were original and fresh beyond anything I had ever heard in such meetings; nothing commonplace or stale about them, making one feel that they were not the thoughts of some commentator he was giving us at second hand, but the product of his own genius and great talents, uttered with real earnestness and sincerity."

"He must have possessed a wonderful command of language," remarked her friend.

"That was one thing that charmed us. His flow of language, appropriate and select, was like a river. It seemed as if he had only to open his mouth, and thoughts flowed out clothed in language that was all aglow. Many, many times I heard the remark, 'he speaks as easily as he breathes.' Well," she continued, after a pause, "he was substantially just such a speaker then as he was afterwards in public life, bating the dignity that age and experience impart."

In this connection we should speak of him as a debater in the lyceum. He was older and more experienced at Hiram than he was at Chester, and his efforts in debate were accordingly more manly. The Illinois lady, from whom we have already quoted, says, "In the lyceum he early took rank far above the others as a speaker and debater." His interest in public matters was growing with the excitement of the times. The infamous fugitive-slave law, for the restoration of runaway slaves to their masters, had been enacted by Congress, as a compromise measure, and no people of the country felt more outraged by the attempts to enforce the Act than the people of the Western Reserve. The excitement became intense. Young men partook of it in common with older citizens. It pervaded the higher schools. It was as strong in the Eclectic Institute as elsewhere

School and village lyceums received an impetus from it. James was an uncompromising foe to slavery before; if possible, he was more so now. The excitement fired him up in debate. He was more denunciatory than ever of slavery. He had been a great admirer of Daniel Webster, but his advocacy of the fugitive-slave bill awakened his contempt. He was not a young man to conceal his feelings, and so his utterance was emphatic.

"A covenant with death, and an agreement with hell," he exclaimed, quoting from Isaiah, "that will destroy the authors of it. The cry of the oppressed and down-trodden will appeal to the Almighty for retribution, like that of the blood of Abel. The lightning of divine wrath will yet shiver the old, gnarled tree of slavery to pieces, leaving neither root nor branch!"

When James became assistant teacher, he had for a pupil, in his Greek class, Miss Lucretia Rudolph, the young lady in whom he was so much interested at Chester. Her father removed to Hiram, in order to give her a better opportunity to acquire a thorough education.

James was glad to meet her; and he was happy to welcome so talented a scholar as pupil. He had no expectation that she would ever stand in a closer relation to him than pupil. But the weeks and months rolled on, and she became one of his permanent scholars, not only in Greek, but in other branches as well, in all of them developing a scholarship that won his admiration. At the same time, her many social and moral qualities impressed him, and the impression deepened from month to month. The result was, before he closed his connection with the school, that a mutual attachment grew up between them, and she engaged to become his wife when he had completed his course of study, and was settled. He was twenty two years of age, and Miss Rudolph was one year his junior.

This was one of the most important steps that James had taken, and it proved to be one of the most fortunate. Those who prophesied that the engagement would interfere with his studies did not fully understand or appreciate the solidity of his character nor the inflexibility of his purpose. Such love affairs are often deprecated because so many young men allow them to interfere with their life-purpose, thus disclosing weakness and puerile ideas. With James, the love affair became an aid to the controlling purpose of his life, and, at the same time, served to refine his coarser qualities by passing them through the fire of a pure and exalted passion. True love is sweeter and higher than the brightest talents, and when its pure and elevating influence refines the latter, they shine with a fairer lustre than ever. This was eminently true of James.

Notwithstanding James was so bashful and retiring when he first went to Chester to commence his studies, he became one of the most social and genial students at Hiram. He was the life of the social circle. Unlike many ripe students, whose minds are wholly absorbed in their studies, he could unbend himself, and enter into a social occasion with zest, bringing his talents, his acquisitions, his wit and humor, to contribute to the enjoyment of all. The lady in Illinois, from whom we have twice quoted, says on this point:

"During the month of June, the entire school went in carriages to their annual grove-meeting, at Randolph, some twenty-five miles away. On this trip he was the life of the party, occasionally bursting out in an eloquent strain at the sight of a bird or a trailing vine, or a venerable giant of the forest. He would repeat poetry by the hour, having a very retentive memory."

The reader learns from this, that it was not "small talk," nor mere slang and folly, that he contributed to a social time, but sensible, instructive material. He had no sympathy for, or patience with, young men who dabbled in silly, trifling conversation and acts, to entertain associates. To him it was evidence of such inherent weakness, and absence of common sense, that it aroused his contempt. One who was intimate with him in social gatherings at Hiram makes a remark that discloses an important element of his popularity. "There was a cordiality in his disposition which won quickly the favor and esteem of others. He had a happy habit of shaking hands, and would give a hearty grip, which betokened a kind-hearted feeling for all." The same writer says, what confirms the foregoing statements respecting his recognized abilities, "In those days both the faculty and pupils were in the habit of calling him 'the second Webster,' and the remark was common, 'He will fill the White House, yet.'"

There was one branch of the fine arts that he pursued, to gratify a taste in that direction, which should receive a passing notice. It was mezzotint drawing. He became so proficient in the art that he was appointed teacher of the same. The lady from whom we have quoted was one of his pupils, and she writes:

"One of his gifts was that of mezzotint drawing, and he gave instructions in this branch. I was one of his pupils in this, and have now the picture of a cross, upon which he did some shading and put on the finishing touches. Upon the margin is written, in the hand of the noted teacher, his own name and his pupil's. There are, also, two other drawings, one of a large European bird on the bough of a tree, and the other a churchyard scene in winter, done by him at that time."

Thus the versatility of his talents, enforced by his intense application, appeared to win in almost any undertaking. Without his severe application, his versatility would not have availed much. He reduced that old maxim thoroughly to practice, "Accomplish, or never attempt," because his application was invincible. Here was the secret of his success in teaching. He was just as good a teacher as scholar. Before the completion of his academic course, the trustees made his success a subject of serious consideration.

"We must secure his return to Hiram as soon as he gets through college," said the chairman. "He will make a popular and successful professor."

"That is true," replied another trustee. "In what department would you put him?"

'Any department that is open. He will fill any

department admirably. I have noticed that when we conclude that he is particularly suited to one position, he soon surprises us by filling another equally well."

"It will certainly be for the popularity of the school to instal him over a prominent professorship here," added the chairman; "and I dare say it will be agreeable to his feelings."

The subject was not dropped here. Both the principal and chairman of the board interviewed James upon the subject; and when he left the Institute for college, it was well understood that he would return at the close of his college course. The present president of the institution says:

"I shall not here speak of him as a teacher further than to say, in two years' service he had demonstrated his great ability in that capacity, had won the hearts of the students generally, and had wrought in the minds of the school authorities the conviction that his further service would be indispensable on his return from college."

On his success as a teacher, when preparing for college, the Illinois lady, who was his pupil, writes:

"He was a most entertaining teacher,—ready with illustrations, and possessing in a marked degree, the power of exciting the interest of the scholars, and afterwards making clear to them the lessons. In the arithmetic class there were ninety pupils, and I cannot recollect a time when there was any flagging in the interest. There were never any cases of unruly conduct, or a disposition to shirk. With scholars who were slow of comprehension, or to whom recitations were a burden, on account of their modest and retiring disposition, he was especially attentive, and by encouraging words and gentle assistance would manage to put all at their ease, and awaken in them a confidence in themselves."

A leading lawyer of Cleveland, Ohio, Hon. J. H. Rhodes, referring to his connection with the school, at the time James was studying and teaching, in a public assembly, said, —

"I remember a circumstance that had much to do with my remaining at Hiram. I was a little homesick, and one day I went into the large hall of the college building, and the tall, muscular, tow-headed man in charge there, who was teaching algebra, came up to me, and, seeing a cloud over my face, threw his arms about me in an ardent way. Immediately the home-sickness disappeared. The tow-headed man has not so much hair to-day as he had then. Hard knocks in public life have uprooted a heap of his hair."

"Going to Bethany College, I suppose," remarked the principal to him. That was the college established by Alexander Campbell, founder of the sect called Disciples.

"I had intended to go there until recently," James answered.

"What has changed your purpose? That college is of our denomination, you know."

"Yes, I know; but I have been thinking that it might be better for me to enlarge my observation by going beyond our sect."

"That may be; you want more room, do you?"

"I know the Disciples' church pretty well. Perhaps I had better know something outside of it. It seems narrow to me to tie myself down to the limits of my own denomination. Besides, will it not be of real value to me to connect myself with a New England college?"

"Perhaps so; I agree with you in the main; too contracted a sphere will not be well for you. That idea is well worth considering. You will be qualified to enter college two years in advance; at least, you can enter some colleges two years in advance. What college have you in mind?"

"I have not decided upon any particular one, yet. I am going to write to Yale College, Williams College, and Brown University, stating the ground I have been over, and inquiring whether I can enter as Junior, learning the expense, and other things."

"That is a good plan. Then you will know definitely where to go, and you can prepare accordingly."

James did write to the presidents of Yale College, New Haven, Ct., Williams College, Williamstown, Mass., and to the president of Brown University, Providence, R. I., also; and each one of the presidents replied to his inquiries. The substance of the answers, together with his decision, may be learned from a letter which James wrote to a friend one week before he started for college, as follows:

"There are three reasons why I have decided not to go to Bethany: First, the course of study is not so extensive or thorough as in eastern colleges; second, Bethany leans too heavily toward slavery; third, I am the son of Disciple parents, am one myself, and have had but little acquaintance with people of other views, and having always lived in the west, I think it will make me more liberal, both in my religious and general views and sentiments, to go into a new circle, where I shall be under new influences. These considerations led me to conclude to go to some New England college. I therefore wrote to the presidents of Brown University, Yale, and Williams, setting forth the amount of study I had done, and asking how long it would take me to finish their course.

"Their answers are now before me. All tell me I can graduate in two years. They are all brief business notes, but President Hopkins concludes with this sentence: 'If you come here we shall be glad to do what we can for you.' Other things being so nearly equal, this sentence, which seems to be a kind of friendly grasp of the hand, has settled the question for me. I shall start for Williams next week."

James always did like to have people carry their hearts in their hands, as he did; and Dr. Hopkins came so near to it that he put his heart in his pen, when he wrote, and James accepted his hearty handshake.

"How is it, James, about funds? You cannot have enough money laid up for your college expenses," his brother said to him, several weeks before he closed his studies at Hiram, just at the time when James was revolving the subject with some anxiety. True, he had trusted to Providence so much, and Providence had provided for him so unexpectedly at times, and so generously always, that he was disposed to trust for the wherewith to pay expenses in college. His brother's question was timely. He always thought that Providence managed the affair.

"No, I have not more than half enough," James replied; "but I shall teach in the winter, and perhaps I can find some kind of labor to perform in term time. I always have been able to pay my way."

"But if you enter two years in advance, I would not advise you to labor in term time. You will have enough to do."

"How can I pay my way, unless I do work?"

"I will loan you money to meet your expenses."

"And wait long enough for me to pay it?"

"Yes. When you get through college you can teach, and it will not take you long to pay the debt."

"Suppose I should die; where will you get your pay?"

"That is my risk."

"It ought not to be your risk. It is not right that you should lose the money on my account."

"It is, if I consent to it."

"It occurs to me," continued James, after a pause, "that I can arrange it in this way. You can loan me the money, and I will get my life insured for five hundred dollars. This will protect you in case of my death."

"I will agree to that, if it suits you any better."

"Well, it does. I shall be satisfied with that method; and I shall be relieved of some anxiety. I want to make my two years in college the most profitable of any two years of my course of study."

James took out an insurance upon his life, and when he carried it to his brother he remarked:

"If I live I shall pay you, and if I die you will suffer no loss."

What James accomplished during the three years he was at Hiram Institute, may be briefly stated, thus: The usual preparatory studies, requiring four years, together with the studies of the first two years in college, — the studies of six years in all, — he mastered in three years. At the same time he paid his own bills by janitor and carpenter work, and teaching, and, in addition, laid up a small amount for college expenses.

CHAPTER XXI.

IN COLLEGE.

AT the close of the summer term at Williams College, candidates for admission, who presented themselves, were examined. James presented himself to Dr. Hopkins very different, in his personal appearance, from the well-worded and polished letter that he wrote to him. One describes him — "As a tall, awkward youth, with a great shock of light hair, rising nearly erect from a broad, high forehead, and an open, kindly, and thoughtful face, which showed no traces of his long struggle with poverty and privation." His dress was thoroughly western, and very poor at that. It was evident to Dr. Hopkins that the young stranger before him did not spend much time at his toilet; that he cared more for an education than he did for dress. Of course, Dr. Hopkins did not recognize him.

"My name is Garfield, from Ohio," said James. That was enough. Dr. Hopkins recalled the capital letter which the young man wrote. His heart was in his hand at once, and he repeated the cordial hand-shake that James felt when he read in the doctor's letter, "If you come here, we shall be glad to do what we can for you." James felt at home at once. It was such a kind, fatherly greeting, that he felt almost as if he had arrived *home.* He never had a natural father whom he could remember, but now he had found an intellectual father, surely, and he was never happier in his life. Yet a reverential awe possessed his soul as he stood before the president of the college, whose massive head and overhanging brow denoted a giant in intellect. James was perfectly satisfied that he had come to the right place, now; he had no wish to be elsewhere. He had read Dr. Hopkins' Lectures on the "Evidences of Christianity," and now the author impressed him just as the book did when he read it. The impression of *greatness* was uppermost.

James passed the examination without any difficulty, and was admitted to the Junior class. Indeed, his examination was regarded as superior. He was qualified to stand abreast with the Juniors, who had spent Freshman and Sophomore years in the colleges. And this fact illustrates the principle of *thoroughness,* for which we have said James was distinguished. In a great measure he had been his own teacher in the advanced studies that he must master in order to enter the Junior class; yet he was *thoroughly* prepared.

"You can have access to the college library, if you remain here during the summer vacation," said Dr. Hopkins to him. "If you enjoy reading, you will have a good opportunity to indulge your taste for it."

"I shall remain here during vacation, and shall be thankful for the privilege of using the library," answered James. "I have not had the time to read what I desire, hitherto, as I have had to labor and teach, to pay my bills. It will be a treat for me to spend a few weeks in reading, with nothing else to do."

Dr. Hopkins gave him excellent advice, and words of encouragement, not only for vacation, but for term time, as well; and James found himself revelling among books, within a few days. He had never seen a library of such dimensions as that into which he was now introduced, and his voracious mental appetite could now partake of a "square meal." One of the authors whom he desired to know was Shakespeare. He had read only such extracts from his writings as he had met with in other volumes. Therefore he took up a volume containing Shakespeare's entire works with peculiar satisfaction. He read and studied it, studied and read it, committing portions of it to memory, and fairly made the contents of the book his own. His great familiarity with the works of Shakespeare dates from that period. Certain English poets, also, he read and studied, for the first time; and he committed a number of poems to memory, which he always retained. Works of fiction he rejected from principle. When he joined the Disciples' church he resolved to read no novels. His decision was in accordance with the practice of that church. On the whole, that vacation in the college library was a very profitable one to James. It was just what he needed after so many years of hard study in the sciences and classics.

It was well for him, too, to be relieved from the strain of study and pecuniary support, that had taxed him heavily from the outset. He had no carpenter's job on hand, or class to teach, for his support. For exercise, the beauty and grandeur of the scenery lured him into the fields and over the mountains. The wild, mountainous country around presented a striking contrast with the level, monotonous landscape of the Western Reserve. He enjoyed explorations of the region; climbing Greylock to its summit that he might take in the view, plunging into forests, and ranging fields, until the country for miles around was almost as familiar to him as Orange township, Ohio. By the time the college term opened, he was as familiar with the locality as any of the students.

"Hill, what do you think of that westerner?" said one of the juniors to his classmate, Hill, a few days after the term began. "Got acquainted with him?"

"Not exactly; haven't had time yet. Have you?"

"A little acquainted; not much, though."

"He is not a slave to the *fashions*, I conclude;" alluding to his rather uncouth dress.

"No; he gives tailors a wide berth, in my judgment: but he is none the worse for that. Put him into a tasty garb, and he would be a splendid-looking fellow."

"That's so: but neither his character nor scholarship would be improved by the change. If dress would improve these, some of our fellows would patronize tailors more than butchers, a great deal."

"I think I shall like him, judging from a slight acquaintance. A little western in his speech."

"Western provincialisms?"

"Yes; though not bad. Evidently he is one of the fellows who will go through thick and thin to acquire an education. There must be considerable to him, or he never could enter a New England college two years in advance, especially if he prepared at the west."

"Do you know where, in the west, he fitted for college?"

"At a little place on the Western Reserve somewhere; an academy that belongs to a sect called Disciples. So one of the boys says."

"Disciples! I never heard of that sect before, except the one in New Testament times. A disciple will work in well, here;" trying to be humorous.

This conversation shows quite well the circumstances in which James was brought into contact with the students. That they should scrutinize his apparel and appearance, is not strange. James expected that, and the thought caused him some embarrassment. He knew very well that his dress must appear shabby to young men who consulted tailors, and that his speech was marred by provincialisms that must sound queerly to them. So he very naturally dreaded the introduction to college life. Yet he proved as much of a philosopher here as elsewhere, and made the best of the situation. He was happily disappointed in his intercourse with students. He found no pride or caste among them. They treated him kindly, and gave him a hearty welcome to their companionship. Within a few weeks he ranked among the "best fellows" of the college. The college boys soon found that the "Great West" had turned out a great scholar; that the student who had the least to do with tailors was a rare fellow; and they treated him accordingly. James never had any reason to complain of his treatment by the faculty and students of Williams College.

"He is one of the most accurate scholars I ever knew," said Hill to Leavitt, some weeks after James entered college; "he never misses anything, and he never fails to answer a question."

"That is because he knows it all," replied Leavitt. "He gave me some account of his methods of study in preparing for college. He did it all himself, pretty much. He sticks to anything until he understands it fully; that gives him the advantage now. He is one of the best-read students in college, and all that he ever read is at his tongue's end."

"He showed *that* in the debate last Saturday," continued Hill. "His ability as a debater is superior; nobody in this college can compete with him." Reference was here made to a debate in the Philologian society of the college.

"A born speaker, I think. It is just as easy for him to speak as it is to recite; and that is easy enough."

"I predict," continued Hill, "that he will stand at the head of our class, notwithstanding he entered two years in advance."

"It looks so now. 'All signs fail in a dry time,' it is said, but the signs certainly point that way."

That these young men were not partial, or mistaken, in their estimate of James, is evident from the following communication, penned by a classmate recently, after the lapse of twenty-five years:

"In a class of forty or more, he immediately took a stand above all others for accurate scholarship in every branch, but particularly distinguishing himself as a writer, reasoner, and debater. He was remarkable for going to the bottom of every subject which came before him, and seeing and presenting it in entirely a new light. His essays written at that time, not of the commonplace character too common in college compositions, can even now be read with pleasure and admiration. While an indefatigable worker, he was by no means a bookworm or recluse, but one of the most companionable of men, highly gifted, and entertaining in conversation, ready to enjoy and give a joke, and having a special faculty for drawing out the knowledge of those with whom he conversed, thus enriching his own stock of information from the acquirements of others. Even then he showed that magnetic power, which he afterwards exhibited in a remarkable degree in public life, of surrounding himself with men of various talents, and of employing each to the best advantage in his sphere. When questions for discussion arose in the college societies, Garfield would give each of his allies a point to investigate; books and documents from all the libraries would be overhauled; and the mass of facts thus obtained being brought together, Garfield would analyze the whole, assign each of the associates his part, and they would go into the battle to conquer. He was always in earnest, and persistent in carrying his point, often against apparently insurmountable obstacles; and in college election contests (which are often more intense than national elections) he was always successful."

James had taxed himself so long to his utmost capacity by advanced and extra studies, crowding six years' labor into three, that it was easy for him now to lead his class. He did add German to the regular studies of the college, and he became so proficient in it within one year, that he could converse considerably in the language. But all this was little labor in comparison with his work at Hiram. He found much time to read, and to engage in the sports of the Campus. The latter he enjoyed with a keen relish; no one entered into them more heartily than he did. His college mates now recall with what enthusiasm he participated in their games. This was indispensable for his health now, as he had no labor with plane or hammer to perform.

The "Williams Quarterly" was a magazine supported by the college. James took great interest in it, and his compositions frequently adorned its pages, both prose and poetry. The following was from his pen in 1854:—

"AUTUMN.

"Old Autumn, thou art here! Upon the earth
And in the heavens the signs of death are hung;
For o'er the earth's brown breast stalks pale decay,
And 'mong the lowering clouds the wild winds wail,
And sighing sadly, shout the solemn dirge
O'er Summer's fairest flowers, all faded now.
The Winter god, descending from the skies,
Has reached the mountain tops, and decked their brows
With glittering frosty crowns, and breathed his breath
Among the trumpet pines, that herald forth
His coming.

"Before the driving blast
The mountain oak bows down his hoary head,
And flings his withered locks to the rough gales
That fiercely roar among his branches bare,
Uplifted to the dark, unpitying heavens.

The skies have put their mourning garments on,
And hung their funeral drapery on the clouds.
Dead Nature soon will wear her shroud of snow,
And lie entombed in Winter's icy grave!

"Thus passes life. As heavy age comes on
The joys of youth — bright beauties of the Spring
Grow dim and faded, and the long, dark night
Of death's chill winter comes. But as the Spring
Rebuilds the ruined wrecks of Winter's waste,
And cheers the gloomy earth with joyous light,
So o'er the tomb the star of hope shall rise,
And usher in an ever-during day."

"Garfield, what are you going to do with yourself this vacation?" inquired Bolter, just as the fall term was closing.

"I am considering that question, now. How should I make it teaching penmanship, do you think?"

"You would do well at it; and the vacation is long enough for you to teach about ten lessons."

James was a good penman, for that day, and he had taken charge of a writing-class in school, for a time. The style of his penmanship would not be regarded with favor now by teachers in that department; nevertheless it was a broad, clear, business style, that country people, at least, were then pleased with.

"Think I could readily get a class?" continued James.

"No doubt of it. Strike right out into the country almost anywhere, and you will find the way open."

"I am quite inclined to take a trip into New Hampshire, to see what I can do. I have some distant relatives there: my mother was born there."

"Well, if you go where your mother was born, you will not be likely to get into bad company, though there is enough of it in New Hampshire."

"Acquainted there?"

"As much as I want to be. There is too much of the pro-slavery democracy there for me; but they need to improve their penmanship awfully, Garfield. It won't interfere with *your* business."

The conversation proceeded in a kind of semi-jovial way until the bell rang for recitation. The upshot was that James opened a writing-school in Pownal, Vermont, instead of in New Hampshire. He met with some party who directed his steps to this small town, where he taught a large class in penmanship, in the village school-house. It proved a profitable venture to him, both financially and socially. He added quite a little sum to his private treasury, besides making many warm friends and enlarging the sphere of his observation and experience.

As he spent the next winter vacation in New York state, we may relate the circumstances here. He went to Poestenkill, a country village about six miles from Troy, N. Y., where there was a Disciples' church, over which a preacher by the name of Streeter was settled. Here he opened a school of penmanship, thereby earning a few dollars, in addition to paying his expenses. His efforts in the religious conference meeting were so marked that the pastor invited him to occupy his pulpit on the Sabbath; and the invitation was accepted. Having preached once, the people demanded that he should preach again; and he did. It was the common opinion that he would become the most renowned preacher in the Disciples' church," no one doubting that he was expecting to fill the sacred office.

James became acquainted with several of the teachers and school-committee at Troy, and when he was there one day, Rev. Mr. Brooks, one of the committee, surprised him by saying:

"We have a vacancy in the high-school, and I would like to have you take the situation. It is an easy place, and a good salary of twelve hundred dollars."

"You want me to begin now, I suppose?"

"Yes; next week the term begins."

"I should be obliged to relinquish the idea of graduating at Williams."

"That would be necessary, of course; and perhaps that may be best for you."

"No; it seems best for me to graduate, at any rate; that has been my strong desire for several years, and to abandon the purpose now, when I am just on the eve of realizing my hopes, would be very unwise."

"You understand your own business best," continued Mr. Brooks; "but we should be very glad to employ you, and only wish that you could see it for your interest to accept our proposition."

"There is another difficulty in the way," James replied. "I feel under some obligations to Hiram Institute, where I prepared for college. There was no bargain with me, and yet the trustees expect me to return, and take a position as teacher. That is a young institution, struggling to live, and I have a desire to give my small influence to it."

"You need not decide to-day; think of it longer; you may view the matter differently after a little thought," Mr. Brooks urged.

"No; I may just as well decide now. Your offer is a tempting one; I could soon pay my debts on that salary. I cannot expect any such salary at Hiram, and I thank you with all my heart for the offer. But my ambition has been to win an honorable diploma at an Eastern college, and then devote my energies to the institute that has done so much for me. I must decline your alluring offer."

James arrived at this decision quickly, because accepting the offer would interfere with the accomplishment of the great purpose of his life. He had no difficulty, at any time, in rejecting any proposition that came between him and a collegiate education.

His refusal of the tempting offer was the more remarkable because he was in straitened circumstances at the time. His brother, who had promised to loan him money, had become embarrassed, so that further aid from that quarter was out of the question. He needed a new suit of clothes very much, but he had not the money to purchase them. One of his friends in Poestenkill, knowing this, went to a tailor of his acquaintance in Troy, Mr. P. S. Haskell, and said:

"We have a young man in our village, a rare fellow, who is poor, but honest, and he wants a suit of clothes. He is struggling to go through Williams College, and finds it hard sledding. Can you do anything for him?"

"Yes; I am willing to help such a young man to a

suit of clothes. I will let him have a suit of clothes on credit," the tailor replied promptly.

"You will get every cent of your pay in time, I'm sure of that. The young man preaches some now, and he preaches grandly."

"What is his name?"

"James A. Garfield. His home is in Ohio."

"Well, send him along."

On the following day James called upon the tailor, frankly told him his circumstances, and promised to pay him for the clothes as early as possible. He could not fix the date.

"Very well," said Mr. Haskell, who was thoroughly pleased with James' appearance. "Take your own time; don't worry yourself about the debt. Go on with your education; and when you have some money that you have no other use for, pay me." James got his suit of clothes, returned to college, and paid the debt in due time, to the entire satisfaction of the tailor.

After returning to college, James looked about for pecuniary relief. Debts on his second year had already accumulated, and now it was certain that he would receive no loans to meet them from his brother. He thought of the cordial and friendly doctor who examined him about six years before, and encouraged him to acquire an education, — Dr. J. P. Robinson, now of Cleveland, Ohio. He sat down and wrote to the jolly doctor, stating his pressing wants and future purposes, telling him of his life insurance, and of his expected connection with Hiram Institute as teacher, when he would be able to liquidate the debt. It is enough to say that Dr. Robinson cheerfully loaned him the money.

At the close of his first collegiate year, James visited his mother in Ohio. She was then living with her daughter, who was married and settled in Solon. It is not necessary to rehearse the details of this visit: the reader can imagine the mutual joy it occasioned much better than we can describe it. Imagination cannot exaggerate the satisfaction his mother found in meeting her son again, so near the ministry, where she had come to think his field of usefulness would be found.

In college, James' anti-slavery sentiments grew stronger, if possible. Charles Sumner was in congress, dealing heavy blows against slavery, assailing the fugitive-slave bill with great power and effect, claiming that "freedom is national, and slavery sectional," denouncing the "crime against Kansas," and losing no opportunity to expose the guilt and horrors of southern bondage. Outside of congress he made speeches, urging that the whig party should attack and overthrow American slavery. James admired the fearless, grand public career of Sumner, and also despised the criminal support the democratic party gave to slavery, and the truckling, timid, compromising course of the leaders of the whig party. Then, in the fall of 1855, John Z. Goodrich, who was a member of congress from western Massachusetts, delivered a political address in Williamstown upon the history of the Kansas-Nebraska struggle, and the efforts of the handful of republicans then in congress to defeat the Missouri compromise. James was profoundly impressed by the facts and logic of that speech, and he said to a classmate, on leaving the hall, —

"This subject is new to me; I am going to know all about it."

He sent for documents, studied them thoroughly, and was fully prepared to join the new republican party, and also to support John C. Fremont for president of the United States. The students called a meeting in support of Fremont, and James was invited to address them. The scope and power of his speech, packed with facts and history, showed that he had canvassed the subject with his accustomed ability; and even his classmates, who knew him so well, were surprised.

"The country will hear from him yet, and slavery will get some hard knocks from him," remarked a classmate.

Just afterwards the country was thrown into the greatest excitement by the cowardly attack of Preston Brooks, of South Carolina, upon Charles Sumner. Enraged by his attacks upon slavery, and urged forward, no doubt, by southern ruffians, Brooks attacked him with a heavy cane, while Sumner was writing at his desk in the United States senate. Brooks intended to kill him on the spot, and his villainous purpose was nearly accomplished.

On receipt of the news at Williams College, the students called an indignation meeting, at which James, boiling over with indignant remonstrance against such an outrage, delivered the most telling and powerful speech that had fallen from his lips up to that time. His fellow-students listened with wonder and admiration. They were so completely charmed by his fervor and eloquence that they sat in breathless attention until he closed, when their loud applause rang through the building, repeated again and again in the wildest enthusiasm.

"The uncompromising foe to slavery!" exclaimed one of his admirers.

"Old Williams will be prouder of her student than she is to-day, even," remarked another.

And many were the words of surprise and gratification expressed, and many the prophecies concerning the future renown of young Garfield.

We said that James rejected fiction from his reading, on principle. When about half through his college course he found that his mind was suffering from excess of solid food. Mental dyspepsia was the consequence. His mind was not assimilating what he read, and was losing its power of application. He was advised to read fiction moderately. "Romance is as valuable a part of intellectual food as salad of a dinner. In its place, its discipline to the mind is equal to that of science in its place." He finally accepted the theory, read one volume of fiction each month, and soon found his mind returning to its former elasticity. Some of the works of Walter Scott, Cooper, Dickens, and Thackeray, not to mention others, became the cure of his mental malady. His method of taking notes in reading was systematically continued in college. Historical references, mythological allusions, technical terms, and other things, not well understood at the time, were noted, and afterwards looked up in the library, so that nothing should remain doubtful or obscure in his mind. "The ground his mind traversed he carefully cleared and ploughed before leaving it for fresh fields."

James graduated in 1856, bearing off the honors of his class. Dr. Hopkins had established the "metaphysical oration" as the highest honor at commencement, and James won it, by the universal consent of the faculty and students. In the performance of his part at commencement, he fully sustained his well earned reputation for scholarship and eloquence. Both teachers and classmates fully expected, when he left college, that his name would appear conspicuously in the future history of his country.

Dr. Hopkins wrote of him, eight years after James graduated:

"The course of General Garfield has been one which the young men of the country may well emulate. . . . A rise so rapid in both civil and military life is, perhaps, without example in the country. . . . Obtaining his education almost wholly by his own exertions, and having reached the age when he could fully appreciate the highest studies, General Garfield gave himself to study with a zest and delight wholly unknown to those who find in it a routine. A religious man and a man of principle, he pursued, of his own accord, the ends proposed by the institution. He was prompt, frank, manly, social, in his tendencies; combining active exercise with habits of study, and thus did for himself what it is the object of a college to enable every young man to do,—he made himself a MAN. There never was a time when we more needed those who would follow his example."

Mr. Chadbourne, who is now president of Williams College, and who was professor when James was a student, writes:

"He graduated in 1856, soon after I began my work here as professor. The students who came under my instruction then made a much stronger impression upon me than those of a later day, since my attention has been called to other interests than those of the lecture-room. But Garfield, as a student, was one who would at any time impress himself upon the memory of his instructors, by his manliness and excellence of character. He was one whom his teachers would never suspect as guilty of a dishonest or mean act, and one whom a dishonest or mean man would not approach. College life is, in some respects, a severe test of character. False notions of honor often prevail among students, so that, under sanction of "college customs," things are sometimes done by young men which they would scorn to do in other places. There was manliness and honesty about Garfield that gave him power to see and do what was for his own good, and the honor of the college. His life as a student was pure and noble. His moral and religious character, and marked intellectual ability, gave great promise of success in the world. His course since he entered active life has seemed to move on in the same line in which he moved here. He has been distinguished for hard work, clear insight into great questions of public interest, strong convictions, and manly courage. I know of no better example among our public men of success fairly won."

CHAPTER XXII.

RETURN TO HIRAM

HE trustees of Hiram Institute elected Garfield "Teacher of Ancient Languages and Literature" before his return to the school. His welcome back was a hearty one. His acceptance of the position was equally hearty.

His position was now a high and honorable one, although he was but nine years removed from the tow-path of the Ohio and Pennsylvania Canal. Into that nine years were crowded labors, struggles, and triumphs, the like of which we can scarcely find in the annals of human effort.

"I have attained to the height of my ambition," he said to a friend. "I have my diploma from an eastern college, and my position here as instructor; and now I shall devote all my energies to this Institute."

He had no intention of entering the ministry permanently, as many supposed, nor had he aspirations for a political career. He was content to be a teacher at Hiram, ambitious to make the school the pet of the Western Reserve, if possible. He might have secured positions where double the salary was paid; but he was satisfied to teach at Hiram for eight hundred dollars a year. No board of trustees could lure him away by the offer of a princely income. His heart was at Hiram, and he meant that his best efforts should be there.

He brought from Williams College a profound reverence for Dr. Hopkins, the president, as an instructor and scholar of great ability. He profited by the lessons he learned at his feet, and augmented the value of his own labors by imitating him as far as practicable. He was not long in convincing the board that, successful as he was in teaching before entering Williams College, his ability in that sphere was largely increased by his collegiate course. At the end of the first year he was placed at the head of the Institution, with the title, "Chairman of the Board of Instructors," and, one year later, was made PRINCIPAL. In eleven years from the time he left the tow-path of the canal he was installed Principal of the "Eclectic Institute of the Western Reserve," where three hundred young ladies and gentlemen were pursuing a course of education.

One of his successful points, as instructor, was to discover young men of superior talents, and persuade them to acquire a liberal education. Sometimes their fathers would put a veto upon such a project, when he was forced to try his logic and persuasive powers upon them. He called this "capturing boys," and he enjoyed it hugely. There are many bright intellects now adorning the learned professions of the country that would have been unknown to fame but for his persistent efforts in "capturing" them. President Hinsdale, who now presides over Hiram College, was one of them,—one of the ablest and most remarkable scholars of the land. Garfield tells the story of the capture of two boys as follows:

"I have taken more solid comfort in the thing itself, and received more moral recompense and stimulus in after life, from capturing young men for an education than from anything else in the world.

"As I look back over my life thus far, I think of nothing that so fills me with pleasure as the planning of these sieges, the revolving in my mind of plans for scaling the walls of the fortress; of gaining access to the inner soul-life, and at last seeing the besieged party won to a fuller appreciation of himself, to a higher conception of life, and of the part he is to bear in it. The principal guards which I have found it necessary to overcome in gaining these victories are the parents or guardians of the young men themselves. I particularly remember two such instances of capturing young men from their parents. Both of those boys are to-day educators, of wide reputation,—one president of a college, the other high in the ranks of graded-school managers. Neither, in my opinion, would to-day have been above the commonest walks of life unless I, or some one else, had captured him. There is a period in every young man's life when a very small thing will turn him one way or the the other. He is distrustful of himself, and uncertain as to what he should do. His parents are poor, perhaps, and argue that he has more education than they ever obtained, and that it is enough. These parents are sometimes a little too anxious in regard to what their boys are going to do when they get through with their college course. They talk to the young man too much, and I have noticed that the boy who will make the best man is sometimes most ready to doubt himself. I always remember the turning period in my own life, and pity a young man at this stage from the bottom of my heart. One of the young men I refer to came to me on the closing day of the spring term, and bade me good-by at my study. I noticed that he awkwardly lingered after I expected him to go, and had turned to my writing again. 'I suppose you will be back again in the fall, Henry?' I said, to fill in the vacuum. He did not answer, and turning towards him, I noticed that his eyes were filled with tears, and that his countenance was undergoing contortions of pain.

"He at length managed to stammer out, 'No, I am not coming back to Hiram any more. Father says I have got education enough, and that he needs me to work on the farm; that education don't help along a farmer any.'

"'Is your father here?' I asked, almost as much affected by the statement as the boy himself. He was a peculiarly bright boy, one of those strong, awkward, bashful, blonde, large-headed fellows, such as make men. He was not a prodigy, by any means; but he knew what work meant, and when he had won a thing by true endeavor, he knew its value."

"'Yes, father is here, and is taking my things home for good,' said the boy, more affected than ever

"'Well, don't feel badly,' I said. 'Please tell him Mr. Garfield would like to see him at his study, before he leaves the village. Don't tell him that it is about you, but simply that I want to see him.' In the course of half an hour the old gentleman, a robust specimen of a Western Reserve Yankee, came into the room, and awkwardly sat down. I knew something of the man before, and I thought I knew how to begin. I shot right at the bull's eye immediately.

"'So you have come up to take Henry home with you, have you?' The old gentleman answered, 'Yes.' 'I sent for you because I wanted to have a little talk with you about Henry's future. He is coming back again in the fall, I hope?'

"'Wal, I think not. I don't reckon I can afford to send him any more. He's got eddication enough for a farmer already, and I notice that when they git too much they sorter git lazy. Yer eddicated farmers are humbugs. Henry's got so far 'long now that he'd rather hev his head in a book than be workin'. He don't take no interest in the stock nor in the farm improvements. Everybody else is dependent in this world on the farmer, and I think that we've got too many eddicated fellows setting around now for the farmers to support.'

"'I am sorry to hear you talk so,' I said: 'for really I consider Henry one of the brightest and most faithful students I have ever had. I have taken a very deep interest in him. What I wanted to say to you was, that the matter of educating him has largely been a constant outgo thus far, but if he is permitted to come next fall term, he will be far enough advanced so that he can teach school in the winter, and begin to help himself and you along. He can earn very little on the farm in the winter, and he can get very good wages teaching. How does that strike you?'

"The idea was a new and good one to him. He simply remarked, 'Do you really think he can teach next winter?'

"'I should think so, certainly,' I replied. 'But if he cannot do so then, he can in a short time, anyhow.'

"'Wal, I will think on it. He wants to come back bad enough, and I guess I'll have to let him. I never thought of it that way afore.'

"I knew I was safe. It was the financial question that troubled the old gentleman, and I knew that would be overcome when Henry got to teaching, and could earn his money himself. He would then be so far along, too, that he could fight his own battles. He came all right the next fall, and, after finishing at Hiram, graduated at an Eastern college."

"Well, how did you manage the campaign for capturing the other young man?" Garfield was asked.

"Well, that was a different case. I knew that this youth was going to leave mainly for financial reasons also, but I understood his father well enough to know that the matter must be managed with exceeding delicacy. He was a man of very strong religious convictions, and I thought he might be approached from that side of his character; so when I got the letter of the son, telling me, in the saddest language that he could master, that he could not come back to school any more, but must be content to be simply a farmer, much as it was against his inclination, I revolved the matter in my mind, and decided to send an appointment to preach in the little country church where the old gentleman attended. I took for a subject the parable of the talents, and in the course of my discourse dwelt specially upon the fact that children were the talents which had been intrusted to parents, and if these talents were not increased and developed there was a fearful trust neglected. After church I called upon the parents of the boy I was besieging, and I saw that something was weighing upon their minds. At length the subject of the discourse was taken up and gone over again, and in due course the young man himself was discussed, and I gave my opinion that he should by all means be encouraged and assisted in taking a thorough course of study. I gave my opinion that there was nothing more important to the parent than to do all in his power for the child. The next term the young man again appeared upon Hiram Hill, and remained pretty continuously till graduation."

He was wonderfully magnetic. He never failed to win students to himself. President Hinsdale says of him:

"Naturally, Garfield, the teacher, drew his pupils to himself with extraordinary power. Never have I seen such devotion to another teacher. An old Hiram student, now holding a responsible office in the public schools of Cleveland, speaking of the old times before Garfield went to college, says in a private letter: 'Then began to grow up in me an admiration and love for Garfield that has never abated, and the like of which I have never known. A bow of recognition or a single word from him was to me an inspiration.' And such would be the general testimony. In all this there was method; not the method of crafty art, as the cynical might say, but the method of nature, the method of a great mind and noble heart. I take my leave of this Hiram teacher with affirming my conviction that, other things being equal, Garfield has never been greater than he was in Hiram from 1857 to 1861. He left the quiet of the academy for the roar of the field and the forum at the age of thirty, but not until he had demonstrated his fitness for the highest educational work and honors."

The following facts and incidents will illustrate some of his methods and qualities as a teacher.

One day a pupil made a sad failure in the class, at least on a portion of the lesson, when Garfield roguishly pointed to a soiled place in one corner of the recitation-room, where the water had trickled through the plastering, and run down upon the wall.

"Look there," he said, laughing at the same time, and eliciting a smile from each member of the class. That was all he said; but the rebuke was keen and sharp, coming in that way from him. Such was his usual method. Occasionally, however, when he perceived a really rebellious spirit that meant mischief, he was severe and withering in his method of treatment.

He assigned a certain task to a student at one time, when the latter said:

"I doubt whether I can do it. I do not think I am equal to it."

"Not equal to it?"

"No, sir."

"Darsie!" answered Garfield; "when I get intc a place that I can easily fill, I always feel like shoving out of it into one that requires of me more exertion."

In this single sentence was one of the secrets of his success; and Darsie saw it at once. Garfield had risen rapidly by setting his standard high, and, bringing himself up to it.

Akin to this, he said to the students, on one occasion, —

"I shall give you a series of lectures upon history, beginning next week. I do this not alone to assist you; the preparation for the lectures will *compel* me to study history."

It was not the mere announcement that was interesting; it was a method of his to show his pupils the best plan of study. He could do more and better work under a necessity than otherwise; and so can every one. It was his custom to lecture on the topics he desired to study particularly, that he might derive the benefit of a two-fold object. He wanted his pupils to appreciate the advantage of it.

"How in the world can he time his steps so as to take the last one just as the bell stops?" remarked a student, referring to his coming into the chapel exercises and taking his seat precisely as the bell ceased.

"Hard telling," replied Darsie; "but he is always on the stairs in the last half of the last minute, and glides into his seat just as the last tap of the bell is struck." The last stroke of the bell was indicated by a little more vigorous pull of the rope.

"And what seems marvellous to me is, that he never fails. I couldn't time my steps like that," added the student.

Garfield insisted upon *punctuality* everywhere,—at prayers, recitation, lectures, all engagements. He demanded *promptness* as an essential duty. He made his pupils feel the importance of these qualities. But he would not require of them what he did not practise himself. He was the last man to preach what he did not practise. So he illustrated every day, by personal example, the lessons which he taught respecting these virtues.

Returning from a neighboring town one morning, where he lectured on the previous evening, he entered his recitation room late. Another teacher, supposing he would not return in season to hear the recitation, had taken his class. As he entered, a pupil was answering a question. While in the act of removing his overcoat, and precisely as the pupil's answer ceased, Garfield put another question in the same line, as if the previous question were put by himself. He smiled, the teacher laughed and bowed himself out of the room, and the class roared. It was a happy termination of a single act of tardiness.

He was accustomed to lecture to his pupils upon "manners," "elements of success," and kindred topics. One day his topic was the "Turning Point of Life," in which he said,

"The comb of the roof at the court-house at Ravenna (capital of Portage county, of which Hiram was a town) divides the drops of rain, sending those that fall on the south side to the Gulf of Mexico, and those on the opposite side, into the Gulf of St. Lawrence, so that a mere breath of air, or the flutter of a bird's wing, may determine their destiny. It is so with your lives, my young friends. A passing event, perhaps of trifling importance in your view, the choice of a book or a companion, a stirring thought, a right resolve, the associations of an hour, may prove the turning point of your lives."

During his connection with the school as principal his lectures were numerous. He lectured upon the natural sciences, reading, books, government, and occasional "topics of the times." He delivered many lectures in Portage county, and in neighboring counties, before literary societies; lectures upon geology, illustrated by charts of his own making, "Character and Writings of Sir Walter Scott," "Character of the German People," and "Carlyle's Frederic the Great." He was the most popular lecturer in Ohio. Crossing swords with William Denton, the skeptic, brought him into great notoriety. He held a debate with Denton on the question of "Whether all life upon the earth was developed by processes of law, or had been introduced by successive creative acts." Denton held the development theory; Garfield that of intelligent, providential action. The discussion lasted five days and evenings, embraced twenty speeches on the part of each of the disputants, and was remarkable as a sustained and severe intellectual effort. It won laurels for Garfield as a debater and a man of giant intellect.

Says Rev. J. L. Darsie, who was one of his pupils, "His lectures to the school were upon all sorts of subjects, and were generally the result of his readings and observation. One season he took a trip, and, on his return, gave a very interesting series on "The Chain of Lakes," including Niagara, Thousand Islands and sub-historic points. One lecture on ærolites I shall never forget. He gave several upon Ordnance, about the time of the attack upon Fort Sumter. Æsthetics came in for a share of treatment, with others on the personal habits of the students ; and they were very effective. He lectured upon any and every scientific subject."

A large number of students were always in attendance, who paid their way along by teaching school in the winter. To these he gave lectures on the art of teaching. Mr. Darsie says: "At each lecture he appointed one or two pupils to bring in a review of the lecture in writing, on a succeeding morning, and these reviews were read to the school. I now recall one of the most successful journalists of our land, who began his training here. In all he said or did, Garfield had the remarkable power of impressing himself and his thoughts upon his hearers, by his manners, gestures, tone of voice, and the freshness of his style. It was customary to act plays on commencement occasions, and the drama, in its more moral and high toned phases, was encouraged. Often the play was original, and always subject to the strictures of the faculty, as were all the public performances. Garfield, when a student, was one of the most successful in delineating character. He could impersonate almost any character, and was amazingly successful in this role."

He delivered also many extemporaneous speeches on social and literary occasions, and even in political campaigns. He studied law, also, while he was teacher at Hiram, doing it by the improvement of odd moments, and by burning midnight-oil. He was admitted to the bar before he exchanged the quiet of teaching for the roar of battle. He studied law, "not so much, with the intention of becoming a lawyer as to acquaint himself with the principles of law. He had no idea of abandoning his chosen profession to spend his energies in law-practice, but the principles of law were needed to round his knowledge, and increase his power."

As a Christian man, his influence was grand and ennobling, and his labors as a preacher are to be added to the mass of his other labors. He often preached in the Disciples' church at Hiram, and at one time he preached regularly at Solon and Newburg, whither he went on Saturday night, returning on Monday morning. He preached more or less throughout the county. Preaching and lecturing in other towns, near and remote, spread a knowledge of the school, and made it popular. He required his pupils to observe the highest standard of moral conduct, and his counsel here was frequent and direct. His favorite hymn at chapel-service was, "Ho! reapers of Life's Harvest," etc., and he joined in the singing with a will. He often requested the students to sing this hymn at morning devotions, allowing them to sit until they came to the last verse, when he would rap upon the desk with his knuckles, and the school would rise and sing the last verse standing.

He married Miss Rudolph, the lady to whom he was engaged before entering college, on November 11, 1858. Her efficient co-operation enabled him to accomplish so large an amount of labor. Often in the preparation of a lecture or speech, his wife and Miss Booth would explore the library for him, or examine certain books which he designated. The number of books that he perused in a year was almost incredible. Going from the library with his arms full of volumes was a common spectacle. Mr. Darsie has seen him on his way to the library, in the rain, returning ten or twelve volumes, a student walking by his side, holding an umbrella over his head. Some books awakened his enthusiasm; he read them more than once. Such books as "Tom Brown's School Days" won his admiration. He told his pupils that every one of them ought to read the work carefully. Macaulay's writings, and Mill's, and works of kindred ability and value, he particularly enjoyed and recommended.

In those days, Commencement exercises brought together from five to ten thousand people. They came from fifty miles around. A large tent was pitched over a stage, on which the literary exercises were performed. Booths for refreshments were erected here and there, and often showmen would appear upon the ground. Roughs and intoxicated persons sometimes appeared in large numbers, causing disturbance, and sadly marring the harmony of the occasion. But after Garfield became principal these scenes stopped. The pointing of his finger, or the waving of his hand, when disturbance broke out in any quarter, quelled it at once. Roughs appeared to understand that his authority could not be trifled with on such occasions.

We shall close this chapter by another quotation from Rev. Mr. Darsie:

"No matter how old the pupils were, Garfield always called us by our first names, and kept himself on the most familiar terms with all. He played with us freely, scuffled with us sometimes, walked with us in walking to and fro, and we treated him out of the class just about as we did one another. Yet he was a most strict disciplinarian, and enforced the rules like a martinet. He combined an affectionate and confiding manner with respect for order, in a most successful way. If he wanted to speak to a pupil, either for reproof or approbation, he would generally manage to get one arm around him, and draw him close up to him. He had a peculiar way of shaking hands, too, giving a twist to your arm, and drawing you right up to him. This sympathetic manner has helped him to advancement. When I was janitor he used sometimes to stop me and ask my opinion about this and that, as if seriously advising with me. I can see now that my opinion could not have been of any value, and that he probably asked me, partly to increase my self-respect and partly to show me that he felt an interest in me. I certainly was his friend all the firmer for it.

"I remember once asking him what was the best way to pursue a certain study, and he said, 'Use several text-books; get the views of different authors as you advance; in that way you can plough a broader furrow. I always study in that way.' He tried hard to have us observe carefully and accurately. He broke out one day in the midst of a lesson with, 'Henry, how many posts are there under the building downstairs?' Henry expressed his opinion, and the question went round the class, hardly one getting it right. Then it was, 'How many boot-scrapers are there at the door?' 'How many windows in the building?' 'How many trees in the field?' 'What were the colors of particular rooms, and the peculiarities of any familiar objects?' He was the keenest observer I ever saw. I think he observed, and numbered, every button on our coats. A friend of mine was walking with him through Cleveland, one day, when Garfield stopped and darted down a cellar-way, asking his companion to follow, and briefly stopping to explain himself. The sign, 'Saws and Files' was over the door, and in the depths was heard a regular clicking sound. 'I think this fellow is cutting files,' said he, 'and I have never seen a file cut.' Down they went, and, sure enough, there was a man recutting an old file, and they stayed there ten minutes and found out all about the process. Garfield would never go by anything without understanding it."

CHAPTER XXIII.

FROM PEACE TO WAR.

IT is impossible for a public speaker of Garfield's power to keep out of politics. In political campaigns the public demand his efforts; men will not take *no* for an answer. It was so with Garfield. He was impressed into the service by leading citizens of his county. In the autumn after his return to Hiram, before he hardly had time to become settled in his great work, his efforts on the platform were sought; and the new Republican party, on the anti-slavery basis, with its first candidate, John C. Fremont, a man of Garfield's stamp in vigor, courage, and force of character, was exceedingly taking to him. Nobody had to tease him long for a speech. Often he went in the evening to make a speech, five, six, ten miles distant, returning after the address. Usually he took a student with him for company and improvement. As soon as they started he would open conversation, seldom upon the subject of his discourse, but upon some topic of real value to the student. Going and returning, his conversation was continued without the least abatement.

Alphonso Hart, a stalwart Democrat of Ravenna,

delivered a speech in Hiram, full of slavery and Democratic sophistries and errors. Garfield heard it, with many Republican citizens.

"Reply to it, Mr. Garfield," appealed an influential citizen to him. "Floor him."

"That can easily be done," Garfield answered; "but is it wise?"

"It is always wise to refute error and wrong anywhere."

"I confess that I should enjoy handling him without gloves for an hour."

"Handle him, then," urged the citizen. "It will do the Republican party a world of good."

Other citizens put in their pleas for him to answer Hart.

"You are just the one to do it."

"Everybody wants you should answer him."

"It will make votes for Fremont."

"Come, now, do gratify the public desire."

In this way, Garfield was beset with pleas to answer the Democratic orator; and he consented. The meeting was in the Disciples church, and it was packed to its utmost capacity. Garfield's reply was devoid of all bitterness, but was powerful with logic and facts. He hauled over the record of the Democratic party, with its endorsement of slavery with all its horrors, and he made that record appear black enough. The effort was both able and triumphant, and the fame of it rapidly spread throughout the county. Appeals for more speeches came in from all the region about, and finally a discussion was arranged between Garfield and Hart, to take place at

Garrettsville on a given day. Crowds flocked to hear the debate. Garfield was in his element on that day, for he had posted himself thoroughly upon the history of the Democratic party, and the aims of its southern leaders to make slavery national. His antagonist was completely discomfited in the discussion. He had counted without his host. He was floored. Garfield's success lifted him at once into enviable notoriety as a political debater and orator, and, from that time, remarks like the following were common:

"He must go to the legislature."

"We must send him to congress."

"Just the man to follow that old anti-slavery war-horse, Giddings."

"You'll see him President, yet."

And so the enthusiastic awakening expended itself, in a measure, upon Garfield's supposed future career. One year later, the position of representative to the State legislature was tendered him.

"No; my work is here in the Institute. I have no ambition to enter political life. I must decline the proposition." Garfield thus replied out of an honest heart

Again and again he was urged to accept the position, but to every one his answer was the same.

"My work is here, and my heart is here, and my DUTY is here." No appeals could move him.

In 1859, the faculty of Williams College invited him to deliver the master's oration on Commencement day. It was a rare compliment the faculty paid him by this invitation, for it was but three years after he had graduated. Accepting the invitation, and pre paring himself carefully for the occasion, he left Hiram for Williamstown, Massachusetts, accompanied by his wife, taking the first pleasure-trip of his life. He descended the St. Lawrence river to Quebec, and then crossed the New England states to his destination. A warm welcome awaited him there. Nor were the numerous friends who gathered disappointed in the orator of the day. His praises were on every lip.

On his return, when he had reached Mentor, in his own state, a delegation of citizens met him with an unexpected proposition.

"We want you to become a candidate for state senator."

"Indeed!" exclaimed Garfield, very much surprised by the proposition. "I thought Mr. Prentiss was the man."

"Mr. Prentiss has just died, very suddenly."

Mr. Prentiss was a man well advanced in life, a very popular citizen of Ravenna, whose re-election had been determined upon. But his sudden death frustrated their plans; and now all hearts turned tc the young principal of Hiram Institute.

"You are the first choice of the leading Republicans of the district."

"I thank you sincerely for thinking of me, and, really, it is a temptation to receive this offer; but I do not see how I can consistently consent."

"Your name will enable us to carry the district for the Republicans easily," urged another one of the delegation. "I hope you will not decline without giving the subiect some thought."

"Yes, but my thought is of the Institute. How can I accept your proposition and discharge my duties to the school?"

"Your duties in the senate will keep you away but a few weeks. Suppose you take the subject into consideration, confer with the faculty, and let us have your decision a week hence."

The last speaker knew that some members of the faculty and board of trustees were anxious that he should accept the nomination.

To this last suggestion Garfield yielded, and the matter was laid before the faculty and trustees. To his surprise all of them urged him to consent to the use of his name. Teachers volunteered to do extra work in his absence, and all were willing to contribute service, so as to make it possible for him to go.

Garfield was pressed into this political service, and received the nomination. He was present by request, at the nominating convention, and while the business was in progress, a delegate who saw the youthful candidate on that day for the first time, remarked to a leading Republican:

"Don't you make a mistake in putting forward so young a man for senator?"

"Only young in years; he is not young in ability," was the prompt reply.

"I don't know about that; unless his looks belie him, his experience in public life must be rather limited."

"You wait and see. We shall hear from him when this business is through, and you will be satisfied that his head is old, though his body is young."

After nomination, according to the custom that prevailed, Garfield accepted it in a characteristic speech. The delegate who doubted the wisdom of the nomination immediately said to the Republican to whom his doubts were expressed,

"I am perfectly satisfied; he is a power."

Garfield was elected by a very large majority, and took his seat in the state senate, January, 1860. It was a time of great excitement. The south was threatening secession and civil war, if a Republican should be elected president in the approaching campaign. The north was fully aroused to check the incursions of slavery, by a bold and victorious advance. Garfield was just the man to occupy a seat in the state senate at such a time, though he was the youngest member of the body. There was another able young man in the senate with him, as radical as himself, Jacob D. Cox, afterwards major-general, governor of Ohio, and Secretary of the Interior. The two roomed together, and were as intimate as brothers. Some of the members called them "Damon and Pythias." There was still another young man, Professor Munroe of Oberlin College, an institution that was founded on anti-slavery principles, and whose teachers were as one with Garfield on the great national question that overtopped all others — liberty. Cox himself was the son-in-law of an Oberlin professor. These three senators stood shoulder to shoulder against slavery, and were called the "radical triumvirate."

Garfield took rank at once with the ablest speakers in that body. President Hinsdale says, "He was a valuable man on committees and in party councils

No senator was more frequently called to his councils by the president of the senate when knotty points of order were to be untied or cut."

In a previous chapter we learned that Garfield visited Columbus with his mother, and saw the legislature in session. Little did he dream, or his mother. that in less than ten years he would be a leading member of that senate, his eloquence ringing through those halls, and his wise counsels and patriotic efforts preparing the state to oppose rebellion with great power; yet so it was. One of the most marvellous examples of success on record!

During his second term in the senate, 1861, he was confronted by the gravest questions that state or nation ever had to deal with. Lincoln had been elected president, the southern states were preparing to secede, and civil war was imminent. "Shall Ohio prepare for war?" "Has a state the right to secede?" "Can a state be coerced?" "Shall we punish treason?" These were among the questions the young senator was compelled to discuss. Almost night and day he labored to qualify himself to discuss them intelligently and ably. Night after night, until eleven, twelve, and even one o'clock, he spent in the state library, studying these and kindred questions. Whenever he spoke upon them, he spoke pointedly, and with great power. He led the senate in its patriotic stand against secession and compromise with slavery. He denounced Buchanan, the Democratic president, who was favoring the secessionists, and characterized Cobb, who robbed the national treasury, and Floyd, who stole the arms from every northern arsenal, and

Toucey, who sent the ships of the navy as far away as possible — all members of the Democratic cabinet — he characterized them as traitors to their country. In a speech that blazed with fervid eloquence, he told a Democratic senator, Judge Key, of Cincinnati, "to remember whose cabinet it was that had embraced traitors among its most distinguished members, and sent them forth from its most secret sessions to betray their knowledge to their country's ruin!"

When congress very unwisely proposed a "Constitutional Amendment," prohibiting further legislation upon slavery in the states, — a measure designed to placate the secessionists, — Garfield denounced it in the Ohio senate as a compromise with traitors, an unpatriotic and base surrender to the slave oligarchy. He declared that his arm should wither in its socket before it should be lifted in favor of a measure that virtually abandoned liberty, and left slavery master of the situation. "The events now transpiring make it clear that this is no time for any such amendment," he exclaimed. "Would you give up the forts and other government property, or would you fight to maintain your right to them?"

When the vote was taken, Garfield, with six others, recorded their names against the "base surrender." He opposed the meeting of the famous Washington Peace Commissioners until after the inauguration of Mr. Lincoln; he protested against all such "peace measures" as cowardly and futile, preferring himself to stand by the old flag, and *fight* for human rights.

Before this, he was satisfied that war could not be averted. Late one night he said to his room-mate:

"Cox, war is inevitable."

"That is sure as you live," answered Cox.

"You and I must fight."

"Or prove ourselves cowards."

"Here, then, we pledge our lives to our country in this hour of peril." And they clasped hands silently, such emotions stirring their breasts as patriots only feel in the solemn hour of danger.

News of the firing upon Fort Sumter was followed immediately by a call from President Lincoln for seventy-five thousand men. The call was read in the Ohio senate, crowded with patriotic spectators, whose tumultuous applause seconded the President's demand. As soon as the deafening cheers had subsided, Garfield sprang to his feet, and in a short speech, of almost surpassing eloquence and power, moved,—

"That Ohio contribute twenty thousand men, and three million dollars, as the quota of the state."

The motion was carried amid the wildest demonstrations of devotion to the country.

Governor Dennison, of Ohio, sent Garfield to Missouri to obtain five thousand stand of arms, a portion of those which General Lyon removed from the arsenal at St. Louis. He was successful in his mission, shipped the guns, and saw them safely delivered at Columbus.

After the fall of Sumter, Governor Dennison sent him to Cleveland, to organize the seventh and eighth regiments of Ohio infantry. Having organized them, the governor offered him the colonelcy of one of them; but he declined the offer because he lacked "military experience." He promised to take a subordinate position, however, provided a West Point graduate was placed in command. The result was, that the governor appointed him lieutenant-colonel, and sent him to the Western Reserve to recruit a regiment, promising him a West Pointer to command it, if one could be found. Garfield suggested his old friend and schoolmate, Captain Hazen, then in the regular army; but when the governor sent to the war department for his transfer, General Scott refused to release him. So the Forty-second Ohio regiment, recruited by Garfield, and embracing a large number of Hiram students, went into camp at Columbus without a colonel. It was in these circumstances, and after repeated requests from officers and members of the regiment, that Garfield consented to take the command.

He proved himself as victorious in war as he had been successful in peace. In less than one month after he went into action with his regiment, under the orders of General Buell, he fought the battle of Middle Creek, January 10, 1862, driving the rebel General Marshall, whose forces largely outnumbered his, out of his entrenchments, compelling him to retreat into Virginia. Other victories followed, in what was called the "Sandy Valley campaign," eliciting from the commanding-general a congratulatory order, in which he spoke of the expedition as "calling into action the highest qualities of a soldier — fortitude, perseverance, courage." For his bravery and military skill in this campaign, the authorities at Washington made Garfield a brigadier-general, dating his commission back to January 10, 1862, the day of the battle of Middle Creek. As Garfield was the youngest member of the Ohio senate, so now he became the youngest brigadier-general in the army.

Subsequently he was made major-general "for gallant and meritorious services at the battle of Chickamauga." The antecedents of that famous battle, under General Rosecrans, show that the victory was due more to the sagacity, plans, and courage of General Garfield than to any other officer. Within about one year and a half, he rose from a lieutenant-colonelcy to a major-generalship. Several incidents, connected with his war record, deserve special attention here.

The thoughtful consideration that he devoted to issues of importance appeared in the current of his thoughts and acts after he had determined to enter the army. He went to his home at night thinking of his dear mother and dearer wife and child, as well as the small property he should leave them if he laid down his life on the battle-field. Opening the Bible which his mother gave him, to see what it would say to him upon the subject, he read, and read, and every passage seemed like the voice of God, saying to him, "Go! Go!" Far into the night he thought and read, and read and thought, more and more satisfied that his decision was in the path of duty; and, before the dawn of morning, he wrote to a near friend as follows:

"I have had a curious interest in watching the process, in my own mind, by which the fabric of my life is being demolished and reconstructed, to meet the new condition of affairs. One by one my old plans and aims, modes of thought and feeling, are found to be inconsistent with present duty, and are set aside to give place to the new structure of military life. It is not without a regret, almost tearful at times, that I look upon the ruins. But if, as the result of the broken plans and shattered individual lives of thousands of American citizens, we can see on the ruins of our own national errors a new and enduring fabric arise, based on larger freedom and higher justice, it will be a small sacrifice indeed. For myself, I am contented with such a prospect, and, regarding my life as given to the country, am only anxious to make as much of it as possible before the mortgage upon it is foreclosed."

When he went into camp, to drill his regiment before joining the army, his thoroughness and systematic way of doing things, as well as his tact and use of carpenters' tools, came into immediate use. He was ignorant of military tactics, and so he sat down first to the task of instructing himself before he undertook the instruction of his regiment. "Bringing his saw and jack-plane again into play, he fashioned companies, officers, and non-commissioned officers, out of maple blocks, and, with these wooden-headed troops, thoroughly mastered the infantry tactics in his quarters. Then he organized a school for the officers of his regiment, requiring thorough recitation in the tactics, and illustrating the manœuvres by the blocks he had prepared for his own instruction. This done, he instituted regimental, company, squad, skirmish, and bayonet drill, and kept his men at these exercises from six to eight hours a day, until it was universally admitted that no better drilled or disciplined regiment could be found in Ohio."

His decision and force of character, so noticeable in his early life, were illustrated by the promptness and energy with which he met a singular disappointment on the day his regiment left Columbus for the seat of war. By some mistake or misunderstanding he had not reached the depot when the train started. Coming up within five minutes, he remarked to the superintendent of the road, "I was never behind time before in my life, and I will not be now;" and he chartered an engine, was off in a few minutes, and overtook his regiment in less than one hour.

Colonel Garfield's orders were, to open communication with Colonel Cranor, and form a junction with his forces, although his command did not number half that of the enemy. The first indispensable thing to be done was to find a trusty messenger, to bear despatches to Colonel Cranor. He must be a man who would die rather than betray his trust; for Colonel Cranor was a hundred miles away, and the messenger must go through a region inhabited by disloyal people, and infested by guerillas. He applied to Colonel Moore, of the Fourteenth Kentucky.

"Have you a man who will die rather than fail or betray us?"

"I think I have," the colonel replied, after a little reflection; "John Jordan."

The man was called, a strong-looking fellow, tall and lean, with a squeaking voice, his speech the uncouth dialect of the mountains, where he was born and reared, subject to the hardest toil and privation. He knew much of nature, in whose lap he was dandled, but very little of books, except the "Course of Time" and the Bible. Some officers would have thought him too simple for a spy, or expert messenger, but Garfield read him in a minute, — a rude, unlettered, trusty, Christian man.

"Why did you come into the war?" at last asked the colonel.

"To do my sheer fur the kentry, gin'ral," answered the man. "And I didn't druv no barg'in wi' th' Lord. I guv him my life squar' out; and ef he's a mind ter tuck it in on this tramp, why, it's a' his'n; I've nothin' ter say ag'in it."

"You mean that you've come into the war not expecting to get out of it?"

"That's so, gin'ral."

"Will you die, rather than let the despatch be taken?"

"I wull."

"Very well; I will trust you."

Colonel Garfield wrote his despatch on tissue-paper, rolled it into the form of a bullet, coated it with warm lead, and delivered it to Jordan. At the same time he provided him with a carbine, a brace of revolvers, and the fleetest horse in the regiment. Jordan started upon his perilous journey at night, after the moon was down. He was to ride by night, and hide in the woods, or rest in loyal families, if they could be found, by day.

Before Jordan returned, another incident transpired, showing how great service Garfield's life on the canal was to him in another direction. One day, a loyal scout presented himself at his headquarters, and grasping Colonel Garfield's hand, exclaimed, in a jolly way, —

"Jim!"

Garfield looked at him with surprise, for a moment, but did not recognize him.

"Who are you?" he inquired.

"Yer old companion, Jim," answered the scout.

"*My* old companion!" ejaculated Garfield.

"Yis, yer old companion! Yer see I was a scout in West Virginia, under Rosecrans; and hearing of the Sandy Valley expedition, and that James A. Garfield, of Ohio, had command of it, I thought as how that must be my old companion on the canal boat; and so I made tracks for yer."

"Harry!" exclaimed Garfield, shaking his hand heartily, as he recognized one of Captain Letcher's crew, whose name was Henry S. Brown, but known as "*Harry*" on the boat. The marks of a very dissipated life had obliterated the traces of his former self, so that it was not strange that Garfield did not recognize him. Brown was strongly attached to "Jim," on the canal, and now he desired, above all things, to serve him.

"Colonel Garfield," at length Brown said, laying aside the familiar title by which he was known on the canal boat, and addressing him respectfully, as any loyal soldier would address a superior officer, "Colonel Garfield, I'm at yer service."

"Just the man I want for a scout," answered Garfield, heartily. He had confidence in Brown for that business, and trusted him at once. He knew the country thoroughly; and Garfield sent him ahead of his column to make the circuit of the rebel camp, and learn, if possible, the strength and position of Mar shall's army. He was directed, also, to sweep through the mountain border of Virginia, to learn if the loyal forces were threatened from that quarter. Brown departed, and Garfield moved forward.

On the following night, as Garfield lay in sound sleep, about midnight, Jordan came riding into camp from his dangerous trip. Alighting from his foaming steed, he rushed into his commander's quarters, and shook him until he awoke.

"What! back safe?" exclaimed Garfield, as soon as he recognized Jordan. "Have you seen Colonel Cranor?"

"Yes, colonel; he can't be mor'n two days ahind o' me, nohow."

"God bless you, Jordan! You have done us great service," said Garfield, warmly.

"I thank you, colonel," answered Jordan, his voice trembling; "that's more pay'n I expected."

He had returned safely; but the Providence which so wonderfully guarded his way out seemed to leave him to find his own way back; for, as he expressed it, "The Lord he cared more for the despatch nor he cared for me; and it was nat'ral he shu'd; 'cause my life only counts one, but the despatch — it stood for all Kentucky."

The use of Jordan and Brown for scouts initiated Garfield into the condition of a successful "secret service." When he became chief of General Rosecrans' staff he organized a "secret service," which Rosecrans called "the eyes of the army;" and it was acknowledged to be the most complete and efficient scout system of the war.

The *Atlantic Monthly*, of October, 1865, contained a detailed account of Jordan's wonderful trip, and it closed by leaving the hero in some unknown graveyard — dead. But, two years afterwards, he turned up, and wrote to General Garfield that he was dead only on paper, and that he still had a life to give to his country.

We have seen that Garfield was a born leader among the companions of his youth, and that the magnetism of his personal presence inspired hearts around him with a kindred spirit. When he became a teacher, we have seen that he excelled other teachers in awakening the enthusiasm of his pupils, and leading them to pursue their studies, or a life purpose, with singular devotion. It was equally so in the army. In the first victorious battle that he fought — that of Middle Creek — many incidents transpired to establish this fact.

Colonel Garfield had a hundred of his Hiram students in his command. As soon as he discovered where the main rebel force lay he ordered the Hiram students to cross the rapid stream, and climb the ridge opposite, whence the rebel fire had been the hottest, his object being to bring on a battle. As if imitating their brave commander, who never seemed to heed danger, or to think of himself, the students responded with a cheer, and were soon up to their waists in the cold, wintry river. Once over, they started up the rocky ascent with a yell, clinging to the trees and underbrush to support themselves. When not more than half way up the ridge, two thousand rebel rifles opened upon them; but on they went, until the very summit was reached, when suddenly the hill was alive with rebel soldiers, springing from ambush, and pouring a deadly fire into the little Spartan band. For an instant the students faltered, but the shout of their leader, Captain Williams, rallied them.

"Every man to a tree! Give them as good as they send, boys!"

The order was obeyed, and behind the huge oaks and maples the boys stood and fired, picking off the confederates, one by one. As yet, not one of the Hiram boys had fallen. But the rebels charge upon them, and drive them down the hill, two of their number falling, one to rise no more. A Hiram boy turns to his wounded comrade, to bear him away, when a rebel, within thirty feet, fires, and the bullet strikes a tree just above his head. The Hiram student takes deliberate aim, and sends that rebel to his account. But he cannot bear away his comrade, for the rebels are upon him. He joins his retreating companions just as the voice of the heroic Captain Williams is heard again, above the din of battle:

"To the trees again, my boys! We may as well die here as in Ohio!"

To the trees they go, and succeed in turning back the rebel advance, and driving them up the hill. Passing the wounded Hiram boy, a confederate said to him.

"Boy, guv me yer musket."

"Not the gun, but the contents," shouted the brave fellow; and the confederate fell dead at his feet.

Another rebel raised his weapon to brain the

prostrate student, when the latter seized the dead rebel's gun, at his feet, and shot him so quickly that the rebel scarcely knew what hurt him. One hour afterwards the boys had borne their bleeding hero to camp, where the surgeon proceeded to amputate his limb.

"Oh, what will mother do?" exclaimed the patriot, in the midst of his agony. His mother was poor, dependent upon her son for support. Two weeks later the story of Charles Carlton, of Franklin, Ohio, was told in the Ohio senate, and it aroused the state to lead off in framing statutes to aid the widows and mothers of its soldiers.

Colonel Garfield ordered five hundred soldiers forward to support the Hiram valiants. With a shout they plunged into the stream, holding their cartridge-boxes above their heads.

"Hurrah for Williams, and the Hiram boys!"

But four thousand muskets, and twelve pieces of artillery, concentrated a fearful fire upon them.

"This will never do," cried Garfield; "who will volunteer to carry the other mountain?"

"We will," answered Colonel Moore, of the Twenty-second Kentucky. "We know every inch of the ground."

"Go in, then, and give them Hail Columbia!" Garfield shouted.

And they did; a similar fight on the other ridge, the loyal troops behind trees, picking off the rebels whose heads peered above the rocks. Cooler men never served in war.

"Do you see that reb?" said one comrade to another. "Hit him while I'm loading."

Another was raising his cartridge to his mouth when a rebel bullet cut away the powder, leaving the lead in his fingers. Shielding his arm with his body, he said, as he reloaded, —

"There, see if you can hit that!"

Another took out a piece of hard tack, and a ball cut it to pieces in his hand.

He coolly swallowed the remnant, and fired at his foe. One was brought down by a rebel bullet in his knee; but, with rifle still in hand, he watched for the man who shot him. The rebel's head soon appeared above the rock, and the two fired at the same moment. The loyal soldier was hit fatally in the mouth. When his comrades were bearing him away, he spoke out, —

"Never mind; that secesh is done for."

When the confederate was found, on the following day, the upper part of his head was shot away by the other's fatal charge.

So the battle raged, the loyal forces advancing, and then retreating, until the fate of the little Union army seemed to hang in the balance, when Garfield, standing on a rock that was scarred by a thousand bullets, and from which he could take in the whole scene, with his head uncovered, and his hair streaming in the wind, his face upturned in earnest prayer for Sheldon and his forces (expected reinforcements), turned to his hundred men, held back as reserves, exclaiming, as he tossed his outer coat into a tree, —

"Come on, boys! *we* must give them Hail Columbia!"

And they rushed to the succor of the forlorn hope,

just as the sun was sinking behind the western hills; when lo! a look to the northward revealed to Garfield the star-spangled banner waving among the trees! It was Sheldon and his reinforcements, just in season to turn the tide of battle. The rebel commander sounded "retreat!" but had scarcely given the order when six loyal bullets pierced his body, and he fell dead.

"God bless you, boys; you have saved Kentucky!" shouted Garfield to his troops, when they ceased pursuing the retreating confederates.

We learned before, that President Lincoln made Garfield brigader-general for gallant services in this battle. The President was much depressed at the time of this victory, because of repeated disasters to our arms in the "Department of the East." A distinguished army officer was present with him when he received the news of this victory, and Mr. Lincoln said to the officer, —

"Why did Garfield, in two weeks, do what would have taken one of your regular officers two months to accomplish?"

"Because he was not educated at West Point," replied the West Pointer, laughingly.

"No," answered Mr. Lincoln, "that was not the reason. It was because, when he was a boy, he had to work for a living."

After the battle of Middle Creek, Garfield's soldiers were exhausted, and short of rations. The roads were well-nigh impassable, because of the deep mud, and the Big Sandy was swollen to a torrent, rendering the delivery of supplies difficult. Something must be done. Garfield proposed to go down the river to hurry up supplies, but the oldest boatmen refused, saying, "Impossible, it can't be done!"

Brown, the scout, had returned, and Garfield opened the subject to him.

"What do you think of it, Brown? The boatmen say that it is sure death; what do you say? You and I know something about boating."

The scout's reply was characteristic. "It's which and tother, Gineral Jim; starvin' or drownin.' I'd rather drown nor starve. So, guv the word, and, dead or alive, I'll git down the river!"

"All right, Harry, we'll go!" And they sprang into a small skiff, and committed their lives to the raging torrent. It was a fearful sail, but they reached the mouth of the Big Sandy in safety · and here Garfield's experience on the canal boat served him well. There he found a small, rickety steamer, named "Sandy Valley," tied up at Catletsburg.

"I am under the necessity of taking possession of your steamer to carry supplies to my troops," Colonel Garfield said to the captain, who was a secessionist, and who, of course, would have preferred that the troops should starve rather than to feed them.

"This craft can't stem such a current, no how; it'll be the death on us," the captain replied. There was some reason for his saying this, for the water in the channel was sixty feet deep, so swollen that trees along the banks were submerged nearly to their tops.

"Nevertheless, I must have this steamer, and I will assume the command:" and so saying, Garfield ordered the captain and crew on board, took his station at the helm, placed Brown at the bow, with a long fending pole, to keep one eye on the floating logs and uprooted trees, and the other on the rebel captain. The steamer was loaded with provisions, and started up the river with Captain (not Colonel just now) Garfield in command. We learned, in the course of our narrative, that once he desired to command some sort of water-craft, and now his early hopes were realized.

When night came on, it was dark and tempestuous, and the captain said, —

"The boat must be tied up to-night; can't live in such a time ; it is madness to keep on."

"But I am captain of this steamer, now," responded Garfield ; "keep to your duty and I will keep to mine. We don't tie up boats in such a crisis as this. Freshen the fires, men, and put on the steam." And he kept the steamer on its way.

Finally, in turning a bend in the river, the steamer swept round and grounded on a bar of quicksand. The usual efforts were made to relieve her, but in vain. And now that tact and sound common sense for which we have seen that Garfield was distinguished from boyhood, came to his rescue.

"Get a line to the opposite shore!" commanded Garfield, particularly addressing the sulky captain.

"A line to that shore!" shouted the rebel captain in reply. "It's death on any man that 'tempts it."

"It can be done, and it *must* be done," cried Garfield; and he leaped into the yawl, calling Brown to follow, and steered for the shore. The wild torrent swept them down the stream a short distance, but they rallied by almost superhuman strength, reached the shore, fastened the line, constructed a windlass, and, in a short time, the steamer was drawn from her bed in the mud, and was on her triumphant way up the stream. From Saturday until nine o'clock Monday morning, Garfield stood at the wheel, night and day; and when he reached Paintsville his troops were reduced almost to their last cracker. His experience with rough men at the "Black-saltery," and on the canal, qualified him to deal with such a rebel as the captain of the "Sandy Valley."

When the steamer drew up to the Union camp, Garfield's men were almost frantic with joy. They cheered and yelled, and seized their brave commander, and would have borne him upon their shoulders to headquarters, had he not resolutely protested against it.

Brown, the scout, came to a melancholy end. General Garfield wrote about him, May 31, 1864, as follows: —

"When we first met he recognized me as an old acquaintance on the Ohio canal. He at once took a sort of enthusiastic pride in me, and with a rough, generous nature, was ready to make any personal sacrifices to aid me to success. He was not trusted by most of our people; indeed, many of them attempted to convince me that he was not only a rascal, but a rebel. I think he had an eye for a good horse, and did not always closely distinguish between *meum* and *tuum*; but my remembrance of him on the canal, together with a feeling that he loved me, made me trust him implicitly. I think he was never perfectly happy till he helped me to navigate the little steamer up the Big Sandy in the high water. Indeed, I could not have done that without his aid. He was about forty years old; a short, stocky, sailor-looking fellow, somewhat bloated with hard drinking; in short, he was a rare combination of good and bad qualities with strong traits, a ruined man; and yet, underneath the ruins, a great deal of generous, self-sacrificing noble-heartedness, which made one deplore his fall, and yet like him. He went north on some personal business, just before I left the Sandy Valley, and I received a dirty note from him, written from Buffalo, in which he said he should meet me somewhere in 'the tide of battle,' and fight by my side again; but I have not heard from him since."

Another says:

"This was in 1864. Ten years afterward, as General Garfield was about to deliver an address at Cornell, a heavy hand was laid upon his shoulder, and, turning about, he saw his ex-scout and old boat-companion. He was even a more perfect ruin than before — with bleared eyes, bloated face, and garments that were half tatters. He had come, he said, while the tears rolled down his cheeks, to that quiet place to die, and now he could die in peace, because he had seen his 'gineral.'

"Garfield gave him money, and got him quarters among some kind people, and left him, telling him to try to be a man: but, in any event, to let him know if he ever needed further help. A year or more passed, and no word came from Brown; but then the superintendent of the public hospital at Buffalo wrote the general that a man was there very sick, who, in his delirium talked of him, of the Ohio Canal, and of the

Sandy Valley expedition. Garfield knew at once that it was Brown, and immediately forwarded funds to the hospital, asking that he should have every possible care and comfort. The letter which acknowledged the remittance announced that the poor fellow had died — died, muttering, in his delirium, the name 'Jim Garfield.'

"Garfield gave him a decent burial, and this was the last of the poor fellow."

General Garfield's tact, sagacity, fidelity, spirit of self-sacrifice, and undaunted courage, so conspicuous in his early life, are illustrated by his famous ride from General Rosecrans to General Thomas, when the army of the Cumberland was almost routed in the famous battle of Chickamauga. It was necessary for General Thomas to know the disaster that had befallen Rosecrans' forces, in order to meet the rebel General Longstreet victoriously. Garfield proposed to undertake the fearful ride. Edmund Kirk, war correspondent of the "New York Tribune," described it as follows:

"Rosecrans hesitates, then says, 'As you will, general;' and then, reaching Garfield his hand, he adds, while his face shows his emotion, 'We may not meet again; good-bye; God bless you!' Though one of the bravest men and ablest soldiers that ever lived, Rosecrans has a heart as tender and gentle as a woman's. He thinks Garfield is going to wellnigh certain death, and he loves him as David loved Jonathan. Again he wrings his hand, and then they part — Rosecrans to the rear, to rally his broken troops. Garfield to a perilous ride in pursuit of Thomas.

"Captain Gaw and two of his orderlies go with Garfield to guide the way. They make a wide detour to avoid the Confederates, and, by the route they take, it is eight miles of tangled forest and open road before they get to Thomas, and at any turn they may come upon the enemy.

"At Rossville they take the Lafayette Road, guiding their way by the sound of the firing, and moving cautiously, for they are now nearing the battle-field. The road here is scarcely more than a lane, flanked on one side by a thick wood, and on the other by an open cotton-field. No troops are in sight, and on they gallop at a rapid pace; and they have left Rossville a thousand yards behind, when suddenly, from along the left of the road, a volley of a thousand Minie-balls falls among them, thick as hail, wounding one horse, killing another, and stretching the two orderlies on the ground lifeless. They have ridden into an ambuscade of a large body of Longstreet's skirmishers and sharpshooters, who, entering the fatal gap in the right centre, have pressed thus far upon the flank of Thomas.

"Garfield is mounted on a magnificent horse, that knows his rider's bridle-hand as well as he knows the route to his fodder. Putting spurs to his side, he leaps the fence into the cotton-field. The opposite fence is lined with gray blouses, and a single glance tells him that they are loading for another volley. He has been in tight places before, but this is the tightest. Putting his lips firmly together, he says to himself, 'Now is your time; be a man, Jim Garfield!' He speaks to his horse, and lays his left hand gently on the rein of the animal. The trained beast yields kindly to his touch; and, putting the rowels into his side, Garfield takes a zigzag course across the cotton-field. It is his only chance; he must tack from side to side, for he is a dead man if they get a steady aim upon him.

"He is riding up an inclined plane of about four hundred yards, and if he can pass the crest, he is in safety. But the gray fellows can load and fire twice, before he reaches the summit, and his death is a thing certain, unless Providence has more work for him to do on this footstool. Up the hill he goes, tacking, when another volley bellows from out the timber. His horse is struck, — a flesh wound, — but the noble animal only leaps forward the faster. Scattering bullets whiz by his head, but he is within a few feet of the summit. Another volley echoes along the hill when he is half over the crest, but in a moment more he is in safety. As he tears down the slope, a small body of mounted blue-coats gallop forward to meet him. At their head is General Dan McCook, his face anxious and pallid. 'My God, Garfield!' he cries, 'I thought you were killed, certain. How you have escaped is a miracle.'

"Garfield's horse has been struck twice, but he is good yet for a score of miles; and at a breakneck pace they go forward through ploughed fields and tangled forests, and over broken and rocky hills, for four weary miles, till they climb a wooded crest, and are within sight of Thomas. In a slight depression of the ground, with a group of officers about him, he stands in the open field, while over him sweeps the storm of shotted fire that falls in thick rain on the high foot-hill which Garfield is crossing. Shot and shell and canister plough up the ground all about Garfield; but in the midst of it he halts, and with uplifted right arm, and eyes full of tears, he shouts, as he catches sight of Thomas, 'There he is! God bless the old hero! he has saved the army!'

"For a moment only he halts, then he plunges down the hill through the fiery storm, and in five minutes is by the side of Thomas. He has come out unscathed from the hurricane of death, for God's good angels have warded off the bullets, but his noble horse staggers a step or two, and then falls dead at the feet of Thomas."

Garfield's terrible ride saved the army of the Cumberland from remediless disaster.

Another incident illustrative of his life-long independence in standing for the right, befriending the down-trodden, and assailing slavery, was his refusal to return a fugitive slave. One of his staff told the story thus:

"One day I noticed a fugitive slave come rushing into camp with a bloody head, and apparently frightened almost to death. He had only passed my tent a moment, when a regular bully of a fellow came riding up, and, with a volley of oaths, began to ask after his 'nigger.' General Garfield was not present, and he passed on to the division commander. This division commander was a sympathizer with the theory that fugitives should be returned to their masters, and that the Union soldiers should be made the instruments for returning them. He accordingly wrote a mandatory order to General Garfield, in whose command the slave was supposed to be hiding, telling him to hunt out and deliver over the property of the outraged citizen. I stated the case as fully as I could to General Garfield, before handing him the order, but did not color my statement in any way. He took the order, and deliberately wrote on it the following endorsement:

"'I respectfully but positively decline to allow my command to search for or deliver up any fugitive slaves. I conceive that they are here for quite another purpose. The command is open, and no obstacles will be placed in the way of search.'

"I read the endorsement and was frightened. I expected that, if returned, the result would be that the general would be court-martialled. I told him my fears. He simply replied: 'The matter may as well be tested first as last. Right is right, and I do not propose to mince matters at all. My soldiers are here for other purposes than hunting and returning fugitive slaves. My people, on the Western Reserve of Ohio, did not send my boys and myself down here to do that kind of business, and they will back me up in my action.' He would not alter the endorsement, and the order was returned. Nothing ever came of the matter further."

In the beginning of our story, we learned that one of Garfield's first teachers told him (patting him on the head), "You may make a general, if you learn well." He did not understand the meaning of it at the time, but he knew all about it afterwards. Nor is it difficult to understand how his early opportunities to study human nature, his ability to read character, his tact and experience in disciplining and drilling a large school, fitted him for a successful general.

CHAPTER XXIV.

TOP OF THE LADDER.

IN the summer of 1862, leading republicans of the nineteenth Ohio congressional district nominated Garfield to represent them in congress. They regarded him as the man above all others in the district qualified to succeed Joshua R. Giddings, of whom they were justly proud. Giddings was superseded four years before by John Hutchins, with whom the republicans were not satisfied. The movement for Garfield was undertaken without his knowledge. He was at the head of his command in Kentucky. The knowledge of his great abilities, and his military fame, led to his nomination. At first he thought he must decline the honor, and fight out the battles of his country. He was very popular in the army, both with officers and soldiers, — his pay, too, was double that of a congressman, and he was poor and needed the greater salary, — and there was no doubt that the highest honors awaited him should he continue on the field until the end of the war. The reader can readily see that to accept the nomination in these circumstances, was an act of great self-denial. But President Lincoln signified his desire for Garfield to enter congress, as a member of military experience and skill was much needed there. The wishes of Lincoln settled the doubts of Garfield, and he accepted the nomination, was triumphantly elected, and took his seat in the national house of representatives in December, 1863, after two years and three months of service in the army.

During this time the trustees of Hiram Institute had not abandoned the idea of his return to the institution. While a member of the Ohio senate, he continued his connection with the school, when the senate was not in session. One interesting item of his thoroughness in teaching belongs to this part of his career. He was teaching a class how to write letters, and having taught them how to address different classes of friends and relatives, how to superscribe letters, etc., illustrating the same on the blackboard, he requested each one to write a letter to him at Columbus. In due time the letters were written and forwarded. Subsequently they were returned to the authors, corrected.

During his first two years in congress, his name appeared on the catalogue of Hiram Institute as "Advisory Principal and Lecturer." He remained a member of the board until his death. For seventeen years he served his district as national representative, and became the acknowledged leader of the national house of representatives; the pride of his native state, Ohio, and an honor to the republic.

One of the first important measures that came up, after he entered congress, was a bounty bill—offering men a sum of money, in addition to the regular army pay, to become soldiers, instead of drafting and forcing them to serve. The bounty bill was very popular with his own party, and drafting was very unpopular. General Garfield did not consider the popularity or unpopularity of the measure at all, but he opposed it with all his might, on the ground that bounties recruited the army with unreliable soldiers, necessitated an expense that the government could not long endure; and besides, he claimed that the government had a right to the services of every able-bodied male citizen, from eighteen to forty-five years of age, and they should be drafted to the extent of the country's need. When the vote was taken, Garfield voted against his own party, with only a single member of it to stand with him. A few days thereafter, Secretary Chase said to him:

"General Garfield! I was proud of your vote the other day. Your position is impregnable; but let me tell you, it is rather risky business for a member of congress to vote against his own party."

"Risky business," exclaimed Garfield, "for a man to stand upon his conscience! His constituents may leave him at home, but what is that compared with trampling upon his convictions?"

A few days afterwards, President Lincoln went before the military committee, of which Garfield was a member, and told them what he did not dare to breathe to the country:

"In one hundred days, three hundred and eighty thousand soldiers will be withdrawn from our army, by expiration of the time of their enlistment. Unless congress shall authorize me to fill up the vacancy by draft, I shall be compelled to recall Sherman from Atlanta, and Grant from the Peninsula."

Some of the committee endeavored to dissuade him from such a measure, saying that it would endanger his re-election, to adopt a measure so unpopular. Mr. Lincoln stretched his tall form up to its full height and exclaimed, —

"Gentlemen, it is not necessary that I should be re-elected, but it is necessary that I should put down this rebellion. If you will give me this law, I will put it down before my successor takes his office."

A draft-law for five hundred thousand men was reported to the House, when Garfield made one of his most eloquent and patriotic speeches in its favor, carrying it by storm. Congress and the whole country soon came to feel that Garfield was right.

A few months later, Alexander Long, Democratic member of the house from Ohio, in sympathy with the authors of the rebellion, rose in his seat, and proposed to recognize the southern confederacy. This treasonable act caused Garfield's patriotic blood to boil in his veins, and he sprang to his feet and delivered one of the most powerful philippics ever heard in the American congress. Calling attention to the traitor of the American revolution, — Benedict Arnold, — he said, —

"But now, when tens of thousands of brave souls have gone up to God under the shadow of the flag; when thousands more, maimed and shattered in the contest, are sadly awaiting the deliverance of death; now, when three years of terrific warfare have raged over us; when our armies have pushed the rebellion back over mountains and rivers, and crowded it into narrow limits, until a wall of fire girds it; now, when the uplifted hand of a majestic people is about to hurl the bolts of its conquering power upon the rebellion; now, in the quiet of this hall, hatched in the lowest depths of a similar dark treason, there rises a Benedict Arnold, and proposes to surrender all up, body and spirit, the nation and the flag, its genius and its honor, now and forever, to the accursed traitors to our country! And that proposition comes — God forgive and pity my beloved state — it comes from a citizen of the time-honored and loyal commonwealth of Ohio!

"I implore you, brethren in this house, to believe that not many births ever gave pangs to my mother state such as she suffered when that traitor was born! I beg you not to believe that on the soil of that state another such a growth has ever deformed the face of nature, and darkened the light of God's day."

This single paragraph shows the spirit of this noble effort.

President Lincoln vetoed a bill, in 1864, providing for the organization of civil governments in Arkansas and Louisiana, and appointed military governors. Many Republicans criticized him severely; among them, Garfield. His constituents disapproved of his course, and resolved not to renominate him. The convention of his congressional district, the nineteenth of Ohio, met, and General Garfield was called upon for an explanation. When he went upon the plat form, the delegates expected to hear an apology from him; but instead, he boldly defended his course, and that of Wade and Davis, who criticized the president sharply in the New York *Tribune;* and he gave the reasons for his action, adding:

"I have nothing whatever to retract, and I cannot change my honest convictions for the sake of a seat in congress. I have great respect for the opinions of my constituents, but greater regard for my own conscience. If I can serve you as an independent representative, acting upon my own judgment and convictions, I would be glad to do so; but if not, I do not want your nomination; I would prefer to be an independent private citizen."

It was the coolest, plainest, most fearless speech, probably, that was ever made before a nominating convention in Ohio. Garfield withdrew from the hall as soon as he closed his speech. No sooner had he withdrawn, than a delegate arose and said:

"Mr. President, the man who has the courage to face a convention like that deserves a nomination. I move that General Garfield be nominated by acclamation."

The motion was carried so quickly, and by such a round of applause, that General Garfield heard it before he reached the hotel.

General Garfield prosecuted a European tour in the summer of 1868, for his health. On his return, he found his own congressional district running wild with the heresy of paying the national debt in greenbacks. The convention to nominate a congressional candidate was pending; and his constituents knew that he believed in paying the debt with honest money—gold. Friends told him that his renomination would be opposed on that ground. They proposed to give him a public reception, but charged him not to express his views on that subject in his speech. When called out, however, he struck at once upon that exciting theme, referring to the information he had received concerning their desire to pay the national debt in greenbacks, and said:

"Much as I value your opinions, I here denounce this theory that has worked its way into the state as dishonest, unwise and unpatriotic; and if I were offered a nomination and election for my natural life, from this district, on this platform, I should spurn it. If you should ever raise the question of renominating me, let it be understood you can have my services only on the ground of the honest payment of this debt, and these bonds, in coin, according to the letter and spirit of the contract."

On the fourteenth day of April, 1865, President Lincoln was assassinated. The following morning New York city presented a scene of the most perilous excitement. Placards were pasted up in New York, Brooklyn, and Jersey City, calling upon loyal citizens to meet around Wall-Street Exchange at eleven o'clock. Thousands came, armed with revolvers and knives, ready to avenge the death of the martyred President. Fifty thousand men gathered there, their blood boiling with the fires of patriotism.

There were few in the multitude who would not strike down the rebel sympathizer who should dare speak a word against Lincoln. One such remarked to another, "Lincoln ought to have been shot long ago." He was not suffered to repeat it. A portable gallows was carried through the crowd, lifted above their heads, the bearers muttering, "VENGEANCE!" as they went. The prospect was that the office of the "World," a disloyal journal, and some prominent sympathizers with the rebellious South, would be swallowed in the raging sea of passion. The wave of popular indignation was swollen by the harangues of public speakers. In the midst of the terrible excitement, a telegram from Washington was read, — SEWARD IS DYING." For an instant, vengeance and death upon every paper and every man opposed to Lincoln seemed to move the mighty crowd. Possibly the scene of the French revolution would have been reproduced in the streets of New York, had not a man of commanding figure, bearing a small flag in his hand, stepped forward and beckoned to the excited throng.

"Another telegram trom Washington!" cried hundreds of voices. It was the silence of death that followed. It seemed as if every listener held his breath to hear.

Lifting his right arm toward heaven, in a clear, distinct, steady, ponderous voice, that the multitude could hear, the speaker said:

"Fellow-citizens: Clouds and darkness are round about Him. His pavilion is dark waters and thick clouds of the skies! Justice and judgment are the habitation of His throne! Mercy and truth shall go before His face! Fellow-citizens: God reigns, and the Government at Washington still lives!"

The speaker was GENERAL GARFIELD. The effect of his remarkable effort was miraculous. Another said of it: —

"As the boiling wave subsides and settles to the sea when some strong wind beats it down, so the tumult of the people sank and became still. As the rod draws the electricity from the air, and conducts it safely to the ground, so this man had drawn the fury from that frantic crowd, and guided it to more tranquil thoughts than vengeance. It was as if some divinity had spoken through him. It was a triumph of eloquence, a flash of inspiration such as seldom comes to any man, and to not more than one man in a century. Webster, nor Choate, nor Everett, nor Seward, ever reached it. Demosthenes never equalled it. The man for the crisis had come, and his words were more potent than Napoleon's guns at Paris."

This incident illustrates several of the qualities of Garfield's character that we have seen in his early life, — his sagacity, tact, quick-witted turn in an emergency; his magnetic power, and familiarity with, and confidence in, the Bible. All along through his public career the attainments, habits, and application of his youth contributed to his marvellous success.

As his character and abilities added dignity to the office of janitor and teacher in his early manhood, so they dignified all the offices that he filled throughout his public career.

In scholarship and familiarity with general literature Garfield stood without a peer in Congress. Mr. Townsend said of him: "Since John Quincy Adams, no President has had Garfield's scholarship, which is fully up to this age of wider facts." A Washington writer said: "Few public men in this city keep up literary studies General Garfield is one of the few.'

Another said, " Garfield is a man of infinite resources. He is one of the half-dozen men in Congress who read books." President Hinsdale said, "He has great power of logical analysis, and stands with the first in power of rhetorical exposition. He has the instincts and habits of a scholar. As a student, he loves to roam in every field of knowledge. He delights in creations of the imagination, poetry, fiction, and art; loves the abstract things of philosophy; takes a keen interest in scientific research; gathers into his capacious storehouse the facts of history and politics, and throws over the whole the life and power of his own originality. . . . No public man of the last ten years has more won upon our scholars, scientists, men of letters, and the cultivated classes generally. . . . His moral character is the fit crown of his physical and intellectual nature. His mind is pure, his heart kind, his nature and habits simple, his generosity unbounded. An old friend told me the other day, "I have never found anything to compare with Garfield's heart."

Smalley said, —

"There is probably no living political orator whose efforts before large audiences are so effective. He appeals directly to the reason of men, and only after carrying his hearers along on a strong tide of argument to irresistible conclusions, does he address himself to their feelings. . . . He has a powerful voice, great personal magnetism, and a style of address that wins confidence at the outset, and he is master of the art of binding together facts and logic into a solid sheaf of argument. At times he seems to lift his audience up and shake it with strong emotion, so powerful is his eloquence."

The following are some original sentiments and maxims, from his numerous public addresses, just the thoughts for every youth of the land to ponder:

"There is no more common thought among young people than that foolish one, that by and by something will turn up by which they will suddenly achieve fame or fortune. No, young gentlemen; things don't turn up in this world unless somebody turns them up."

"I feel a profounder reverence for a boy than a man. I never meet a ragged boy on the street without feeling that I owe him a salute, for I know not what possibilities may be buttoned up under his shabby coat."

"There is scarcely a more pitiable sight than to see here and there learned men, so called, who have graduated in our own and the universities of Europe with high honors, and yet who could not harness a horse, or make out a bill of sale, if the world depended upon it."

"Luck is an *ignis fatuus.* You may follow it to ruin, but not to success."

"Be fit for more than the one thing you are now doing."

"If the power to do hard work is not talent, it is the best possible substitute for it."

"Every character is the joint product of nature and nurture."

"For the noblest man that lives there still remains a conflict."

"The privilege of being a young man is a great privilege, and the privilege of growing up to be an independent man, in middle life, is a greater."

"I would rather be beaten in right than succeed in wrong."

"Whatever you win in life you must conquer by your own efforts, and then it is yours — a part of yourself."

"If there be one thing upon this earth that mankind love and admire more than another, it is a brave man, — it is a man who dares look the devil in the face, and tell him he is a devil."

"The student should study himself, his relation to society, to nature, and to art, and above all, in all, and through all these, he should study the relations of himself, society, nature, and art to God, the Author of them all."

"Great ideas travel slowly, and for a time noiselessly, as the gods whose feet were shod with wool."

"Truth is so related and correlated that no department of her realm is wholly isolated."

"I would rather be defeated than make capital out of my religion."

"Ideas are the great warriors of the world, and a war that has no ideas behind it is simply brutality."

"It is a fearful thing for one man to stand up in the face of his brother man and refuse to keep his pledge; but it is a forty-five million times worse thing for a nation to do it. It breaks the mainspring of faith."

"The flowers that bloom over the garden wall of party politics are the sweetest and most fragrant that bloom in the gardens of this world."

"It was not one man who killed Abraham Lincoln; it was the embodied spirit of treason and slavery, inspired with fearful and despairing hate, that struck him down in the moment of the nation's supremest joy."

"When two hundred and fifty thousand brave spirits passed from the field of honor through that thin veil to the presence of God, and when at last its parting folds admitted the martyr-president to the company of the dead heroes of the republic, the nation stood so near the veil that the whispers of God were heard by the children of men."

. . . . .

His great popularity and usefulness as a representative very naturally suggested his name to the Republicans of Ohio, when a United States Senator was to be elected by the legislature, in January, 1880, to succeed Mr. Thurman. When the subject was opened to Garfield, he remarked:

"Just as you please; if my friends think it best, I shall make no objection."

"We want you should go to Columbus when the election is pending."

"I cannot consent to any such plan. I shall not lift my finger for the office. I never sought an office yet, except that of janitor at Hiram Institute. If the people want me, they will elect me."

"Very true," urged his friends; "it is no engineering or finessing that we desire you to do at Columbus. We only want you to be where your friends can see you and confer with you."

"And that will be construed into work for the office, the very appearance of which is distasteful to me. I decline peremptorily to go to Columbus." This was Garfield's characteristic decision and reply.

When the legislature assembled, the feeling was so strong for Garfield that all other candidates withdrew, and he was nominated by acclamation at the party caucus, and unanimously elected.

After the election was over, he visited Columbus, and addressed both branches of the legislature in joint convention. The closing paragraph of his remarkable speech illustrates the courage and independence of the man; qualities that have recommended him to the confidence and support of the people. He said:

"During the twenty years that I have been in public life, almost eighteen of it in the congress of the United States, I have tried to do one thing. Whether I was mistaken or otherwise, it has been the plan of my life to follow my convictions, at whatever personal cost to myself. I have represented for many years a district in congress whose approbation I greatly desired; but though it may seem, perhaps, a little egotistical to say it, I yet desired still more the approbation of one person, and his name was Garfield. He is the only man that I am compelled to sleep with, and eat with, and live with, and die with; and if I could not have his approbation I should have had bad companionship."

In view of this last triumph, President Hinsdale said:

"He has commanded success. His ability, knowledge, mastery of questions, generosity of nature, devotion to the public good, and honesty of purpose, have done the work. He has never had a political 'machine.' He has never forgotten the day of small things. It is difficult to see how a political triumph could be more complete or more gratifying than his election to the senate. No bargains, no 'slate,' no 'grocery,' at Columbus. He did not even go to the capital city. Such things are inspiring to those who think politics in a bad way. He is a man of positive convictions, freely uttered. Politically, he may be called a 'man of war;' and yet few men, or none, begrudge him his triumph. Democrats vied with Republicans the other day, in Washington, in their congratulations; some of them were as anxious for his election as any Republican could be. It is said that he will go to the senate without an enemy on either side of the chamber. These things are honorable to all parties. They show that manhood is more than party."

And so James, the hero of our tale, stood upon the highest round of the ladder of fame, save one!

The final step to the top of the ladder followed quickly; so quickly that he had not time to take his seat in the United States senate. He had but just planted his feet upon the highest round of the ladder, save one, when the call to come up higher — to the top — was heard from Maine to the Golden Gate.

The National Republican Convention, five months later, assembled to nominate a candidate for the presidency of the United States. James A. Garfield was a member of that convention, and his magnetic presence was the occasion of much enthusiasm and applause. Although he was not a candidate for the position, whenever he arose to speak, or moved about in the vast audience, he was greeted with hearty cheers. He was evidently *en rapport* with the crowded assembly After thirty-four ineffectual ballots, about fifty members of the convention cast their votes for James A. Garfield in the thirty-fifth ballot. The announcement created a furore of excitement, as it indicated a breaking up of the factions, and a probable union of all upon the most popular Republican in the convention Instantly the delegates of one state seized their banner with a shout (the delegates of each state sat together, their banner bearing the name of their state), bore it proudly forward, and placed it over the head of the aforesaid patriot and statesman, followed by other delegations, and still others, until seven hundred delegates upon the floor, and fifteen thousand spectators in the galleries, joined in the remarkable demonstration, and cheer upon cheer rent the air, as the banners, one after another, were placed in triumph over the head of their hero, declaring to the world, without the use of language, that James A. Garfield was the choice of the convention for President of the United States; the magnificent ovation terminating by the several bands striking up "Rally Round the Flag," fifteen thousand voices joining in the chorus, and a section of artillery outside contributing its thundering bass to the outburst of joy. It was a wild, tumultuous scene of excitement, the spontaneous outburst of patriotic devotion to the country, such as never transpired in any political assembly before, and, probably, never will again. It was something more, and different from the usual excitement and passion of political assemblies; it was an inspiration of the hour, begotten and moved by more than mortal impulse,—the interposition of Him who has guided and saved our country from its birth!

That spontaneous burst of enthusiasm really nominated General Garfield for President. The thirty-sixth ballot, that followed immediately, was only a method of registering the decision of that supreme moment.

The news of General Garfield's nomination flew with the speed of electricity over the land, creating unbounded joy from Plymouth Rock to the Pacific Slope. The disappointments and animosities of a heated contest vanished at once before the conceded worth and popularity of the candidate. Partisans forgot the men of their choice, in their gladness that union and harmony signalized the close of the most remarkable political convention on record.

HE WAS ELECTED PRESIDENT OF THE UNITED STATES ON THE SECOND DAY OF NOVEMBER, EIGHTEEN HUNDRED AND EIGHTY.

He carried twenty of the thirty-eight states, securing 213 of the 369 electors. In his native town of Orange every ballot was cast for him.

The time between the election and inauguration of General Garfield was characterized by good feeling and general hopefulness. The almost unprecedented excitement of the political campaign subsided into national tranquillity and peace, in which the two great political parties seemed to be more harmonious than ever. Mr. Garfield's popularity won the esteem of leading men who opposed his election, and some of them publicly declared their entire confidence in the man and their profound respect for his great talents. The striking change from the bitterness of an exciting political campaign, for two or three months previous to the election, to the cheerful acquiescence in the result, and the general good-will towards the President-elect, was an event worthy of record.

CHAPTER XXV.

IN THE WHITE HOUSE.

HE Fourth of March, 1881 — the day of the inauguration of General Garfield as President of the United States — will be remembered for its bleak, uncomfortable, stormy morning, threatening to spoil the preparations for a grand military and civic display. About ten o'clock, however, the storm subsided, and the clouds partially broke. The city was crowded with visitors from different sections of the country, among them many civic organizations and military companies which had come to join in the procession. The wide-spread interest in the occasion was due to the fame of the President-elect and the era of good feeling that succeeded his election. Not only his personal friends, but many others in every part of the land, exerted themselves to make the occasion memorable, beyond all similar demonstrations. General Garfield's college classmates were there, to the number of twenty, to congratulate him upon his remarkable public career. On the evening of March third, they tendered to him a reception at Wormley's Hotel in Washington, renewing old friendships around the festive board, each member of the class feeling himself honored in the high honor the country had bestowed upon his gifted classmate. In response to a toast on that occasion, General Garfield said:—

"CLASSMATES: To me there is something exceedingly pathetic in this reunion. In every eye before me I see the light of friendship and love, and I am sure it is reflected back to each one of you from my inmost heart. For twenty-two years, with the exception of the last few days, I have been in the public service. To-night I am a private citizen. To-morrow I shall be called to assume new responsibilities, and on the day after, the broadside of the world's wrath will strike. It will strike hard. I know it, and you will know it. Whatever may happen to me in the future, I shall feel that I can always fall back upon the shoulders and hearts of the class of '56 for their approval of that which is right, and for their charitable judgment wherein I may come short in the discharge of my public duties. You may write down in your books now the largest percentage of blunders which you think I will be likely to make, and you will be sure to find in the end that I have made more than you have calculated—many more.

"This honor comes to me unsought. I have never had the presidential fever—not even for a day; nor have I it to-night. I have no feeling of elation in view of the position I am called upon to fill. I would thank God were I to-day a free lance in the House or the Senate. But it is not to be, and I will go forward to meet the responsibilities and discharge the duties that are before me with all the firmness and ability I can command. I hope you will be able conscientiously to approve my conduct; and when I return to private life, I wish you to give me another class-meeting."

The ceremony of inauguration was arranged for twelve o'clock, noon. Before that hour arrived, more than one hundred thousand people thronged the streets of the city to witness the unusual display. Every State of the Union was represented in the seething multitude; and hundreds of public men were present — senators, representatives, governors, judges, lawyers, clergymen, and authors. A large number of veterans of the late war were there to honor their beloved comrade of other days who was going up higher.

The ceremony was to take place at the Capitol, and preparations were made at the White House, whence the presidential party would be escorted.

At half-past ten o'clock a chorus of bugles announced the arrival of President Hayes and President-elect Garfield from the hotel, who were received in the ante-room by Mr. Pendleton, and for a brief moment the ladies and gentlemen and other invited friends in the House greeted each other in the red room. Col. Casey then announced that everything was ready, and assigned the party to carriages in the following order: First, Gen. Garfield's mother and wife, Mrs. Hayes, Mollie Garfield and Fanny Hayes; second, Mrs. Dr. Davis, Mrs. Herron of Cincinnati, Mr. and Mrs. Andrews and Miss Bullard of Cleveland; third, Mrs. Mason and three daughters of Cleveland; fourth, Harry, Jimmy and Irving Garfield and Scott Hayes; fifth, Messrs. Swaim and Rockwell, Mrs. Deschler and Mrs. Greene of Cleveland; sixth, Miss Cook, Dr. and Mrs. Noble of Columbia. A magnificent four-in-hand of bays then drove up, drawing an open barouche, into which stepped President Hayes and Gen. Garfield, accompanied by Senators Anthony and Bayard, who were driven off a short distance, and were followed by a carriage containing Vice-President-elect Arthur and Senator Pendleton drawn by a beautiful four-in-hand of grays. The presidential party was halted an instant while the Cleveland troupe filed in ahead, and the Cleveland Grays fell in immediately in the rear. As they passed down the avenue they were greeted with cheers and waving of handkerchiefs from the assembled thousands, who, by this time, lined every avenue from end to end.

At the Capitol an imposing scene was presented. After the presidential party had filed into the senate chamber, the gorgeous diplomatic corps, headed by Sir Edward Thornton, preceded by Secretary Evarts, entered and occupied the best seats on the right of the Vice-President. All the legations in Washington were represented. All appeared in court dress, except the Mexican and the Chilian legations, who were in evening costume.

The Supreme Court then appeared in robes and took front seats reserved for it. Messrs. Waite, Harlan, Field, Miller, Bradley, and Woods, and ex-Judges Strong and Swayne were present.

The procession was formed with President Hayes and President-elect Garfield at the head, and proceeded through the corridor and rotunda to the east front, where the platform was erected from which the vast assemblage would listen to the inaugural address. When the dignitaries with their families were finally arranged, silence was maintained for a few moments that the group might be photographed. Then Mr. Garfield stepped to the front and delivered his noble inaugural address, in tones so clear and eloquent that the multitude, even in the distance, heard. Before he closed his address the clouds broke above him, and pure sunlight fell in benediction on his head. As he concluded, Judge Waite, of the Supreme Court, presented the Bible to him on which the Presidents are sworn, and proceeded to administer the oath. At the conclusion, President Garfield reverently kissed the sacred volume, and returned it to the judge. Then, turning to his aged mother, who had wept tears of joy during the delivery of his address, he imprinted a kiss upon her cheek, and another upon that of his wife, the two persons, next to himself, most deeply interested in the transaction of that memorable hour. The President and his attendants withdrew amidst the wildest demonstrations of joy by the concourse of people.

Immediately followed the imposing military and civic procession, which was said to be more elaborate and grand than anything of the kind ever witnessed in the capital of the nation. It was three hours passing a given point, and was reviewed by President Garfield from a stand erected in front of the presidential mansion.

An eye-witness describes the scene as follows:

"One hundred thousand people stood in Pennsylvania avenue, between the Treasury and the Capitol grounds, and gave acclaim to Garfield as he passed. The buildings were splendidly decorated. There was a flag and a dozen fluttering handkerchiefs at every window. All vehicles were excluded from the avenue, and the people hemmed in the procession ten deep on each side.

"The route was around the south side of the Capitol to Pennsylvania avenue, thence to the Treasury department, and so on past the White House. During the time between twelve and half-past one o'clock, Pennsylvania avenue presented a remarkable sight, either from the Treasury department or the Capitol. The crowd was continuous from First to Fifteenth street, and, as the time for the procession to move approached, the crowd increased so that there seemed hardly room for the military column to enter. The movement was promptly at one o'clock, the programme being well carried out. The regular troops led the way with Sherman at their head. Behind Sherman were three four-horse carriages, containing Presidents Garfield and Hayes, Vice-Presidents Arthur and Wheeler, and Senators Pendleton and Bayard. In addition to the Cleveland troop, General Garfield was attended by the Columbia Commandery of Knights Templars of this city, of which he is a member. When the head of the procession reached the Treasury department, the avenue, for its whole mile length, was literally packed with people. There was a pause at this point to enable the President to leave the column and proceed to the grand stand in front of the White House, where he stood hours in witnessing the passage of the great military and civic concourse, which was over three hours in passing a given point. The route was then continued up Pennsylvania avenue to Washington circle, along K street to Vermont avenue, and past the Thomas statue down Massachusetts avenue to Mount Vernon square, where the procession finally dispersed."

After the review, President Garfield gave a reception to the Williams' Alumni Association of Washington, and visiting alumni, in the East Room of the Executive Mansion. Over fifty were present, twenty of whom were the President's classmates whom he met on the previous evening. Ex-President Hopkins was among the number, and he was selected to present the congratulations of the alumni to the president. The latter responded with much emotion to Dr. Hopkins' words of confidence and esteem; and his brief but eloquent speech will long be remembered by the sons of his Alma Mater.

The day closed with a costly display of fireworks, illuminations, and other demonstrations of general joy; and President Garfield and his family were occupants of the White House.

Perhaps no President ever assumed the duties of his high office under more favorable auspices than Mr. Garfield. The announcement of his cabinet gave general satisfaction; and the citizens from Maine to California appeared to feel that *he* would be President, and not some one else. His administration thus began favorably, with the expectations of the people on tiptoe, and their confidence as honest as their hopefulness. The brilliant record of his public life, and even the remarkable record of his youth and eaıly manhood, were well known throughout the country; and upon these the enthusiasm of his constituents and others rested. That personal magnetism which drew the associates of his early life to him, and the admirers of his later life, in public and in private, seemed to attract the hearts of American citizens, from the moment he became the Chief Executive.

There was one trouble, however, which he encountered early in his administration, and which arose within his own party. In making a nomination of the collector of customs at the port of New York, the President found the senators of that state, especially Mr. Conkling, opposed to his choice. Those senators maintained that the act of the President was a wrong to the collector who was to be removed, was contrary to the true principles of civil service, and would be hurtful to the interests of the Republican party. It was, accordingly, well understood that they were firmly opposed to the nomination, and would use their influence against it whenever it should be voted on in the senate. President Garfield, however, adhered to his choice. He claimed that, while the senators from New York had a perfect moral right to their opinions, and a clear constitutional right to exert themselves for the defeat of his nominee, he, in turn, must be the judge concerning his own acts. He therefore refused to withdraw the nomination, affirming that the act was just, and for the welfare of both the country and the party. So the contest became more and more serious. Senators Conkling and Platt saw fit suddenly to resign their seats. The scene of action was thus transferred to the legislature at Albany, where the two senators became candidates for re-election. But after many weeks of bitter contention, the strife was ended by the defeat of the senators, and the election, in their place, of others, who were in accord with the administration. The nomination of the collector was confirmed in the senate by an overwhelming vote. In many respects, it was a signal triumph for the President. In it, all the people and press of the country were, with remarkable unanimity, on his side.

CHAPTER XXVI.

ASSASSINATION.

WHILE the contest was going on in the New York legislature over Senator Conkling's re-election, an attempt was made upon the President's life, which startled and shocked the nation. He had arranged a journey to New England, for the purpose of attending the Commencement at Williams College, Williamstown, Mass.; the annual meeting of the American Institute of Instruction at St. Albans, Vt.; extending his trip into Maine, where he would be the guest of Mr. Blaine, Secretary of State; thence into New Hampshire, in response to an invitation by the legislature of that state, then in session; returning through Boston to Washington; hoping thereby to recruit his somewhat exhausted energies by a brief respite from official duties. On Saturday morning, July 2, he left the Executive Mansion at a few minutes past nine o'clock, in his carriage with Secretary Blaine, for the Baltimore and Potomac Railroad Depot. At twenty minutes past nine o'clock he entered the depot, arm in arm with Mr. Blaine, when two pistol-shots were fired in quick succession, the first one sending a ball through the right coat-sleeve of the President, doing no damage, the second one driving a ball deep into his body above the third rib. The unexpected shot well-nigh paralyzed the bystanders. Mr. Blaine turned to seize the assassin, but found him already in the hands of an officer. As he turned back, the President sank heavily upon the floor, and the fearful tidings spread through the city: "*The President has been assassinated!*" The telegraphic wires took up the terrible news and conveyed it over the country, startling every town, village, and hamlet as they never were startled except by the assassination of President Lincoln. By twelve o'clock, the entire country was apprised of the appalling calamity, except in sections beyond the reach of telegraphs and telephones. The dreadful news flashed over the Atlantic cable, astounding and affecting Europeans almost as sensibly as it did Americans. Surprise and grief were universal. "It was a marvellous tribute," said George William Curtis. "In Europe, it was respect for a powerful state; in America, it was affection for a simple and manly character." The deed was done "in the most peaceful and prosperous moment that this country has known for half a century," as Mr. Curtis wrote; "and the shot was fired absolutely at a man without personal enemies, and a President whom even his political opponents respect." The manifestations of unfeigned sorrow were gauged by this remarkable fact. The South seemed to vie with the North in profound grief over the fearful crime and heartfelt sympathy for the illustrious sufferer. In their dire extremity and deep sorrow, Christian men and women, led by the ministers of religion, gathered in places of prayer, to invoke, upon their knees and in tears, the interposition of God, to save and restore their beloved ruler. Around Christian hearthstones knelt family groups, tearful and hushed as if a great personal sorrow were theirs, to join in fervent supplication to God for the preservation of the President's life. Perhaps so much united, earnest prayer for one man, ascending from even the remotest hamlet of the nation, was never offered at the throne of grace.

But to return to the wounded President. Physicians and surgeons were speedily summoned; and, within an hour, he was removed to the White House in an extremely prostrated and critical condition. The presidential party, consisting of Secretaries Lincoln, Windom and Hunt, and Postmaster-General James, with their wives, were already seated in the special car provided for them, when the cry reached them, "The President is shot." At first they could not credit the tidings: the crime was too awful to be believed. As soon as they recovered from the shock, however, and were really convinced that an attempt had been made to assassinate the President, they abandoned the car and repaired to the executive mansion, to render all possible assistance.

The President was still conscious while prostrate upon the floor at the depot, and fearing that the intelligence of his injury might overcome his wife in her feeble state of health, he dictated to Colonel Rockwell, who was at his side, the following despatch to her at Long Branch:—

Mrs. Garfield, Elberon, New Jersey:

The President wishes me to say to you from him that he has been seriously hurt — how seriously he cannot yet say. He is himself, and hopes you will come to him soon. He sends his love to you. A. F. ROCKWELL.

It should be stated that Mrs. Garfield was recovering from a severe sickness of several weeks, and a few days before, the President accompanied her to Long Branch to hasten her restoration. Her life was despaired of for a time, and her husband's watchful and tender care of her, night and day, when her life hung quivering in the balance, in connection with official duties, made a heavy draft upon his strength.

By the time the ambulance reached the White House, soldiers from the garrison at the Arsenal were performing sentinel duty there, that the policemen might be at their respective posts of duty in the city, where the excitement was intense. A correspondent of the New York *Times*, who was an eye-witness, said, that when the President "was tenderly lifted from the vehicle with the pallor of death stamped upon his countenance, glancing up to the window, he saw some familiar faces, and with a smile which those who saw it will never forget, he raised his right hand and gave the military salute, which seemed to say, 'Long live the republic.'"

Soon after the President was laid upon his bed in the presidential mansion, his nervous prostration passed away and he became composed and cheerful, greeting members of his cabinet, and other intimate friends present, with a cordial pressure of the hand and words of cheer. He was so much like himself, genial, calm and hopeful, that both friends and physicians thought it was the harbinger of recovery. Once he said to Mr. Blaine, who was sitting at his bedside, "What motive do you think that man could have in trying to assassinate me?" Mr. Blaine answered, "I do not know, Mr. President. He says he had no motive. He must be insane." The President responded to this, with a smile, "I suppose he thought it would be a glorious thing to emulate the pirate chief." At another time his son James was sobbing at his bedside, when he addressed him lovingly, "Don't be alarmed, Jimmy; the upper story is all right; it is only the hull that is a little damaged." He was somewhat impatient for the arrival of his wife, as were all the friends present, and when Colonel Rockwell announced that she had left Long Branch on a special train, he responded with much emotion, "God bless the dear woman! I hope the shock will not break her down." Dr. Bliss stated, that often, during the afternoon, he became even jocular, conversing more than the physicians thought for his good, but doing it, evidently, to encourage the depressed friends around him. He told Dr. Bliss that he desired to be kept accurately informed about his condition. "Conceal nothing from me," he said, "for, remember, I am not afraid to die." About four o'clock in the afternoon, the evidence of internal hemorrhage became unmistakable, and it was feared he might not live until Mrs. Garfield arrived. Dr. Bliss and his medical associates were making an examination, when he inquired what the prospects were. "Are they bad, doctor? Don't be afraid; tell me frankly. I am ready for the worst." "Mr. President," answered Dr. B., "your condition is extremely critical. I do not think you can live many hours." The President calmly and seriously responded, "God's will be done, doctor! I am ready to go, if my time has come."

The despatch of the President to his wife, dictated at the depot, did not disclose the nature of the wound. Other dispatches to other parties advised keeping her in ignorance of the real condition of her husband. But when Judge-Advocate-General Swaim of the army, who was at the Elberon House, Long Branch, received a telegram in advance of that sent by the President, he approached Mrs. Garfield with the design of partially breaking the news only, and starting her off as speedily as possible to Washington. But the moment he entered the room and drew near to her, she inquired, with apparent anxiety, "What is the matter?" as if she read bad news in his countenance. "The President has met with an accident," he answered. "Is he dead?" Mrs. Garfield responded at once. "No!" was all the answer he could make before she inquired, "What was the accident?" "I think he was shot," replied General Swaim. "I think he must have been fooling with a pistol, and doubtless he shot himself. I can't think it is anything very serious." Mrs. Garfield said, with animation, as if suspecting that he was concealing the truth, "It is impossible that he could have shot himself. He has been shot. Tell me the truth." Seeing that it was useless to evade her questions, Judge Swaim told her the story so far as he knew it.

Mrs. Garfield received the truth with the composure of a true Christian, and at once gave orders to her attendants about packing. General Swaim said, "No executive officer of a ship could have prepared for action more speedily and directly than did Mrs. Garfield prepare for her departure to Washington."

A special train started with her at 12.30; and but for an accident twenty miles from Washington, she would have been with her husband at six o'clock. As it was, going at the rate of from forty to fifty miles an hour, she was at the White House before seven o'clock. Her excitement and protracted fast caused her to partially faint, as her son Harry and other friends helped her from the carriage and up the steps; and it was thought best for her to take some tea and food before meeting her husband. But before she accomplished this purpose, word was brought to Colonel Rockwell, who had accompanied her to the dining-hall, that the President was fast sinking, and Mrs. Garfield must hurry to him at once. The President had repeatedly asked, during the afternoon, "What time is it?" "Do you know where the train is, now?" "How long before my wife will reach here?" And when the carriage drove to the door, hearing it, he remarked, "That's my wife." Evidently he thought that a very narrow margin of time was left for what might prove their final meeting.

It was clear that Mrs. Garfield summoned all her force of character to enable her to meet her husband with a cheerful and hopeful heart. It was evident, also, that he did the same. The room was cleared, physicians and all attendants going out, that Mrs. Garfield and her children might meet him alone. Their interview lasted fifteen minutes, when physicians and attendants were readmitted. The communion of loving hearts in those fifteen minutes is known only to them and their God. The history of it never was printed. No reporter ever presumed to lift the veil, and divulge the secrets of that quarter of an hour. No one desired to do it. With tearful eyes and burdened hearts, tens of thousands, in loving and tender sympathy with the devoted wife, were satisfied to say, "Thank God for that meeting!"

From that moment, the President seemed to rally. Their mutual love, confidence and fortitude appeared to assure each other. The two most hopeful and resolute persons in the White House, from that time, were the President and his wife. They put courage and hopefulness into everybody else. "Wipe away your tears, if you are going in there," said Mrs. Garfield to her daughter Mollie, as she met her at the door. This noble spirit was assuring to all who came in contact with them.

A little later, the President said to Mrs. James, who sat by him, "Do you know where Mrs. Garfield is now?"

"Oh, yes," Mrs. James said, "she is close by, watching and praying for her husband."

He looked up to the lady with an anxious face, and said, "I want her to go to bed. Will you tell her that I say, if she will undress and go to bed, I will turn right over, and I feel sure that when I know she is in bed I can go to sleep, and sleep all night? Tell her," he exclaimed, with sudden energy, "that I *will* sleep all night, if she will only do what I ask."

Mrs. James conveyed the message to Mrs. Garfield, who said to her at once, "Go back, and tell him that I am undressing."

She returned with the answer, and the President turned over on his right side, and dropped into a quiet sleep almost instantly.

An hour later, the President said to Dr. Bliss, "What are the indications?" Dr. Bliss answered, "There is a chance of recovery." "Well, then," responded the President, cheerfully, "we will take that chance."

Sunday, July 3, was a day of anxiety and tears to the American people. The churches were filled with mourning thousands, and the burden of sermons and prayers was the great sorrow that had fallen upon the nation. July 4 was such an independence day as the country never saw. No one had a heart to engage in the festivities of the day. Many well-arranged celebrations were abandoned. George William Curtis spoke eloquently and touchingly of the day, as follows:—

"But the emotion and the spectacle of this year are without parallel. In every household there was a hushed and tender silence, as if one dearly loved lay dying. In every great city and retired village the public festivities were stayed, and the assembly of joy and pride and congratulation was solemnized into a reverent congregation of heads bowed in prayer. In foreign countries, American gayety was suspended. In the British Parliament, Whig and Tory and Radical listened to catch from the lips of the Prime Minister the latest tidings from one sufferer. From the French republic, and from the old empire of Japan, and the new kingdom of Bulgaria, from Parnell, the Irish agitator, and from the Lord Mayor of Dublin, came messages of sympathy and sorrow. Sovereigns and princes, the people and the nobles, joined in earnest hope for the life of the Republican President. The press of all Christendom told the mournful story, and moralized as it told. In this country, the popular grief was absolutely unanimous. One tender, overpowering thought called a truce even to party contention. Old and young, men and women of all nationalities and of all preferences, their differences forgotten, waited all day for news, watched the flags and every sign that might be significant, and lay down, praying, to sleep, thanking God that, as yet, the worst had not come."

But the assassin — how about him? His name is Charles J. Guiteau, an eccentric, pettifogging lawyer, about forty years of age, of a weak, disordered mind, who had tried in vain to get an appointment to a foreign consulate. In his chagrin, poverty and disappointment, as some suppose, reason was partially dethroned, and he committed the crime in his desperation. Others suppose that, since he sympathized with Mr. Conkling and Vice-President Arthur, in their opposition to the Garfield administration, relating to the New York appointment, he made himself believe that, President Garfield out of the way, and Mr. Arthur in his place, the appointment could readily be secured. Be that as it may, he coolly perpetrated the deed, and within an hour was safely lodged in the District jail.

Detective McElfresh, who took the prisoner to jail, reports the following conversation with him, while being conducted thither : —

"I asked him, 'Where are you from?'

"'I am a native-born American — born in Chicago — and am a lawyer and a theologian.'

"'Why did you do this?'

"'I did it to save the Republican party.'

"'What are your politics?'

"'I am a stalwart among the stalwarts. With Garfield out of the way, we can carry all the Northern States; and with him in the way, we can't carry a single one.'"

Upon learning that McElfresh was a detective, Guiteau said: "You stick to me, and have me put in the third story, front, at the jail. General Sherman is coming down to take charge. Arthur and all those men are my friends, and I'll have you made Chief of Police. When you go back to the depot, you will find that I left two bundles of papers at the news-stand, which will explain all."

"Is there anybody else with you in this matter?"

"Not a living soul. I have contemplated the thing for the last six weeks, and would have shot him when he went away with Mrs. Garfield, but I looked at her, and she looked so bad that I changed my mind."

The following letter was found in the street soon after his arrest, unsealed, and the envelope addressed thus: "Please deliver at once to General Sherman, or his first assistant in charge of the War Department: —

"*To General Sherman:*

"I have just shot the President. I shot him several times, as I wished him to go as easily as possible. His death was a political necessity. I am a lawyer, theologian and politician. I am a stalwart of the stalwarts. I was with General Grant and the rest of our men in New York during the canvass. I am going to the jail. Please order out your troops and take possession of the jail at once. Very respectfully,

CHARLES GUITEAU."

The profound sympathy and sorrow of the people of this and other countries was manifested by telegrams from every quarter, letters of condolence, and resolutions of public bodies and organizations, conveying to the President expressions of grief and prayer for his recovery. They were received by hundreds in a day, for a time. Hon. B. R. Bruce, late member of Congress from Mississippi, and now register, received hundreds of letters and telegrams from Mississippi, from both Republicans and Democrats, denouncing the attempt upon the President's life, and expressing sincere hopes of his recovery. The Vicksburg *Herald* (Miss.) accompanied its words of sympathy with this statement: "No President since the war has so gained on the good feeling of the Southern people as President Garfield." In Arkansas, the fourteenth day of July was observed as a day of fasting and prayer for the recovery of President Garfield, the day having been appointed by Governor Churchill. Governor Blackburn of Kentucky also appointed the fourteenth day of July, as a day of fasting and prayer for the same object, and the day was very generally observed. The Queen of England, King of Spain,

King of Belgium, Emperors of Russia, Japan and China, and Germany, and other foreign rulers, sent despatches full of sorrow and expressions of good-will. Some of them repeated their telegrams on receipt of more favorable news respecting the President's recovery. Victoria said: —

"I wish to express my great satisfaction at the very favorable accounts of the President, and hope that he will soon be considered out of danger."

Even the Indians of our country, in whose welfare the President had been so deeply interested, were profoundly touched by the appalling news; and on receipt of the intelligence that hopes of his recovery were entertained, Moses, the chief of the Confederate tribes of Washington Territory, sent the following: —

"Tell the Great Chief at Washington that it makes our hearts sad to hear of the cowardly attempt made on his life. Chief Moses and all of his people offer their warmest sympathy to the Great Father and his family. He has always been a good friend to the Indians. We are glad to hear that he is recovering, and hope his life may be spared."

All classes, parties and sects, except some Mormons and Socialists, appeared to feel deeply the calamity to the nation, and to indulge the most heartfelt desire that the President's life might be spared. It was a demonstration of esteem and confidence, as honorable to the citizens of our country as it must have been grateful to the President and his family. The patriotic words of the illustrious sufferer, in the outbreak of the late "War of the Rebellion," have peculiar significance now to every thoughtful American: "I regard my life as given to my country. I am only anxious to make as much of it as possible, before the mortgage on it is foreclosed."

The gloom of our National Independence was somewhat lifted by the more favorable condition of the President. From that time he slowly but steadily gained, all the while being buoyant in spirits, and feeling that his recovery was assured. Twice he experienced serious relapses, during the first five or six weeks of his sickness, going down to the very brink of death, causing general alarm and sorrow everywhere. From these relapses he rallied, to suffer on, while the sympathies of his devoted countrymen were drawn out more and more, and their prayers for his recovery went up to heaven with increasing fervor.

But another and still more serious relapse awaited him on the twenty-sixth day of August, destroying the hopes of the physicians and attending friends. The bullet-wound was doing well, discharging healthy pus freely; but an ugly abscess, occasioned by pus-poisoning, appeared upon the neck, and the stomach ceased to assimilate or retain food. At 4 o'clock P. M., on the twenty-sixth day of August, he appeared to be rapidly sinking. He was unconscious, and breathed heavily, like one suffering in the last stages of apoplexy. A consultation of the doctors resulted in the decision that the last ray of hope had vanished, and a few hours more would put the seal of death upon all that was mortal of the illustrious President. Two of the medical attendants were delegated to break the sad conclusion to Mrs. Garfield, whose expectation of his recovery had scarcely been eclipsed

It was an hour of dreadful depression in the Executive Mansion, and few were the eyes that refused to weep. The doctors dreaded to bear the terrible message to Mrs. Garfield, — a message that would dash her last hope, and possibly overcome her hitherto trusting and heroic spirit. What was their surprise, however, to find that her truly noble soul was equal to the occasion, and seemed to rise higher and grander upon the wings of faith!

That was a desolate night in Washington — Friday of August twenty-sixth — and the mourners went about the streets, or lay sleepless in their beds. The general expectation was, that the pall of death would rest upon the White House before another rising sun. About two o'clock on Saturday morning, the President, aroused from his unconscious state, and seeing his wife watching at his bedside, spoke feebly, "Go to bed, my dear, and try to get some rest." She pleaded to remain, when he responded, "Is it true that we shall be separated so soon? You'd better stay, then."

Morning brought no relief, except that the patient still lived. Telegraphic despatches had borne the tidings over the land — "no hope!" In many localities the report of the President's death was current. The Atlantic cable bore such a message to Great Britain, and a notice of his death, with a biographical sketch, appeared in a Liverpool daily on Saturday. The queen was deeply affected by this unexpected relapse, and immediately sent a cablegram to Mrs. Garfield: "I am most deeply grieved at the sad news received, and would express my sincere sympathy." She knew full well the anguish of that loving heart, whose idol was apparently to be removed, for she had been in that vale of sorrow herself, the memory of which was still fresh and vivid. She broke through the barriers of royalty and addressed herself directly to Mrs. Garfield, as one mourning widow speaks to a sister about to become like herself. It was the warm, tender hand-grasp of real sympathy across the sea, for which the nation itself is glad. Long live the queen!

On Saturday, the churches of Washington consulted together, through representatives, and it was decided to observe the following day as one of fasting and prayer in behalf of the President, who still lived. Christians felt that, since human care and medical skill were exhausted, and the wisest counsellors had said "we can do no more," it was time for believers in prayer to gather in their places of worship, and implore God to interpose and spare the patient, whom medical science could not save. Telegrams were flashed over the country, inviting Christians of every name to spend Sunday, August 28, in supplication for the recovery of the President. The response was general and sympathetic. True, a volume of prayer had been going up to God from church and family altars, as well as from secret places, for his restoration, from the day he was shot, but no such concert of prayer had been proposed. A daily paper of Boston, on Monday, August 29, said, under the heading, "A Nation on its Knees:"

"Through the length and breadth of the land there were few pulpits of any denomination of Christians in which no reference was made to President Garfield's condition on Sunday, and few worshipping assemblies in which earnest prayer was not offered for his recov ery. There was no need of any special summons to this service. It was the spontaneous and natural expression of the national feeling. The heavy tidings of Saturday had prepared all for the worst. The physicians had abandoned hope, and all human help seemed to have been tried and to have failed; and in an agony of prayer the whole nation, with one consent, directed its entreaties to Him who holds men and nations in His hands. Never before, probably, have so many prayers been offered at one time in behalf of one man. Those who have faith in prayer must have had their confidence strengthened by the thought of such a solemn unity of petition; and those who have little faith in religious things can hardly have failed to be impressed by it. To many minds, the strange and marked improvement in the President's condition, reported during the day, must have seemed a fresh reason for belief in the efficacy of prayer. Whether these countless prayers are answered in the way in which those who offered them desire, or not, only good can come from this deepened sense of the nation's dependence upon God."

While the Christian men and women of the country were yet upon their knees, the President rallied from the extreme prostration of Friday and Saturday; his stomach resumed its functions, his pulse fell, and he said in a stronger voice than he had used for a week, "I am better; I shall live." The talk of a day of national thanksgiving was renewed with increased interest. This subject was announced by Governor Foster of Ohio, when hope of his recovery was first awakened after he was shot, by the following card:

"GOVERNOR'S OFFICE, COLUMBUS, O., July 10.

"Present indications strongly encourage the hope that the resident will recover from the effects of the horrible attempt upon s life. It must occur to all that it would be most fitting for the overnors of the several States and Territories to issue proclaations setting apart a day to be generally agreed upon for ianksgiving and praise to Almighty God for the blessed deliverıce of our President, and for this great evidence of His goodness this nation. If this suggestion meets your approbation, permit e to name the Governors of New York, Pennsylvania, Kentucky, [aryland, and Ohio, as a committee to fix upon a day to be so ɔserved. Please reply.

(Signed) CHARLES FOSTER."

The suggestion was a proof of the strong place the resident occupied in the affections ot the people; ıd there was evidence that every state in the Union ould unite in such an expression of gratitude to God, his life were spared. North and South, East and /est, the interest was profoundly impressive; in no ırt of the country was it more beautiful than in the outh. The *Atlanta Constitution* came to us with ıis delightful tribute:—

"An element that contributes largely to increase ıe sympathy of the Southern people is the happy ımily relations of the President. It was remembered ɔw, upon the occasion of the inauguration, he turned om the applauding crowd to kiss his wife and his hite-haired mother; and many a Southern wife and ıother wrung their hands in grief when the news of is assassination was received, and cried: 'Oh, what ill his wife do? How will his mother bear it?' racious little hints, shining here and there through ıe bewildering dullness of political discussions, have given the people a tolerably clear idea of the exquisite beauty and harmony of the President's family relations, in such charming contrast to the showy shoddyism of the capital, and this knowledge has had a potent effect on the public mind. It is no small or unimportant thing that, in the midst of conditions altogether heartless, and surrounded by influences calculated to destroy reverence for the family hearth, the home life of the President of the Republic should be ideally perfect, and the fact that it is, brings him and his family very close to the hearts of the American people. But it is not necessary to endeavor to account for or to explain Southern manifestations of sympathy for the stricken President. They were spontaneous and they are not fleeting We know a little girl — the daughter of a Confederate officer who fought through the war — who, upon being told last Sunday morning that the President was still alive, quietly replied, 'I know it. I prayed last night that he might live.' The child had prayed with faith, and was certain her prayer would be answered. This Sunday morning there is every indication that the President will be spared to his family and to the country, but to the stricken man — to fair-faced wife and white-haired mother — the South, standing in the shadow of great troubles of her own, still sends forth her sympathy."

A Democratic member of Congress, Representative Hurd, in publicly expressing his unfeigned grief over the President's critical condition, told this story: —

"It happened once that I — a young member —

was called upon to close on the Democratic side a debate which Mr. Garfield was to close the next morning on behalf of the Republicans. I felt the responsibility; I was extremely anxious to make a reply which would do credit to myself and not disgrace my party; and I went to Garfield that night and pointed out my dilemma. I did not feel equal to the occasion of making an impromptu response to a speech which he was fully prepared to make. Like the man he is — like a brother, I might say — he told me what he was going to say, the whole tenor of his argument, and thus gave me the benefit of twenty-four hours' study in which to reply to him. You can understand my admiration, my love, my anxiety for that man." Then he added, "I stumped my state against him last year, but, from my knowledge of the man, I feel that he was never guilty of a dishonest or ungenerous act."

An Illinois editor said: —

"The statement, that President Garfield has never done better service to the nation than since he was stricken down, is one that will meet an 'amen' in every heart. The Christian fortitude, the perfect submission, the heroic desire to live if possible, but to die bravely and resignedly if he must, the chivalric devotion to and careful thought for his wife and children and mother, have given the country an exhibition of high manhood and nobility of character most salutary. The effect will not be ephemeral. General Garfield on his bed of death, as it promised to be, has elevated the American people. They will not soon forget the lessons he has taught."

This chapter, in which the heroic wife of the Pres: dent is seen to have borne her part with so mucl calmness and faith, would not be complete withou the following picture, which we are permitted to giv our readers from her own hand. It is an extrac from a letter written by Mrs. Garfield to her husban ten years ago; and, coming into the hands of Presi dent Hinsdale of Hiram College, it was published i a late number of *The Student*, issued at that college.

"I am glad to tell you, that out of all the toil an disappointments of the summer just ended I hav risen up to victory; that silence of thought since yo have been away has won for my spirit a triumph I read something like this the other day: 'There i no healthy thought without labor, and thought make the labor happy.' Perhaps this is the way I hav been able to climb up higher. It came to me on morning when I was making bread. I said to mysel 'Here I am, compelled by an inevitable necessity t make our bread this summer. Why not consider it pleasant occupation, and make it so by trying to se what perfect bread I can make?' It seemed like a inspiration, and the whole of life grew brighter. Th very sunshine seemed flowing down through my spiri into the white loaves! and now I believe my table i furnished with better bread than ever before. An this truth, old as creation, seems just now to hav become fully mine — that I need not to be the shirk ing slave to toil, but its regal master, making what ever I do yield me its best fruits. You have bee king of your works so long that maybe you will laug at me for having lived so long without my crown but I am too glad to have found it at all to be entirely disconcerted even by your merriment.

"Now, I wonder if right here does not lie the 'terrible wrong,' or at least some of it, of which the woman suffragists complain. The wrongly educated woman thinks her duties a disgrace, and frets under them, or shirks them if she can. She sees man triumphantly pursuing his vocations, and thinks it is the kind of work he does which makes him grand and regnant; whereas it is not the kind of work at all, but the way in which, and the spirit with which, he does it."

The physicians became satisfied that the malarial air of Washington was very unfavorable to the recovery of the President. From the time he was stricken down, the public were extremely anxious about this danger. It was not until Tuesday, the fifth day of September, however, that he was removed to Long Branch, New Jersey. Preparations were made to remove him upon his bed, with the least possible excitement and motion; and at six o'clock on the morning of that day he was taken from the White House to the special train in waiting, accompanied by his devoted wife and loving daughter, together with his medical attendants and other friends. His two eldest sons left Washington on the day previous to enter Williams College, Williamstown, Mass., and the two youngest remained still at the family home in Mentor, Ohio. The removal of the President was accomplished without injury to him, save extreme weariness, which was anticipated. That was the most remarkable journey in the annals of time: the sick and prostrate ruler of a great nation borne upon his bed at the rate of fifty miles an hour in quest of recovery! At every station along the whole distance, the sympathizing people gathered in large numbers; and, in silence, with uncovered heads and tearful eyes, watched the train as it swept by, representative of fifty millions of people who waited, with bated breath, the result of the perilous experiment. Many eyes were dim with tears when, at the close of the eventful day, they read the account of his journey from the presidential mansion to the sea, the event was so unusual and pathetic. And yet their hearts rejoiced to learn that, without detriment, he was comfortably lodged in Francklyn Cottage, which had been arranged for his reception, at about one o'clock, P. M.

The change appeared to benefit the patient at first, and he enjoyed the sea-air with a keen relish. On the fourth day after his arrival, Dr. Hamilton said to Mrs. Garfield, "I am afraid to tell you how confident I feel of your husband's recovery." The public participated in this confident hope, and there was renewed talk of a national thanksgiving. The interest and joy of the public expressed itself in offers to supply this, that, and the other article that might add comfort and hope to his condition. One man sent him a fine Jersey cow, that he might be supplied with fresh milk. Two little girls in Pennsylvania, reading that the President wanted squirrel broth, sent to him their pet squirrel in a box by express, delighted to give the great and good man any thing they possessed to aid in his recovery. There was no limit to the tangible expressions of tender regard by the people.

The buoyant hopes raised by the removal of the

patient were dashed, however, in a few days, by the undoubted evidence of blood-poisoning, and the presence of an abscess in the right lung. Many thought the last hope was gone. Others still clung to the hope which the patient's great physical vitality and uniform courage inspired. All along, the public, and even the doctors, had depended much upon the physical and moral make-up of the man, to restore him; and there can be no doubt, that, with an ordinary constitution, less will-power, and fewer of those conspicuous qualities, like decision, courage, self-reliance, and persistent purpose, which developed into his noble manhood, he would have died soon after the attempt upon his life. But he grew worse; and, on the seventeenth day of September, appeared to be beyond mortal aid. The medical attendants well-nigh despaired of him, although there was no evidence of speedy dissolution. Two days later, September nineteenth, there appeared slight improvement. He called for a hand-glass, that he might see his face. Mrs. Garfield put it into his hand, and he held it for some moments, viewing himself, when he remarked: "I do not see how it is that a man who looks as well as I do should be so dreadfully weak." In the evening, Colonel Rockwell, his faithful attendant, said: "Things look better; I always told you that the President would get well." Dr. Bliss remarked: "There are no more bad symptoms to mention. We think the lung trouble is a little better; his temperature is normal, and his pulse greatly reduced." General Swaim said: "He is worth all the dead men that can be laid between here and New York. His pulse is firmer, stronger, and has more volume,

His mind is clear, and his stomach right. His pluck and courage are amazing. He comes out of a chill as cheerful as if he were leaving an evening party." Dr. Hamilton remarked to a friend: "It is almost impossible to look upon that cheerful, smiling face, and not feel that he is going to live." Under the impulse of this more buoyant feeling, at ten o'clock, P. M., the following was sent to Minister Lowell in London:—

"The President had another chill of considerable severity this morning, which, following so soon after the chill of last evening, left him very weak indeed. His pulse became more frequent and feeble than at any time since he recovered from the immediate shock of the wound, and his general condition was more alarming during the day. His system has reacted to some extent, and he passed the afternoon and evening comfortably. At this hour he is resting quietly, and no disturbance is expected during the night. There has been, however, no gain whatever in strength, and therefore, there is no decrease of anxiety."

The lights were lowered for the night; Mrs. Garfield and the physicians retired; and the illustrious sleeper was left alone with his watchers

CHAPTER XXVII.

DEATH — FUNERAL CEREMONIES.

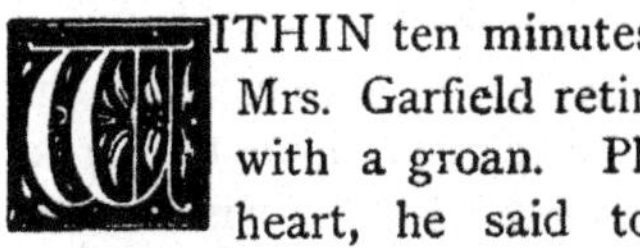ITHIN ten minutes after the physicians and Mrs. Garfield retired, the President awoke with a groan. Placing his hand upon his heart, he said to General Swaim, "Oh, Swaim! what a terrible pain I have here!" Dr. Bliss was summoned from an adjoining room, hastily, and the moment he fastened his eye upon the sufferer, he exclaimed, "My God, Swaim, he is dying; call Mrs. Garfield." From that moment he appeared to be unconscious, although he fixed his eyes upon his wife as she hurriedly entered the room, and seemed to follow her as she moved around to the other side of the bed to take his hand in hers. His eyes were wide open, but dazed; his pulse only fluttered; he gasped, and was no more. At thirty-five minutes past ten o'clock, Dr. Bliss pronounced life extinct! A sudden and terrible change from the hope inspired at ten o'clock! The President of the United States — her favorite son, scholar, and statesman — was dead!

The unutterable sadness of that moment in the Francklyn Cottage can never be put upon paper. The idol of the family and nation had ceased to live, and the witnesses of the dying scene were silent and in tears. Through that little company of friends, as representatives, the American people wept with the widow by that lifeless form.

A few moments of hushed silence, broken only by irrepressible sobs, and Mrs. Garfield slipped out of the chamber of death into her own room. She knew, by blessed experience, where to go for help in her sorrow; and, alone with Him whose grace is sufficient for all, to be made equal to the loss. In ten minutes she returned and took her seat by her dear, departed husband, calm, self-possessed, and heroic, as if she had laid a part of her crushing grief upon the Great Burden-Bearer. On being asked what her wishes were respecting the disposition of the body, she replied that she "could not consider that subject until morning." For two hours she kept her place at the bed-side of the painless sleeper, then retired sadly to her room, not to slumber, but to pace the floor until dawn.

The cabinet were near by, except Secretaries Blaine and Lincoln, who were *en route* for Long Branch from New England, and they were immediately summoned. About midnight they sent the following telegram to Vice-President Arthur, who was at his home in New York City:—

"It becomes our painful duty to inform you of the death of President Garfield, and to advise you to take the oath of office as President of the United States without delay. If it concurs with your judgment, will be very glad if you will come here on the earliest train to-morrow.

"WILLIAM WINDOM, *Secretary of the Treasury.*
"W. H. HUNT, *Secretary of the Navy.*
"THOMAS L. JAMES, *Postmaster-General.*
"WAYNE MACVEAGH, *Attorney-General.*
"S. J. KIRKWOOD, *Secretary of Interior.*"

The next telegram was forwarded to his aged mother at Hiram, Ohio, who was awaiting the issue with maternal solicitude and Christian trust. The next went to his two sons in college, at Williamstown, Mass. :—

"At thirty-five minutes past ten o'clock to-night your father passed peacefully away. Come to Long Branch at once."

Secretaries Blaine and Lincoln were taking the train in Boston about the time the President expired, when the following telegram was handed to Mr. Lincoln : —

"LONG BRANCH, Sept. 19, 1881, 9 P. M.

"The President has passed a comfortable day, and is now resting quietly.

"WAYNE MACVEAGH."

Of course the two secretaries left Boston with increased hope; but that hope perished suddenly, when, at Putnam, Conn., a telegram intercepted them, announcing the President's death.

The news of his death was carried speedily over the country by telegraph, and before one o'clock, the inhabitants of Boston, New York, Washington, Philadelphia, and other large cities and towns, were aroused from their slumbers by the tolling of bells. They knew full well the import of that solemn knell; and tens of thousands exchanged sleep for mourning. The sad intelligence was borne so rapidly over the land and world that, by twelve o'clock on the following day, the bells of towns from Maine to California tolled their melancholy requiem in honor of the dead. From valley, plain and hill-top, far and near, the doleful sound was borne on the wings of the wind, until almost every hamlet heard the tidings and bowed in sorrow. The Canadas joined in the general lamentation, and expressed their heartfelt sympathy by the tolling of bells. And even across the Atlantic, the sad refrain was caught up by English towns, and their church-bells told of their sympathy for our afflicted land, and their respect for the deceased President. The sorrow was universal. How strange that thousands and thousands of bells should unite in tolling the death-knell of one who never heard the sound of a bell until he was more than ten years of age.*

President Garfield died on the anniversary of his promotion to Major-General, SEPTEMBER NINETEENTH, for brave deeds in the battle of Chickamauga. His famous ride in that battle from General Rosecrans to General Thomas, in which he ran the gauntlet of rebel guns for miles, his two orderlies and their horses being shot at his side, was so wonderful as to cause a correspondent of the *New York Tribune*, who was on the ground, to say: "His death was certain, unless Providence had more work for him to do on this footstool." † God had eighteen years more of patriotic work for him to do for his country, and so he emerged from that fearful ordeal with only the smell of fire upon his garments. His countrymen hoped that God had still more and greater work for him in public life, and so would spare him now. But his life was well rounded; he had reached the Pisgah of earthly fame; he had accomplished more at fifty years than most statesmen at seventy; his work was all done, and well done; so God took him, that he might bless the nation more by his death than he could by his life.

* See Chap. VI. † See account of his ride, in Chap. XXIII.

There is a prophetic character in the statement of General Mussey, on the twenty-seventh day of August, when the physicians abandoned all hope of the President's restoration, and so announced to Mrs. Garfield: "He will not live; but he will not die until the nineteenth day of September."

"Why do you make that statement?" he was asked.

"Because it was on the nineteenth day of September, 1863, that General Garfield was made major-general for gallantry in the battle of Chickamauga, and he has often told me that when he died, he thought he should die on the anniversary of his promotion. I claim nothing for his prophecy, but only repeat what he told me several times with an earnestness I shall never forget."

On the arrival of Secretaries Blaine and Lincoln, the Cabinet convened, and with the acquiescence of Mrs. Garfield, arranged for obsequies at Washington on Friday, September twenty-third, and at Cleveland, Ohio, on Monday, September twenty-sixth. Preparations were hastily made for the removal of the body to the Capitol, and in the meantime, a post-mortem examination of the body disclosed what surprised the doctors and the country, — the bullet was found behind the heart, quite distant from the spot where the surgeons located it. They had failed to trace the course of the ball correctly, and, to comprehend fully the fatal extent of the injury. Before the close of Tuesday, Mrs. Garfield received the following telegram of condolence from Queen Victoria: —

"Words cannot express the deep sympathy I feel with you. May God support and comfort you as He alone can."

On Wednesday morning the funeral cortege left Elberon for Washington, accompanied by the new President, Chester A. Arthur, who had taken the oath of office in New York, and Ex-President Grant, with all the members of the Cabinet. The train was deeply draped with mourning emblems, and was met with the symbols of sorrow along the entire route. At the Princeton station, three hundred students from the college stood, with uncovered heads and arms full of flowers, with which they strewed the track and literally covered the funeral car, as the train slacked its speed and moved slowly by. At five o'clock P. M., the casket was deposited in the rotunda of the Capitol, amid the tolling of bells and other sorrowful demonstrations. The Capitol and all the public buildings of the city, together with houses, stores and streets, were elaborately draped with the emblems of grief.

Arrangements were made for the body to lie in state in the rotunda of the Capitol until the time of the funeral on Friday. The lid of the casket was opened immediately after it was deposited upon the catafalque; and the crowd began to enter to view the remains. By the time the lid of the coffin was closed, late on Thursday afternoon, a hundred thousand people had passed in to see the dead President. It became necessary to close the casket on Thursday night, because decomposition was advancing so rapidly. The body had been embalmed, but the decay challenged the embalmer.

and his work proved vain. Before the face of the sleeper was shut from the gaze of men, Mrs. Garfield expressed the wish to be alone with him for a season. She was accompanied to the Capitol by the Attorney-General and other intimate friends. The sentinels and other persons were sent from the rotunda, and every door was locked, save one, through which the stricken widow might pass. As soon as she stepped alone into the rotunda, the guard locked the door behind her; and there she waited in the presence of death. The casket was covered with flowers; and various floral designs of exquisite workmanship—all the tributes of loving friends—spoke to her of beauty and joy where all tears are wiped from the eyes. There was a costly tribute, a most elaborate specimen of the florist's art, from England's queen, accompanied by a mourning card, bearing the following inscription:—

> "Queen Victoria to the memory of the late President Garfield; an expression of her sorrow and sympathy with Mrs. Garfield and the American nation."

For twenty minutes the deeply afflicted woman remained with the dead; when she came forth, pale and wan, but without a tear. There is no doubt that she was met at the coffin by Him who was "a man of sorrows and acquainted with grief;" and that she took leave of her departed husband assured that the all-sufficient One would bear her sorrows and carry her grief. (Is. liii. 4.)

The funeral ceremonies on Friday were short and simple—singing, reading of the scriptures, two prayers, and a brief address by his pastor, Dr. Powers. The singing was the sweetest for the occasion that Washington could furnish, the piece rendered being a favorite hymn of the deceased: "Asleep in Jesus, blessed sleep!" His pastor said: "The cloud so long pending over the nation has at last burst upon our heads. We sit half crushed amid the ruin it has wrought. We remember with joy his faith in the son of God, whose gospel he sometimes himself preached, and which he always truly loved. And we see light and blue sky through cloud structure, and beauty instead of ruin; glory, honor, immortality, spiritual and eternal life, in the place of decay and death. The chief glory of this man, as we think of him now, was his discipleship in the school of Christ. It is as a Christian that we love to think of him, now. It was this which made his life to man an invaluable boon, his death to us an unspeakable loss, his eternity to himself an inheritance incorruptible, undefiled, and that fadeth not away. He was no sectarian. His religion was as broad as the religion of Christ. He was a simple Christian, bound by no sectarian ties, and wholly in fellowship with all pure spirits. He was a christologist rather than a theologist. He had great reverence for the family relations. His example as son, husband and father, is a glory to this nation. He had a most kindly nature. His power over human hearts was deep and strong. He won men to him. He had no enemies. The hand that struck him was not the hand of his enemy, but the enemy of the position, the enemy of the country, the enemy of God. He sought to do right, manward and Godward. He was a grander man than we knew. He wrought even in his pain a better work for the nation than we can now estimate. He fell at the height of his achievements, not from any fault of his; but we may in some sense reverently apply to him the words spoken of his dear Lord: 'He was wounded for our transgressions; he was bruised for our iniquities; the chastisement of our peace was upon him.' As the nations remembered the Macedonian as Alexander the Great, and the Grecian as Aristides the Just, may not this son of America be known as Garfield the Good? Our President rests; he had joy in the glory of work, and he loved to talk of the leisure that did not come to him. Now he has it. This is the clay, precious because of the service it rendered. He is a freed spirit; absent from the body, he is present with the Lord. On the heights whence came his help, he finds repose. What rest has been his for these four days! The brave spirit which has cried in its body, 'I am tired,' is where the wicked cease from troubling, and the weary are at rest. The patient soul which groaned, under the burden of the suffering flesh, 'O, this pain,' is now in a world without pain. Spring comes, the flowers bloom, the buds put forth, the birds sing; autumn rolls round, the birds have long since hushed their voices, the flowers faded and fallen away, the forest foliage assumes a sickly, dying hue; so earthly things pass away and what is true remains with God. The pageant moves, the splendor of arms and the banners glitter in the sunlight, the music of instruments and of orators swells upon the air. The cheers and praises of men resound. But the spring and summer pass by, and the autumn sees a nation of sad eyes and heavy hearts, and what is true remains of God. 'The eternal God is our refuge, and underneath are the everlasting arms.'"

It should not be overlooked that, from the time the President's death was announced, letters and telegrams of sympathy and condolence came to Mrs. Garfield and Secretary Blaine, not only from the distinguished officials of our own country, — governors, senators, judges, representatives, and other public men, — but also from the rulers of almost every country on the globe. The people of every land seemed to feel that they had sustained a loss in the death of the noble man; and their expressions of sympathy were frank and full. The day of the funeral in Cleveland, Monday, September 26th, which President Arthur set apart as a fast, was observed in some foreign countries, where people assembled in large numbers to pay their tribute of respect to the lamented Chief Magistrate of the United States. The courts of England, Belgium, and Spain went into mourning. It was an unusual expression of tender regard, for which the bereaved American people were truly grateful,

At the close of the obsequies in Washington, the remains were conveyed to the train waiting to bear them to Ohio; and a silent and tearful procession followed them to the station, through streets that were thronged with people and mournful with funeral drapery. At five o'clock, all that was mortal of the great man was borne away from the capital, where he was inducted into the presidential office less than seven months before. The entire route from Washington to Cleveland was made memorable by the grateful tributes of citizens gathering in numbers from one to ten thousand at the different railroad stations, with the emblems of their unfeigned sorrow draping every flag and building.

About one o'clock P. M., the funeral train rolled into the depot at Cleveland, presenting a touching spectacle to the assembled multitude there. It was so deeply draped, from the locomotive to the last car, that every particle of brass upon the engine and wood of the cars was concealed by crape. The depot itself was as elaborate in its symbols of death as the train; and the fifty thousand people gathered within sight were moved to tears by the mournful scene. A hearse was in waiting to receive the casket and bear it to the great pavilion that had been erected upon the City Park. It was covered with black, and drawn by four black horses, attended by four colored grooms who served in a similar capacity when the body of President Lincoln was conveyed through the city. As soon as the casket was deposited in its place upon the costly catafalque erected in the centre of the park, the vast concourse of people began to pass around it four abreast, disappointed indeed that the face of their beloved President could not be seen, but glad to pay their honest tribute of respect to his precious memory. Until late in the evening the solemn procession filed past the remains, only a fractional part of the crowd, however, having yet been able to get within the park. Again, at sunrise, on Sabbath morning, the procession took its march, four abreast still, dividing at the foot of the catafalque, and passing it by twos on either side, and thus continued through the day until the military closed the entrance to the park at nine o'clock in the evening. Seventy-five thousand people, composed of all classes, from the highest to the lowest, from the wealthiest to the poorest, had joined the march of honor past the coffin, and yet as many more turned away in sad disappointment.

Monday, the time of the funeral in Cleveland, had been appointed by President Arthur as a day of fasting, humiliation, and prayer; and the governors of most of the states joined in the request. The governors of a few states had appointed Friday, the day of obsequies at Washington, as a fast, before the President's proclamation was issued; still, Monday was regarded as the funeral day for the nation, and Cleveland was the central point to which all hearts turned. Although the capacity of the city to accommodate visitors was overtaxed on Saturday and Sunday, they continued to come on Monday morning by rail and carriage, every sort of vehicle being used to convey them from the surrounding country. What was remarkable to witness were the sad countenances worn by the vast concourse of people, nine out of ten of them wearing some symbol of bereavement, the most common one being a good portrait of the dead man on a piece of black ribbon for males to wear upon their coats. Almost every female wore some emblem of sorrow, a crape bow of black and white upon the neck being the most general. By the time of the funeral ceremonies, at half-past ten o'clock in the morning, two hundred and fifty thousand people were on the streets to witness the pageant moving to the grave.

Perhaps no city in the world was ever draped so beautifully and expensively before. There scarcely could be found a store, shop, or dwelling on which some visible token of respect for the dead did not appear. The streets, too, were arrayed in the deepest mourning, as if loving relatives of the deceased statesman had dressed them for his funeral. Euclid Avenue, six miles long,—one of the longest, widest, and finest avenues in the country,—was draped in the most costly manner from beginning to end. It is lined the whole distance with the richest lawns, in the rear of which stand the most elegant dwellings the city can boast; and the drapery that covered these costly mansions and lawns vied in elegance with the residences themselves. The splendid trees which adorn the avenue on both sides held many sable symbols on their green and thrifty boughs, while every device of floral art appeared in the most appropriate and costly designs. It was through this avenue that the funeral pageant passed to the cemetery; and its wonderful mourning attire was worthy of the sad occasion. The floral tributes in the city, especially in the park and around the catafalque, were too many and elaborate to be described. Fair hands of the city had wrought flowers into the most charming pictures; and other cities and towns had contributed them in equally exquisite forms, till it seemed as if the florists of the world had exhausted their art in furnishing beautiful pieces for the greatest day of sorrow America ever knew. Cincinnati alone forwarded two carloads of floral devices. Enormous arches spanned every entrance to the public squares, and these were covered with black cloth relieved with bands and fringes of white, while flowers wrought into such pictures of beauty as to remind beholders of fairy fingers, lent enchantment to the view. Each arch bore a suitable inscription in white flowers. It is quite impossible to describe the display of flowers. We shall not attempt it, except to say that, perhaps, the most attractive design of all was the pendant from the arch at the western gate. A large cross-hilted sword of evergreen, surmounted by a white dove, formed the basis of the structure, and across it was a ladder of white immortelles. There were eleven rounds to the ladder, emblematical of the different stages of General Garfield's career. On the lower round was inscribed the word "Chester;" on the second, "Hiram;" on the third, "Williams;" on the fourth, "Ohio Senate;" on the fifth, "Colonel;" on the sixth, "General;" on the seventh, "Congress;" on the eighth, "United States Senate;" on the ninth, "President;" on the tenth, "Martyr;" the *eleventh* and topmost round bore no inscription, but was heavily shrouded in crape. The reader of this volume will readily interpret these inscriptions, since they describe our hero going to the "top of the ladder."

The floral designs of the casket were numerous and elegant. None were brought from Washington except the *palms*, that symbol "victory," and Victoria's tribute. All others were the contribution of Ohio; and they were all that the truest love and veneration for the dead could ask.

When the people had assembled for the obsequies on the park, there were present two ex-Presidents of the United States, the Cabinet, and Members of Con gress, prominent officers of the army and navy, Judges of the Supreme Court, Foreign Ministers, Governors and ex-Governors of many of the States, together with other public men of fame from various parts of the country, presenting, perhaps, the most imposing scene of the kind ever witnessed. Mrs. Garfield, with the aged mother of the President, and other members of the family, took their seats near the casket. The mother had not seen the President since she left Washington, a few weeks after his inauguration; and now she could only look upon the coffin which held the form so dear to her. As if moved by an irrepressible yearning of love, she rose and stepped to the head of the casket, and covering her face in the deep folds of mourning in which she was clad, she poured out her soul in silent grief for a moment, and thousands wept with her.

At precisely half-past ten o'clock the services opened by the singing of Beethoven's "Funeral Hymn," by the Cleveland Vocal Society.

"Thou art gone to the grave, but we will not deplore thee,
Tho' sorrow and darkness encompass the tomb;
The Saviour has passed thro' its portals before thee,
And the lamp of His love is thy light thro' the gloom."

Scripture selections were read by Bishop Bedell; prayer was offered by Rev. R. C. Houghton; another hymn was sung by the vocal society; when Rev. Isaac Errett, D.D., of Cincinnati, according to a promise made to the deceased, years ago, proceeded to deliver an able and eloquent sermon from texts that seemed to have been inspired for this special occasion (2 Chronicles xxxv. 23–27; Isaiah iii. 1–3; xl. 6–8).

The sermon was followed by the following favorite hymn of General Garfield: —

"Ho! reapers of life's harvest,
Why stand with rusted blade
Until the night draws round thee
And the day begins to fade?
Why stand ye idle, waiting
For reapers more to come?
The golden morn is passing —
Why sit ye, idle, dumb?

Thrust in your sharpened sickle
And gather in the grain;
The night is fast approaching
And soon will come again.
The master calls for reapers —
And shall he call in vain?
Shall sheaves lie there ungathered
And wasted on the plain?

Mount up the heights of wisdom
And crush each error low;
Keep back no words of knowledge
That human hearts should know.
Be faithful to thy mission,
In service of thy Lord,
And then a golden chaplet
Shall be thy just reward."

Dr. C. S. Pomeroy made the closing prayer, when the remains were immediately borne to the funeral car, which was a very imposing carriage in the form of the temple of liberty, draped in black, and having at each corner a group of tattered Ohio battle-flags, among them, those of the Forty-Second Ohio Regiment, which General Garfield organized and commanded. It was drawn by twelve black horses, four abreast, wearing mourning plumes on their heads, and covered with heavy black cloth ornamented with silver fringe. Each horse was led by a sable-liveried colored groom. The family and distinguished citizens present immediately followed the casket and took their seats in carriages provided for them, and joined the procession. The procession had been forming during the progress of the obsequies, so that it was well under way when the services closed. Lake View Cemetery, where General Garfield had expressed a wish to be buried, was seven miles away, and when the head of the procession reached the place of burial, the end of it was still in the city. And such an impressive pageant no one present ever witnessed before. The emblems of mourning, the brilliant dress of Knight Templars, Masonic Lodges and other civilian societies, the parade of richly caparisoned cavalry and the uniform of military companies, together with the draped and expensive carriages of every description drawn by fine horses finely arrayed in appropriate mourning symbols; and bands of music touching the tender hearts of the multitude with solemn dirges, all this constituted such a funeral cortege as never before followed King or Queen or President to the tomb.

At the cemetery there was singing, prayer, an address by Rev. J. H. Jones, Chaplain of the Forty-Second Ohio Regiment when General Garfield was its commander, and benediction by President Hinsdale, of Hiram College, where the deceased laid the foundation of his education as well as the foundation of his greatness.

Thus closed a day of mourning that has no parallel in American history. For, it should not be forgotten, that funeral services were also held all over the country, in the smallest as well as the largest towns, and the people suspended their industrial pursuits, and repaired to their churches and halls, where, surrounded with sombre draperies and floral tributes, they listened to funeral sermons, eulogies, prayers and hymns, and wept over their national and personal loss. The previous day, too, the Sabbath of rest — was observed in every part of the land by appropriate memorial services. The people assembled in their places of worship, in larger numbers than usual, and listened to fitting sermons upon the death of the President. Thousands of discourses were preached upon this melancholy theme in thousands of churches draped in black and decorated with flowers for the occasion. Altogether it was a memorable Sabbath in the history of our Christian land.

The sorrow and sympathy among all lands were without precedent. The Department of State furnishes the following correspondence: —

TOKIO, Sept. 21.

To Yoshida, Japanese Minister, Washington:

You are instructed to transmit the following message to the Hon. James G. Blaine, Secretary of State:

We have received with feelings of profound sorrow a telegram from our Minister, announcing the death of President Garfield. The favorable reports of his condition we have from time to time received make this sad announcement the more unexpected and painful. In the name of His Majesty, we tender to you and the sadly bereaved family our heartfelt condolence and sympathy.

INOUYE, *Minister for Foreign Affairs.*

To Secretary of State, Washington:

By special command of His Majesty, the King of Italy, now absent in the northern provinces, the Minister of Foreign Affairs communicates to me the expression of the profound regret of His Majesty, and of the Italian nation, for the death of our late chief magistrate. MARSH.

From the Acting Governor-General of Canada:

OTTAWA, Sept. 21.

Be pleased to convey to the President, and through him to the people of the United States, the deep sympathy felt by the government and people of the Dominion of Canada, for the sad loss the people of the United States have sustained in the melancholy death of their late President.

To the Secretary of State, Washington, D. C.:

The Minister of Foreign Affairs telegraphs me that the Sultan and the Ottoman government are profoundly grieved at the death of the President; and His Excellency charges me to present, in the name of His Majesty and the government their sincerest sympathy to Mrs. Garfield, and the government of the United States. ARISTARCHI.

To Secretary Blaine, Washington:

Sympathy in Belgium for the nation, and President Garfield's family, profound and universal. The King, the government legations, and citizens have expressed it. PUTNAM, *Brussels.*

ROME, Sept. 21,

To His Excellency, the Minister for Foreign Affairs, Washington:

The loss of the illustrious President Garfield has roused a deep sorrow to the Holy Father. His Holiness directs me to present his condolence to Your Excellency and to the Government, and his best wishes for the prosperity of the republic.

L. CARDINAL JACOBINI.

To President Arthur:

The Anglo-Jewish Association deplores the loss sustained by the American nation, and offers heartfelt sympathy to the Government and people of the United States, and also to the bereaved family of the late illustrious President.

BARON DE WORMS, M. D.

The *Pall Mall Gazette* said:

A year ago to-day not one Englishman in a thousand had heard Garfield's name. To-day there will scarcely be an Englishman in a thousand who will not read of his death with regret as real and as deep as if he had been a ruler of our own. A communion of sorrow unites the members of the English race to-day more closely than it has ever been since 1776.

GLASGOW, Sept. 26.

The flags were at half-mast, and the bells were tolled for an hour; the principal markets have closed for the afternoon.

MANCHESTER, Sept. 26.

Business was to a great extent suspended to-day. There was a funeral service in the Cathedral.

LONDON, Sept. 21.

Every hour increases the evidence that the present is the most remarkable demonstration of sympathy ever witnessed in Europe.

As we recall, in conclusion, the wonderful career of the man, and ponder the mysterious Providence that confronts us in his removal, and ask the meaning of the deep and universal grief at his burial, we can find no more fitting words with which to close this record, than his own words, in the National House of Representatives, on the occasion of the first anniversary of Lincoln's death. In a speech of rare beauty and eloquence, he said, — what applies with remarkable significance to himself:

"This day will be sadly memorable so long as this nation shall endure, which, God grant, may be 'till the last syllable of recorded time,' when the volume of human history shall be sealed up, and delivered to the Omnipotent Judge.

. . . .

"His character is aptly described in the words of England's great leaureate, written thirty years ago, in which he traces the upward steps of some

'Divinely gifted man,
Whose life in low estate began,
And on a simple village green;

Who breaks his birth's invidious bar,
And grasps the skirts of happy chance,
And breasts the blow of circumstance,
And grapples with his evil star;

Who makes by force his merits known,
And lives to clutch his golden keys,
To mould a mighty State's decrees,
And shape the whisper of the throne.

And moving up from high to higher,
Becomes on Fortune's crowning slope
The pillar of a people's hope,
The centre of a world's desire.'

"Such a life and character will be treasured for ever as the sacred possession of the American people and of mankind.

. . . . .

"Ah, sir, there are times in the history of men and nations when they stand so near the veil that separates mortals from immortals, time from eternity, and men from their God, that they can almost hear the beatings and feel the pulsations of the heart of the Infinite. Through such a time has this nation passed. When two hundred and fifty thousand brave spirits passed from the field of honor through that thin veil to the presence of God, and when at last its parting folds admitted the martyr President to the company of the dead heroes of the Republic, the nation stood so near the veil that the whispers of God were heard by the children of men.

"Awe-stricken by his voice, the American people knelt in tearful reverence and made a solemn covenant with Him and with each other that this nation should be saved from its enemies, that all its glories should be restored, and on the ruins of treason and slavery the temples of freedom and justice should be built, and should survive forever. It remains for us, consecrated to that great event, and under a covenant with God, to keep that faith, to go forward in the great work until it shall be completed.

"Following the lead of that great man, and obeying the high behests of God, let us remember that, —

"'He has sounded forth a trumpet that shall never call retreat;
He is sifting out the hearts of men before His judgment-seat;
Be swift, my soul, to answer him; be jubilant, my feet;
For God is marching on.'"

CHAPTER XXVIII.

MR. BLAINE'S EULOGY ON PRESIDENT GARFIELD.

FOR the second time in this generation the great departments of the Government of the United States are assembled in the Hall of Representatives to do honor to the memory of a murdered President. Lincoln fell at the close of a mighty struggle in which the passions of men had been deeply stirred. The tragical termination of his great life added but another to the lengthened succession of horrors which had marked so many lintels with the blood of the first born. Garfield was slain in a day of peace, when brother had been reconciled to brother, and when anger and hate had been banished from the land. "Whoever shall hereafter draw the portrait of murder, if he will show it as it has been exhibited where such example was last to have been looked for, let him not give it the grim visage of Moloch, the brow knitted by revenge, the face black with settled hate. Let him draw, rather, a decorous, smooth-faced, bloodless demon; not so much an example of human nature in its depravity and in its paroxysms of crime, as an infernal being, a fiend in the ordinary display and development of his character."

From the landing of the Pilgrims at Plymouth till the uprising against Charles the First, about twenty thousand emigrants came from old England to New England. As they came in pursuit of intellectual freedom and ecclesiastical independence rather than for worldly honor and profit, the emigration naturally ceased when the contest for religious liberty began in earnest at home. The man who struck his most effective blow for freedom of conscience by sailing for the colonies in 1620 would have been accounted a deserter to leave after 1640. The opportunity had then come on the soil of England for that great contest which established the authority of Parliament, gave religious freedom to the people, sent Charles to the block, and committed to the hands of Oliver Cromwell the Supreme Executive authority of England. The English emigration was never renewed, and from these twenty thousand men, with a small emigration from Scotland and from France, are descended the vast numbers who have New England blood in their veins.

In 1685 the revocation of the edict of Nantes by Louis XIV. scattered to other countries four hundred thousand Protestants, who were among the most intelligent and enterprising of French subjects — merchants of capital, skilled manufacturers, and handicraftsmen, superior at the time to all others in Europe. A considerable number of these Huguenot French came to America; a few landed in New England and became honorably prominent in its history. Their names have in large part become anglicized, or have disappeared, but their blood is traceable in many of the most reputable families, and their fame is perpetuated in honorable memorials and useful institutions.

From these two sources, the English-Puritan and the French-Huguenot, came the late President — his father, Abram Garfield, being descended from the one, and his mother, Eliza Ballou, from the other.

It was good stock on both sides — none better, none braver, none truer. There was in it an inheritance of courage, of manliness, of imperishable love of liberty, of undying adherence to principle. Garfield was proud of his blood; and, with as much satisfaction as if he were a British nobleman reading his stately ancestral record in Burke's Peerage, he spoke of himself as ninth in descent from those who would not endure the oppression of the Stuarts, and seventh in descent from the brave French Protestants who refused to submit to tyranny even from the Grand Monarch.

General Garfield delighted to dwell on these traits, and, during his only visit to England, he busied himself in discovering every trace of his forefathers in parish registries and on ancient army rolls. Sitting with a friend in the gallery of the House of Commons one night after a long day's labor in this field of research, he said with evident elation that in every war in which for three centuries patriots of English blood had struck sturdy blows for constitutional government and human liberty, his family had been represented. They were at Marston Moor, at Naseby and at Preston; they were at Bunker Hill, at Saratoga, and at Monmouth, and in his own person had battled for the same great cause in the war which preserved the Union of the States.

Losing his father before he was two years old, the early life of Garfield was one of privation, but its poverty has been made indelicately and unjustly prominent. Thousands of readers have imagined him as the ragged, starving child, whose reality too often greets the eye in the squalid sections of our large cities. General Garfield's infancy and youth had none of their destitution, none of their pitiful features appealing to the tender heart and to the open hand of charity. He was a poor boy in the sense in which Henry Clay was a poor boy; in which Andrew Jackson was a poor boy; in which Daniel Webster was a poor boy; in the sense in which a large majority of the eminent men of America in all generations have been poor boys. Before a great multitude of men, in a public speech, Mr. Webster bore this testimony:

"It did not happen to me to be born in a log cabin, but my elder brothers and sisters were born in a log cabin, raised amid the snow-drifts of New Hampshire, at a period so early that when the smoke rose first from its rude chimney and curled over the frozen hills there was no similar evidence of a white man's habitation between it and the settlements on the rivers of Canada. Its remains still exist. I make to it an annual visit. I carry my children to it to teach them the hardships endured by the generations which have gone before them. I love to dwell on the tender recollections, the kindred ties, the early affections, and the touching narratives and incidents which mingle with all I know of this primitive family abode."

With the requisite change of scene the same words would aptly portray the early days of Garfield. The poverty of the frontier, where all are engaged in a common struggle and where a common sympathy and hearty coöperation lighten the burden of each, is a very different poverty, different in kind, different in influence and effect from that conscious and humiliating indigence which is every day forced to contrast itself with neighboring wealth on which it feels a sense of grinding dependence. The poverty of the frontier is indeed no poverty. It is but the beginning of wealth, and has the boundless possibilities of the future always opening before it. No man ever grew up in the agricultural regions of the West where a house-raising, or even a corn-husking, is a matter of common interest and helpfulness, with any other feeling than that of broad-minded, generous independence. This honorable independence marked the youth of Garfield as it marks the youth of millions of the best blood and brain now training for the future citizenship and future government of the republic. Garfield was born heir to land, to the title of freeholder which has been the patent and passport of self-respect with the Anglo-Saxon race ever since Hengist and Horsa landed on the shores of England. His adventure on the canal — an alternative between that and the deck of a Lake Erie schooner — was a farmer boy's device for earning money, just as the New England lad begins a possible great career by sailing before the mast on a coasting vessel or on a merchantman bound to the farther India or to the China Seas.

No manly man feels anything of shame in looking back to early struggles with adverse circumstances, and no man feels a worthier pride than when he has conquered the obstacles to his progress. But no one of noble mould desires to be looked upon as having occupied a menial position, as having been repressed by a feeling of inferiority, or as having suffered the evils of poverty until relief was found at the hand of charity. General Garfield's youth presented no hardships which family love and family energy did not overcome, subjected him to no privations which he did not cheerfully accept, and left no memories save those which were recalled with delight, and transmitted with profit and with pride.

Garfield's early opportunities for securing an education were extremely limited, and yet were sufficient to develop in him an intense desire to learn. He could read at three years of age, and each winter he had the advantage of the district school. He read all the books to be found within the circle of his acquaintance; some of them he got by heart. While yet in childhood he was a constant student of the Bible, and became familiar with its literature. The dignity and earnestness of his speech in his maturer life gave evidence of this early training. At eighteen years of age he was able to teach school, and thenceforward his ambition was to obtain a college education. To this end he bent all his efforts, working in the harvest field, at the carpenter's bench, and, in the winter season, teaching the common schools of the neighborhood.

While thus laboriously occupied he found time to prosecute his studies, and was so successful that at twenty-two years of age he was able to enter the junior class at Williams College, then under the presidency of the venerable and honored Mark Hopkins, who, in the fullness of his powers, survives the eminent pupil to whom he was of inestimable service.

The history of Garfield's life to this period presents no novel features. He had undoubtedly shown perseverance, self-reliance, self-sacrifice, and ambition — qualities which, be it said for the honor of our country, are everywhere to be found among the young men of America. But from his graduation at Williams onward, to the hour of his tragical death, Garfield's career was eminent and exceptional. Slowly working through his educational period, receiving his diploma when twenty-four years of age, he seemed at one bound to spring into conspicuous and brilliant success. Within six years he was successively president of a college, State senator of Ohio, major-general of the Army of the United States, and Representative elect to the National Congress. A combination of honors so varied, so elevated, within a period so brief and to a man so young, is without precedent or parallel in the history of the country.

Garfield's army life was begun with no other military knowledge than such as he had hastily gained from books in the few months preceeding his march to the field. Stepping from civil life to the head of a regiment, the first order he received when ready to cross the Ohio was to assume command of a brigade, and to operate as an independent force in Eastern Kentucky

His immediate duty was to check the advance of Humphrey Marshall, who was marching down the Big Sandy with the intention of occupying in connection with other Confederate forces the entire territory of Kentucky, and of precipitating the State into secession. This was at the close of the year 1861. Seldom, if ever, has a young college professor been thrown into a more embarrassing and discouraging position. He knew just enough of military science, as he expressed it himself, to measure the extent of his ignorance, and with a handful of men he was marching, in rough winter weather, into a strange country, among a hostile population, to confront a largely superior force under the command of a distinguished graduate of West Point, who had seen active and important service in two preceding wars.

The result of the campaign is matter of history. The skill, the endurance, the extraordinary energy shown by Garfield, the courage he imparted to his men, raw and untried as himself, the measures he adopted to increase his force and to create in the enemy's mind exaggerated estimates of his numbers, bore perfect fruit in the routing of Marshall, the capture of his camp, the dispersion of his force, and the emancipation of an important territory from the control of the rebellion. Coming at the close of a long series of disasters to the Union arms, Garfield's victory had an unusual and extraneous importance, and in the popular judgment elevated the young commander to the rank of a military hero. With less than two thousand men in his entire command, with a mobilized force of only eleven hundred, without cannon, he had met an army of five thousand

and defeated them — driving Marshall's forces successively from two strongholds of their own selection, fortified with abundant artillery. Major-General Buell, commanding the Department of the Ohio, an experienced and able soldier of the Regular Army, published an order of thanks and congratulation on the brilliant result of the Big Sandy campaign, which would have turned the head of a less cool and sensible man than Garfield. Buell declared that his services had called into action the highest quality of a soldier, and President Lincoln supplemented these words of praise by the more substantial reward of a brigadier-general's commission, to bear date from the day of this decisive victory over Marshall.

The subsequent military career of Garfield fully sustained its brilliant beginning. With his new commission he was assigned to the command of a brigade in the Army of the Ohio, and took part in the second and decisive day's fight in the great battle of Shiloh. The remainder of the year 1862 was not especially eventful to Garfield, as it was not to the armies with which he was serving. His practical sense was called into exercise in completing the task assigned him by General Buell, of reconstructing bridges and re-establishing lines of railway communication for the Army. His occupation in this useful but not brilliant field was varied by service on courts martial of importance, in which department of duty he won a valuable reputation, attracting the notice and securing the approval of the able and eminent Judge-Advocate-General of the Army. That of itself was warrant to honorable fame; for among the great men who in those trying days gave themselves, with entire devotion, to the service of their country. one who brought to that service the ripest learning, the most fervid eloquence, the most varied attainments, who labored with modesty and shunned applause, who in the day of triumph sat reserved and silent and grateful — as Francis Deak in the hour of Hungary's deliverance — was Joseph Holt, of Kentucky, who in his honorable retirement enjoys the respect and veneration of all who love the Union of the States.

Early in 1863 Garfield was assigned to the highly important and responsible post of chief of staff to General Rosecrans, then at the head of the Army of the Cumberland. Perhaps in a great military campaign no subordinate officer requires sounder judgment and quicker knowledge of men than the chief of staff to the commanding-general. An indiscreet man in such a position can sow more discord, breed more jealousy and disseminate more strife than any other officer in the entire organization. When General Garfield assumed his new duties he found various troubles already well developed and seriously affecting the value and efficiency of the Army of the Cumberland. The energy, the impartiality, and the tact with which he sought to allay these dissensions, and to discharge the duties of his new and trying position will always remain one of the most striking proofs of his great versatility. His military duties closed on the memorable field of Chickamauga, a field which however disastrous to the Union arms gave to him the occasion of winning imperishable laurels. The very rare distinction was accorded him of a great promotion for his bravery on a field that was lost. President Lincoln appointed him a major-general in the Army of the United States for gallant and meritorious conduct in the battle of Chickamauga.

The Army of the Cumberland was reorganized under the command of General Thomas, who promptly offered Garfield one of its divisions. He was extremely desirous to accept the position, but was embarrassed by the fact that he had, a year before, been elected to Congress, and the time when he must take his seat was drawing near. He preferred to remain in the military service, and had within his own breast the largest confidence of success in the wider field which his new rank opened to him. Balancing the arguments on the one side and the other, anxious to determine what was for the best, desirous above all things to do his patriotic duty, he was decisively influenced by the advice of President Lincoln and Secretary Stanton, both of whom assured him that he could, at that time, be of especial value in the House of Representatives. He resigned his commission of major-general on the 5th day of December, 1863, and took his seat in the House of Representatives on the 7th. He had served two years and four months in the Army, and had just completed his thirty-second year.

The Thirty-eighth Congress is pre-eminently entitled in history to the designation of the War Congress. It was elected while the war was flagrant, and every member was chosen upon the issues involved in the continuance of the struggle. The Thirty-seventh Congress had, indeed, legislated to a large extent on war measures, but it was chosen before any one believed that secession of the States would be actually attempted,

The magnitude of the work which fell upon its successor was unprecedented, both in respect to the vast sums of money raised for the support of the Army and Navy, and of the new and extraordinary powers of legislation which it was forced to exercise. Only twenty-four States were represented, and one hundred and eighty-two members were upon its roll. Among these were many distinguished party leaders on both sides, veterans in the public service, with established reputations for ability, and with that skill which comes only from parliamentary experience. Into this assemblage of men Garfield entered without special preparation, and it might almost be said unexpectedly. The question of taking command of a division of troops under General Thomas, or taking his seat in Congress was kept open till the last moment, so late, indeed, that the resignation of his military commission and his appearance in the House were almost contemporaneous. He wore the uniform of a major-general of the United States Army on Saturday, and on Monday in civilian's dress, he answered to the roll-call as a Representative in Congress from the State of Ohio.

He was especially fortunate in the constituency which elected him. Descended almost entirely from New England stock, the men of the Ashtabula district were intensely radical on all questions relating to human rights. Well educated, thrifty, thoroughly intelligent in affairs, acutely discerning of character, not quick to bestow confidence, and slow to withdraw it, they were at once the most helpful and most exacting of supporters. Their tenacious trust in men in whom they have once confided is illustrated by the unparalleled fact that Elisha Whittlesey, Joshua R. Giddings, and James A. Garfield represented the district for fifty-four years.

There is no test of a man's ability in any department of public life more severe than service in the House of Representatives; there is no place where so little deference is paid to reputation previously acquired, or to eminence won outside; no place where so little consideration is shown for the feelings or the failures of beginners. What a man gains in the House he gains by sheer force of his own character, and if he loses and falls back he must expect no mercy, and will receive no sympathy. It is a field in which the survival of the strongest is the recognized rule, and where no pretence can deceive and no glamour can mislead. The real man is discovered, his worth is impartially weighed, his rank is irreversibly decreed.

With possibly a single exception, Garfield was the youngest member in the House when he entered, and was but seven years from his college graduation. But he had not been in his seat sixty days before his ability was recognized and his place conceded. He stepped to the front with the confidence of one who belonged there. The House was crowded with strong men of both parties; nineteen of them have since been transferred to the Senate, and many of them have served with distinction in the gubernatorial chairs of their respective States, and on foreign missions of great consequence; but among them all none grew so rapidly, none so firmly as Garfield. As is said by Trevelyan of his parliamentary hero, Garfield succeeded "because all the world in concert could not have kept him in the background, and because when once in the front he played his part with a prompt intrepidity and a commanding ease that were but the outward symptoms of the immense reserves of energy, on which it was in his power to draw." Indeed the apparently reserved force which Garfield possessed was one of his great characteristics. He never did so well but that it seemed he could easily have done better. He never expended so much strength but that he seemed to be holding additional power at call. This is one of the happiest and rarest distinctions of an effective debater, and often counts for as much in persuading an assembly as the eloquent and elaborate argument.

The great measure of Garfield's fame was filled by his service in the House of Representatives. His military life, illustrated by honorable performance, and rich in promise, was, as he himself felt, prematurely terminated, and necessarily incomplete. Speculation as to what he might have done in a field where the great prizes are so few, cannot be profitable. It is sufficient to say that as a soldier he did his duty bravely; he did it intelligently; he won an enviable fame, and he retired from the service without blot or breath against him. As a lawyer, though admirably equipped for the profession, he can scarcely be said to have entered on its practice. The few efforts he made at the bar were distinguished by the same high order of talent which he exhibited on every field where he was put to the test, and if a man may be accepted as a competent judge of his own capacities and adaptations, the law was the profession to which Garfield should have devoted himself. But fate ordained otherwise, and his reputation in history will rest largely upon his service in the House of Representatives. That service was exceptionally long. He was nine times consecutively chosen to the House, an honor enjoyed probably by not twenty other Representatives of the more than five thousand who have been elected from the organization of the government to this hour.

As a parliamentary orator, as a debater on an issue squarely joined, where the position had been chosen and the ground laid out, Garfield must be assigned a very high rank. More, perhaps, than any man with whom he was associated in public life, he gave careful and systematic study to public questions and he came to every discussion in which he took part, with elaborate and complete preparation. He was a steady and indefatigable worker. Those who imagine that talent or genius can supply the place or achieve the results of labor will find no encouragement in Garfield's life. In preliminary work he was apt, rapid, and skilful. He possessed in a high degree the power of readily absorbing ideas and facts, and, like Dr. Johnson, had the art of getting from a book all that was of value in it by a reading apparently so quick and cursory that it seemed like a mere glance at the table of contents. He was a pre-eminently fair and candid man in debate, took no petty advantage, stooped to no unworthy methods, avoided personal allusions, rarely appealed to prejudice, did not seek to inflame passion. He had a quicker eye for the strong point of his adversary than for his weak point, and on his own side he so marshalled his weighty arguments as to make his hearers forget any possible lack in the complete strength of his position. He had a habit of stating his opponent's side with such amplitude of fairness and such liberality of concession that his followers often complained that he was giving his case away. But never in his prolonged participation in the proceedings of the House did he give his case away, or fail in the judgment of competent and impartial listeners to gain the mastery.

These characteristics, which marked Garfield as a great debater, did not, however, make him a great parliamentary leader. A parliamentary leader, as that term is understood wherever free representative government exists, is necessarily and very strictly the organ of his party. An ardent American defined the instinctive warmth of patriotism when he offered the toast, "Our country, always right, but right or wrong, our country." The parliamentary leader who has a body of followers that will do and dare and die for the cause, is one who believes his party always right, but right or wrong, is for his party. No more important or exacting duty devolves upon him than the selection of the field and the time for contest. He must know not merely how to strike, but where to strike, and when to strike. He often skilfully avoids the strength of his opponent's position and scatters confusion in his ranks by attacking an exposed point when really the righteousness of the cause and the strength of logical entrenchment are against him. He conquers often both against the right and the heavy battalions; as when young Charles Fox, in the days of his toryism, carried the House of Commons against justice, against its immemorial rights, against his own convictions, if, indeed, at that period Fox had convictions, and, in the interest of a corrupt administration, in obedience to a tyrannical sovereign, drove Wilkes from the seat to which the electors of Middlesex had chosen him and installed Luttrell in defiance, not merely of law but of public decency. For an achievement of that kind Garfield was disqualified — disqualified by the texture of his mind, by the honesty of his heart, by his conscience, and by every instinct and aspiration of his nature.

The three most distinguished parliamentary leaders hitherto developed in this country are Mr. Clay, Mr. Douglas, and Mr. Thaddeus Stevens. Each was a man of consummate ability, of great earnestness, of intense personality, differing widely, each from the others, and yet with a signal trait in common — the power to command. In the give and take of daily discussion, in the art of controlling and consolidating reluctant and refractory followers; in the skill to overcome all forms of opposition, and to meet with competency and courage the varying phases of unlooked for assault or unsuspected defection, it would be difficult to rank with these a fourth name in all our Congressional history. But of these Mr. Clay was the greatest. It would, perhaps, be impossible to find in the parliamentary annals of the world a parallel to Mr. Clay, in 1841, when at sixty-four years of age he took the control of the Whig party from the President who had received their suffrages, against the power of Webster in the Cabinet, against the eloquence of Choate in the Senate, against the herculean efforts of Caleb Cushing and Henry A. Wise in the House. In unshared leadership, in the pride and plenitude of power he hurled against John Tyler with deepest scorn the mass of that conquering column which had swept over the land in 1840, and drove his administration to seek shelter behind the lines of his political foes. Mr. Douglas achieved a victory scarcely less wonderful when, in 1854, against the secret desires of a strong administration, against the wise counsel of the older chiefs, against the conservative instincts and even the moral sense of the country, he forced a reluctant Congress into a repeal of the Missouri compromise. Mr. Thaddeus Stevens, in his contests from 1865 to 1868, actually advanced his parliamentary leadership until Congress tied the hands of the President and governed the country by its own will, leaving only perfunctory duties to be discharged by the Executive. With two hundred millions of patronage in his hands at the opening of the contest, aided by the active force of Seward in the Cabinet and the moral power of Chase on the Bench, Andrew Johnson could not command the support of one-third in either House against the Parliamentary uprising of which Thaddeus Stevens was the animating spirit and the unquestioned leader.

From these three great men Garfield differed radically, differed in the quality of his mind, in temperament, in the form and phase of ambition. He could not do what they did, but he could do what they could not, and in the breadth of his Congressional work he left that which will longer exert a potential influence among men, and which, measured by the severe test of posthumous criticism, will secure a more enduring and more enviable fame.

These unfamiliar with Garfield's industry, and ig

norant of the details of his work, may, in some degree, measure them by the annals of Congress. No one of the generation of public men to which he belonged has contributed so much that will be valuable for future reference. His speeches are numerous, many of them brilliant, all of them well studied, carefully phrased, and exhaustive of the subject under consideration. Collected from the scattered pages of ninety royal octavo volumes of Congressional Record, they would present an invaluable compendium of the political history of the most important era through which the national government has ever passed. When the history of this period shall be impartially written, when war legislation, measures of reconstruction, protection of human rights, amendments to the constitution, maintenance of public credit, steps towards specie resumption, true theories of revenue may be reviewed, unsurrounded by prejudice and disconnected from partisanism, the speeches of Garfield will be estimated at their true value, and will be found to comprise a vast magazine of fact and argument, of clear analysis and sound conclusion. Indeed, if no other authority were accessible, his speeches in the House of Representatives from December, 1863, to June, 1880, would give a well connected history and complete defence of the important legislation of the seventeen eventful years that constitute his Parliamentary life. Far beyond that, his speeches would be found to forecast many great measures, yet to be completed — measures which he knew were beyond the public opinion of the hour, but which he confidently believed would secure popular approval within the period of his own lifetime, and by the aid of his own efforts.

Differing, as Garfield does, from the brilliant Parliamentary leaders, it is not easy to find his counterpart anywhere in the record of American public life. He perhaps more nearly resembles Mr. Seward in his supreme faith in the all-conquering power of a principle. He had the love of learning, and the patient industry of investigation, to which John Quincy Adams owed his prominence and his Presidency. He had some of those ponderous elements of mind which distinguished Mr. Webster, and which indeed, in all our public life, have left the great Massachusetts senator without an intellectual peer.

In English parliamentary history, as in our own, the leaders in the House of Commons present points of essential difference from Garfield. But some of his methods recall the best features in the strong, independent course of Sir Robert Peel, and striking resemblances are discernible in that most promising of modern conservatives, who died too early for his country and his fame, Lord George Bentinck. He had all of Burke's love for the Sublime and the Beautiful, with possibly, something of his superabundance; and in his faith and his magnanimity, in his power of statement, in his subtle analysis, in his faultless logic, in his love of literature, in his wealth and world of illustration, one is reminded of that great English statesman of to-day, who, confronted with obstacles that would daunt any but the dauntless, reviled by those whom he would relieve as bitterly as by those whose supposed rights he is forced to invade, still labors with serene courage for the amelioration of Ireland, and for the honor of the English name.

Garfield's nomination to the Presidency, while not predicted or anticipated, was not a surprise to the country. His prominence in Congress, his solid qualities, his wide reputation, strengthened by his then recent election as Senator from Ohio, kept him in the public eye as a man occupying the very highest rank among those entitled to be called statesmen. It was not mere chance that brought him this high honor. "We must," says Mr. Emerson, "reckon success a constitutional trait. If Eric is in robust health and has slept well and is at the top of his condition, and thirty years old at his departure from Greenland, he will steer west and his ship will reach Newfoundland. But take Eric out and put in a stronger and bolder man and the ship will sail six hundred, one thousand, fifteen hundred miles farther and reach Labrador and New England. There is no chance in results."

As a candidate, Garfield steadily grew in popular favor. He was met with a storm of detraction at the very hour of his nomination, and it continued with increasing volume and momentum until the close of his victorious campaign :

> No might nor greatness in mortality
> Can censure 'scape ; backwounding calumny
> The whitest virtue strikes. What king so strong
> Can tie the gall up in the slanderous tongue ?

Under it all he was calm, and strong, and confident ; never lost his self-possession, did no unwise act, spoke no hasty, or ill-considered word. Indeed, nothing in his whole life is more remarkable or more creditable than his bearing through those five full months of vituperation — a prolonged agony of trial to a sensitive man, a constant and cruel draft upon the powers of moral endurance. The great mass of these unjust im putations passed unnoticed, and with the general *débris* of the campaign fell into oblivion. But in a few instances the iron entered his soul, and he died with the injury unforgotten, if not unforgiven.

One aspect of Garfield's candidacy was unprecedented. Never before, in the history of partisan contests in this country, had a successful Presidential candidate spoken freely on passing events and current issues. To attempt anything of the kind seemed novel, rash, and even desperate. The older class of voters recalled the unfortunate Alabama letter, in which Mr. Clay was supposed to have signed his political death warrant. They remembered, also, the hot-tempered effusion by which General Scott lost a large share of his popularity before his nomination, and the unfortunate speeches which rapidly consumed the remainder. The younger voters had seen Mr. Greeley, in a series of vigorous and original addresses, preparing the pathway for his own defeat. Unmindful of these warnings, unheeding the advice of friends, Garfield spoke to large crowds as he journeyed to and from New York, in August, to a great multitude in that city, to delegations and deputations of every kind that called at Mentor during the summer and autumn. With innumerable critics, watchful and eager to catch a phrase that might be turned into odium or ridicule, or a sentence that might be distorted to his own or his party's injury, Garfield did not trip or halt in any one of his seventy speeches. This seems all the more remarkable when it is remembered that he did not write what he said, and yet spoke with such logical consecutiveness of thought, and such admirable precision of phrase, as to defy the accident of misreport and the malignity of misrepresentation.

In the beginning of his Presidential life, Garfield's experience did not yield him pleasure or satisfaction. The duties that engross so large a portion of the President's time were distasteful to him, and were unfavorably contrasted with his legislative work. "I have been dealing all these years with ideas," he impatiently exclaimed one day, "and here I am dealing only with persons. I have been heretofore treating of the fundamental principles of government, and here I am considering all day whether A or B shall be appointed to this or that office." He was earnestly seeking some practical way of correcting the evils arising from the distribution of overgrown and unwieldy patronage — evils always appreciated and often discussed by him, but whose magnitude had been more deeply impressed upon his mind since his accession to the Presidency. Had he lived, a comprehensive improvement in the mode of appointment and in the tenure of office would have been proposed by him, and, with the aid of Congress, no doubt perfected.

But, while many of the Executive duties were not grateful to him, he was assiduous and conscientious in their discharge. From the very outset he exhibited administrative talent of a high order. He grasped the helm of office with the hand of a master. In this respect, indeed, he constantly surprised many who were most intimately associated with him in the government, and especially those who had feared that he might be lacking in the executive faculty. His disposition of business was orderly and rapid. His power of analysis, and his skill in classification, enabled him to dispatch a vast mass of detail with singular promptness and ease. His Cabinet meetings were admirably conducted. His clear presentation of official subjects, his well-considered suggestion of topics on which discussion was invited, his quick decision when all had been heard, combined to show a thoroughness of mental training as rare as his natural ability and his facile adaptation to a new and enlarged field of labor.

With perfect comprehension of all the inheritances of the war, with a cool calculation of the obstacles in his way, impelled always by a generous enthusiasm, Garfield conceived that much might be done by his administration towards restoring harmony between the different sections of the Union. He was anxious to go South and speak to the people. As early as April he had ineffectually endeavored to arrange for a trip to Nashville, whither he had been cordially invited, and he was again disappointed a few weeks later to find that he could not go to South Carolina to attend the centennial celebration of the victory of the Cowpens. But for the autumn he definitely counted on being present at three memorable assemblies in the South, the celebration at Yorktown, the opening of the Cotton Exposition at Atlanta, and the meeting of the Army of the Cumberland, at Chattanooga. He was already turning over in his mind his address for each occasion, and the three taken together, he said to a friend, gave him the exact scope and verge which he needed. At Yorktown he would have before him the associations of a hundred years that bound the South and the North in the sacred memory of a common danger and a common victory. At Atlanta he would present the material interests and the industrial development which appealed to the thrift and independence of every household, and which should unite the two sections by the instinct of self-interest and self-defence. At Chattanooga he would revive memories of the war only to show that, after all its disaster, and all its suffering, the country was stronger and greater, the Union rendered indissoluble, and the future, through the agony and blood of one generation, made brighter and better for all.

Garfield's ambition for the success of his administration was high. With strong caution and conservatism in his nature, he was in no danger of attempting rash experiments or of resorting to the empiricism of statesmanship. But he believed that renewed and closer attention should be given to questions affecting the material interests and commercial prospects of fifty millions of people. He believed that our continental relations, extensive and undeveloped as they are, involved responsibility, and could be cultivated into profitable friendship or be abandoned to harmful indifference or lasting enmity. He believed with equal confidence that an essential forerunner to a new era of national progress must be a feeling of contentment in every section of the Union, and a generous belief that the benefits and burdens of government would be common to all. Himself a conspicuous illustration of what ability and ambition may do under republican institu tions, he loved his country with a passion of patriotic devotion, and every waking thought was given to her advancement. He was an American in all his aspirations, and he looked to the destiny and influence of the United States with the philosophic composure of Jefferson and the demonstrative confidence of John Adams.

The political events which disturbed the President's serenity, for many weeks before that fateful day in July, form an important chapter in his career, and, in his own judgment, involved questions of principle and of right which are vitally essential to the constitutional administration of the Federal Government. It would be out of place here and now to speak the language of controversy; but the events referred to, however they may continue to be source of contention with others, have become, so far as Garfield is concerned, as much a matter of history as his heroism at Chickamauga or his illustrious service in the house. Detail is not needful, and personal antagonism shall not be rekindled by any word uttered to-day. The motives of those opposing him are not to be here adversely interpreted nor their course harshly characterized. But of the dead President this is to be said, and said because his own speech is forever silenced and he can be no more heard except through the fidelity and the love of surviving friends: From the beginning to the end of the controversy he so much deplored, the President was never for one moment actuated by any motive of gain to himself or of loss to others. Least of all men did he harbor revenge, rarely did he even show resentment, and malice was not in his nature. He was congenially employed only in the exchange of good offices and the doing of kindly deeds.

There was not an hour from the beginning of the trouble till the fatal shot entered his body, when the President would not gladly, for the sake of restoring harmony, have retraced any step he had taken if such retracing had merely involved consequences personal to himself. The pride of consistency, or any supposed sense of humiliation that might result from surrendering his position, had not a feather's weight with him. No man was ever less subject to such influences from within or from without. But after the most anxious deliberation and the coolest survey of all the circumstances, he solemnly believed that the true prerogatives of the Executive were involved in the issue which had been raised, and that he would be unfaithful to his supreme obligation if he failed to maintain, in all their vigor, the constitutional rights and dignities of his great office. He believed this in all the convictions of conscience when in sound and vigorous health, and he believed it in his suffering and prostration in the last conscious thought which his wearied mind bestowed on the transitory struggles of life.

More than this need not be said. Less than this could not be said. Justice to the dead, the highest obligation that devolves upon the living, demands the declaration that in all the bearings of the subject, actual or possible, the President was content in his mind, justified in his conscience, immovable in his conclusions.

The religious element in Garfield's character was deep and earnest. In his early youth he espoused the faith of the Disciples, a sect of that great Baptist Communion, which in different ecclesiastical establishments is so numerous and so influential throughout all parts of the United States. But the broadening tendency of his mind and his active spirit of inquiry were early apparent and carried him beyond the dogmas of sect and the restraints of association. In selecting a college in which to continue his education he rejected Bethany, though presided over by Alexander Campbell, the greatest preacher of his church. His reasons were characteristic; first, that Bethany leaned too heavily toward slavery; and, second, that being himself a Disciple and the son of Disciple parents, he had little acquaintance with people of other beliefs, and he thought it would make him more liberal, quoting his own words, both in his religious and general views, to go into a new circle and be under new influences.

The liberal tendency which he anticipated as the result of wider culture was fully realized. He was emancipated from mere sectarian belief, and with eager interest pushed his investigations in the direction of modern progressive thought. He followed with quickening step in the paths of exploration and speculation so fearlessly trodden by Darwin, by Huxley, by Tyndall, and by other living scientists of the radical and advanced type. His own church, binding its disciples by no formulated creed, but accepting the Old and New Testaments as the word of God with unbiased liberty of private interpretation, favored, if it did not stimulate, the spirit of investigation. Its members profess with sincerity, and profess only, to be of one mind and one faith with those who immediately followed the Master, and who were first called Christians at Antioch.

But however high Garfield reasoned of "fixed fate, free will, foreknowledge absolute," he was never separated from the Church of the Disciples in his affections and in his associations. For him it held the ark of the covenant. To him it was the gate of heaven. The world of religious belief is full of solecisms and contradictions. A philosophic observer declares that men by the thousand will die in defence of a creed whose doctrines they do not comprehend and whose tenets they habitually violate. It is equally true that men by the thousand will cling to church organizations with instinctive and undying fidelity when their belief in maturer years is radically different from that which which inspired them as neophytes.

But after this range of speculation, and this latitude of doubt, Garfield came back always with freshness and delight to the simpler instincts of religious faith, which, earliest implanted, longest survive. Not many weeks before his assassination, walking on the banks of the Potomac with a friend, and conversing on those topics of personal religion, concerning which noble natures have an unconquerable reserve, he said that he found the Lord's prayer and the simple petitions learned in infancy infinitely restful to him, not merely in their stated repetition, but in their casual and frequent recall as he went about the daily duties of life. Certain texts of scripture had a very strong hold on his memory and his heart. He heard, while in Edinburgh some years ago, an eminent Scotch preacher who prefaced his sermon with reading the eighth chapter of the Epistle to the Romans, which book had been the subject of careful study with Garfield during all his religious life. He was greatly impressed by the elocution of the preacher and declared that it had imparted a new and deeper meaning to the majestic utterances of Saint Paul. He referred often in after years to that memorable service, and dwelt with exaltation of feeling upon the radiant promise and the assured hope with which the great apostle of the Gentiles was "persuaded that neither death, nor life, nor angels, nor principalities, nor powers, nor things present, nor things to come, nor height, nor depth, nor any other creature, shall be able to separate us from the love of God, which is in Christ Jesus our Lord."

The crowning characteristic of General Garfield's religious opinions, as, indeed, of all his opinions, was his liberality. In all things he had charity. Tolerance was of his nature. He respected in others the qualities which he possessed himself — sincerity of conviction and frankness of expression. With him the inquiry was not so much what a man believes, but does he believe it? The lines of his friendship and his confidence encircled men of every creed, and men of no creed, and to the end of his life, on his ever-lengthening list of friends, were to be found the names of a pious Catholic priest and of an honest-minded and generous-hearted free-thinker.

On the morning of Saturday, July second, the President was a contented and happy man — not in an ordinary degree, but joyfully, almost boyishly happy. On his way to the railroad station to which he drove slowly, in conscious enjoyment of the beautiful morning, with an unwonted sense of leisure and a keen anticipation of pleasure, his talk was all in the grateful and gratulatory vein. He felt that after four months of trial his administration was strong in its grasp of affairs, strong in popular favor and destined to grow stronger; that grave difficulties confronting him at his inauguration had been safely passed; that trouble lay behind him and not before him; that he was soon to meet the wife whom he loved, now recovering from an illness which had but lately disquieted and at times almost unnerved him; that he was going to his Alma Mater to renew the most cherished associations of his young manhood, and to exchange greetings with those whose deepening interest had followed every step of his upward progress, from the day he entered upon his college course until he had attained the loftiest elevation in the gift of his countrymen.

Surely, if happiness can ever come from the honors or triumphs of this world, on that quiet July morning James A. Garfield may well have been a happy man. No foreboding of evil haunted him; no slightest premonition of danger clouded his sky. His terrible fate was upon him in an instant. One moment he stood erect, strong, confident in the years stretching peacefully out before him. The next he lay wounded, bleeding, helpless, doomed to weary weeks of torture, to silence, and the grave.

Great in life, he was surpassingly great in death. For no cause, in the very frenzy of wantonness and wickedness, by the red hand of murder, he was thrust from the full tide of this world's interest, from its hopes, its aspirations, its victories, into the visible presence of death — and he did not quail. Not alone for the one short moment in which, stunned and dazed, he could give up life, hardly aware of its relinquishment, but through days of deadly languor, through weeks of agony, that was not less agony because silently borne, with clear sight and calm courage, he looked into his open grave. What blight and ruin met his anguished eyes, whose lips may tell — what brilliant, broken plans, what baffled, high ambitions, what sundering of strong, warm, manhood's friendships, what bitter rending of sweet household ties! Behind him a proud, expectant nation, a great host of sustaining friends, a cherished and happy mother, wearing the full, rich honors of her early toil and tears; the wife of his youth, whose whole life lay in his; the little boys not yet emerged from childhood's day of frolic; the fair young daughter; the sturdy sons just springing into closest companionship, claiming every day and every day rewarding a father's love and care; and in his heart the eager, rejoicing power to meet all demand. Before him desolation and great darkness! And his soul was not shaken. His countrymen were thrilled with instant, profound, and universal sympathy. Masterful in his mortal weakness, he became the centre of a nation's love, enshrined in the prayers of a world. But all the love and all the sympathy could not share with him his suffering. He trod the wine-press alone. With unfaltering front he faced death. With unfailing tenderness he took leave of life. Above the demoniac hiss of the assassin's bullet he heard the voice of God

With simple resignation he bowed to the Divine decree.

As the end drew near, his early craving for the sea returned. The stately mansion of power had been to him the wearisome hospital of pain, and he begged to be taken from its prison walls, from its oppressive, stifling air, from its homelessness and its hopelessness. Gently, silently, the love of a great people bore the pale sufferer to the longed-for healing of the sea, to live or to die, as God should will, within sight of its heaving billows, within sound of its manifold voices. With wan, fevered face tenderly lifted to the cooling breeze, he looked out wistfully upon the ocean's changing wonders; on its far sails, whitening in the morning light; on its restless waves, rolling shoreward to break and die beneath the noonday sun; on the red clouds of evening, arching low to the horizon; on the serene and shining pathway of the stars. Let us think that his dying eyes read a mystic meaning which only the rapt and parting soul may know. Let us believe that in the silence of the receding world he heard the great waves breaking on a further shore, and felt already upon his wasted brow the breath of the eternal morning.